A Sleepwalker's Guide to Social Media

Dedicated to my brother from what seems like another life, John Stanley Sampson (1960–1984), my ceaselessly caring parents, and my delightful, but sometimes ominously impulsive teenagers, Harry, Daisy and Sam.

A Sleepwalker's Guide to Social Media

TONY D. SAMPSON

polity

Copyright © Tony D. Sampson 2020

The right of Tony D. Sampson to be identified as Author of this Work has been asserted in accordance with the UK Copyright, Designs and Patents Act 1988.

First published in 2020 by Polity Press

Polity Press
65 Bridge Street
Cambridge CB2 1UR, UK

Polity Press
101 Station Landing
Suite 300
Medford, MA 02155, USA

All rights reserved. Except for the quotation of short passages for the purpose of criticism and review, no part of this publication may be reproduced, stored in a retrieval system or transmitted, in any form or by any means, electronic, mechanical, photocopying, recording or otherwise, without the prior permission of the publisher.

ISBN-13: 978-1-5095-3740-2 (hardback)
ISBN-13: 978-1-5095-3741-9 (paperback)

A catalogue record for this book is available from the British Library.

Library of Congress Cataloging-in-Publication Data

Names: Sampson, Tony D., author.
Title: A sleepwalker's guide to social media / Tony D. Sampson.
Description: Medford : Polity, 2020. | Includes bibliographical references and index. | Summary: «A leading scholar›s cutting-edge analysis of the power and impact of social media and its users»-- Provided by publisher.
Identifiers: LCCN 2019054266 (print) | LCCN 2019054267 (ebook) | ISBN 9781509537402 (hardback) | ISBN 9781509537419 (paperback) | ISBN 9781509537426 (epub)
Subjects: LCSH: Social media--Political aspects. | Social media--Social aspects.
Classification: LCC HM742 .S286 2020 (print) | LCC HM742 (ebook) | DDC 302.23/1--dc23
LC record available at https://lccn.loc.gov/2019054266
LC ebook record available at https://lccn.loc.gov/2019054267

Typeset in 11.25 on 13pt Dante MT Pro
by Fakenham Prepress Solutions, Fakenham, Norfolk NR21 8NL
Printed in Great Britain by CPI Group (UK) Ltd, Croydon

The publisher has used its best endeavours to ensure that the URLs for external websites referred to in this book are correct and active at the time of going to press. However, the publisher has no responsibility for the websites and can make no guarantee that a site will remain live or that the content is or will remain appropriate.

Every effort has been made to trace all copyright holders, but if any have been overlooked the publisher will be pleased to include any necessary credits in any subsequent reprint or edition.

For further information on Polity, visit our website:
politybooks.com

Contents

Acknowledgements		vi
Intro		1
1	Feeling Facts and Fakes	11
2	On the Viral Spectra of Somnambulism	40
Coda	Christchurch; El Paso	76
3	The Virality of Experience Capitalism	78
Segue	A Dark [Viral] Refrain	111
4	Immunity, Community and Contagion	114
5	Deeper Entanglements	151
Outro	Disrupting the Dark Refrain	169
Notes		174
Index		203

Acknowledgements

Writing a book can be an incredibly isolating experience. I would therefore like to express much gratitude to all those friends, colleagues and students who have allowed me to share ideas in various discussions, guest talks, keynotes, panels, journal articles, interviews, summer schools, taprooms, restaurants, walks, lectures, supervision and so on. These people include Greg Seigworth, Charlie Tweed, Rebecca Coleman, Charles Talcott, Jussi Parikka, Ryan Bishop, Yigit Soncul, Grant Bollmer, James Ash, Mona Mannevuo, Holly Avella, Darren Kelsey, Jonas Fritsch, Camila Møhring Reestorff, Mikey Georgeson, Vanessa Bartlett, Mateusz Borowski, Małgorzata Sugiera, Tero Karppi, Paolo Davoli, Letizia Rustichelli (Rizosfera), Anastasia Denisova, Francesco Tacchini, Chris Richardson, Nathaniel Tkacz, Kate Hayles, Jamie Bamber, Simon Taylor, Michael Schillmeier, Stefan Herbrechter and Michelle Jamieson.

Special thanks go to all the inspirational speakers at the fourth A&SM conference in east London in 2018, including the concluding panel with Greg, Rebecca, Amit S Rai, Patricia Clough, Darren Ellis, Jessica Ringrose and Ian Tucker.

I would also like to thank the Cultural Engine (Peter Vadden and Giles Tofield) for allowing me the space, time and endless coffee to fuel the writing process.

Intro

A Sleepwalker's Guide to Social Media is a book all about user experience. It is not, however, a study typically focused on a notion of user understood as an individual person. The discussion instead follows a trajectory of critical theoretical work that endeavours to conceive of experience by decentring the human subject from its analytical foci. The approach tends to stress, as such, the collective, mimetic and nonconscious nature of user experience rather than fixing on subjective consciousness. Significantly, though, it is important not to misconstrue the emphasis on impersonal experience as dismissive of personal subjectivity. My approach does not discount the attentive labours of an individual user's cognition. It does not deny the emergence of subjects who *feel* their own sense of rationality as a kind of core self-concept. It does not refuse phenomenal modes of subjective volition or intentionality towards objects. Nevertheless, as will soon become apparent, these more concentrated moments of lucid experience are regarded as a part of a process stirred into action by a *collective nonconscious*. In a nutshell, the subjectivity of the user is the product, not the producer of experience.

Before reading on, it also is important to note that *A Sleepwalker's Guide* builds on previous work by this author addressing the collective nonconscious.[1] It is, as follows, a continuation of a *dystopian media theory*.[2] For readers unfamiliar with this approach, it can speedily be defined as an alternative mode of critical theory, which does not grasp its subject (social media in this case) by way of a conventional ideological critique of media power. It does not follow dialectical movements or indeed look for its subject in symbolic ideas-in-form or media representations. Instead, the dystopian mode of criticality suspiciously follows the movement of often unresolvable and paradoxical mixtures of power, including hard and soft control, oppositional and acquiescent behavioural manipulations, and modes of domination established, simultaneously, by way of slavery and freedom.[3]

Throughout this work, the shadow of certain theorists has loomed large. Readers familiar with Gilles Deleuze and Felix Guattari will no doubt recognize most of the ontological preferences utilized in these pages. It is, nonetheless, the presence of the influential microsociologist, Gabriel Tarde, and the persistent mobilization of his *conceptual persona* of the somnambulist that figures most prominently throughout.[4] The somnambulists are social figures who originated (and initially faded) alongside the rise and fall of nineteenth-century crowd contagion theories, yet have, in recent years, found a new sense of purpose in the analysis of viral networks and the neurocultures of social media.

This new somnambulist coincidentally corresponds with a spate of media headlines declaring that humanity is sleepwalking into numerous world crises (see the discussion in Chapter 2). It is important, however, not simply to grasp the sleepwalkers, as they are often represented in these foreboding newspaper headlines, as dispossessed of rational consciousness. In spite of these popular discourses, which position populations as collectively sleepwalking towards various economic, political, environmental and technological calamities, this book is not solely about sleep, nor indeed does it concern waking the sleepwalker! Along these lines, Frédéric Neyrat proposes that our experience of the digital present may in fact have little to do with sleep.[5] In place of the dulled sense of reverie we might experience when struggling to wake up; those moments when it is difficult to differentiate between the woken surroundings from a lingering dream, Neyrat points to periods of protracted wakefulness. The power is always switched on, or permanently on charge, meaning that digital work and leisure time can indeed occur at any time. Check that email, notification, update, post, tweet ... The platform tells us when to start and when to end a shift. Sleeping isn't easy, with the onset of all these attentional demands, excesses of light, data and infinite linking and smart thinking. Contrary, then, to the popular figure of the involuntarily zombie smartphone user, and apparent rise in cases of so-called sleep texting,[6] Neyrat supposes that digital work requires vigorous cognitive engagements.

But then again, perhaps the digital present is a little fuzzier than this somewhat forced distinction between dreamy sleep and full on wakefulness suggests. Which is to say, such a clear distinction seems to miss a number of paradoxical aspects of the contemporary user experience. This is the main point of bringing back Tarde's somnambulists. They are absurd conceptual personae who do not sit easily on either side of a barrier erected between dreamy or uninterrupted sleep, on one hand, and the prolonged interruptions and wakefulness of digital culture, on the other. What is argued here is a little closer to what Jonathan Crary calls the 'monotonous indistinction of 24/7' digital labour and consumption.[7]

This is a 'zone of insensibility' and memory loss which 'defeats', Crary contends, 'the possibility of experience'.[8] However, again, we need to be careful. The struggle for experience seems to be a lot fuzzier than this account suggests. This indistinction must not simply be restricted to the erosion of day and night or work and leisure time alone. On the contrary, what I will call *experience capitalism* has already breeched the boundaries that separate wakefulness and sleep. Much of what is produced, consumed and discarded is now carried out in these zones of indistinction.

It would seem that we need a somnambulist who can explore these in-betweens, since, like most other kinds of work, digital labour tends not only to interfere with, but also occupies the outer margins of sleep.[9] The neuro-management of collective user experiences by psychological corporations, with their teams of behavioural marketers, data miners and experience designers, similarly works in-between nonconscious and conscious states. To be sure, reading the work of influential experience designers and consumer researchers, we can trace a long-running fascination with appeals to an overriding relational nonconscious state of consumption. Along these lines, experience capitalism might be seen as an extension of earlier appeals made to a theatrical subconscious as a way to affect social influence that leads to mass consumption. It is this new focus on the neurochemically constituted nonconscious states of the user that supposedly processes experience on a visceral register (apparently located in the body–brain relation) before it surfaces as a mechanical habit or moment of inward reflection concerning, for example, an affinity with a brand identity.[10] *The collective nonconscious is the new parasomnia.* As follows, users do not need to be asleep or fully awake to negotiate neurologically premeditated comfort zones of consumption or the increasing pervasiveness of nontask interactions at work.

Tarde's sleepwalkers are indeed central to how this book conjures the concept of the collective nonconscious. They help to bring the concept to life by providing a persona through which it can live and breathe. It is, indeed, through the lives of various sleepwalkers in each chapter that the nonconscious is thought, perceived and felt. The sleepwalkers become intrinsic conceptual personae; philosophical tools able to make interventions into the production of the concept itself.[11] Tarde's somnambulists are, as such, the perfect conceptual personae for the paradoxical ontology of dystopian media theory, since they allow analytical entry to the collective nonconscious of user experience.

Crucially, though, sleepwalkers are not really persons at all. They are *larval subjects* or becoming subjects. They are never quite actualized as fully

Subject-of-becoming [handwritten annotation]

formed subjects. ⌐Sleepwalkers are not social actors or individual nodes in a network, as such. They are rather social relations or collectively felt experiences.¬ Along these lines, then, the experience of the somnambulist helps us to grasp why, although many users may feel wide awake, they cannot become dissociated from their nonconscious associations with the collective. *A Sleepwalker's Guide* marks a point in this author's work wherein the persona of the somnambulist (and its luring by way of the action-at-a-distance of social relationality) begins to encompass a far wider range of concepts of impersonal user experiences, including overlaps with the concepts developed by A. N. Whitehead, Patricia Clough, R. D. Laing, Roger Caillois and Roberto Esposito, for example.

A Dark Refrain of Social Media

A Sleepwalker's Guide uniquely points the antennae of Tarde's conceptual persona towards a particularly dark moment in the social media age. I have to admit, regretfully, although there are a few affirmative propositions (i.e. around the failure of immunopolitics), much of the discussion will not make for an especially joyous read. The previous conclusion of dystopian media theory did not unsurprisingly propose a blooming bed of roses for future user experiences either. *Far from it!* There was already an apparent sense of foreboding; a Huxleyesque orchid garden taking root in digital culture, and therefore a need to ramp up the aforementioned suspicions of critical theory.[12] However, dystopian media theory also needs to explore potential *lines of flight*, offering some insights into the possibilities of revolutionary social media contagion; suggesting something more democratic might always be conceivable. As imperfect and overhyped as earlier examples of social media-fuelled contagions have proven to be, their part in the election of the first black US President in 2008 and the emergence of a nascent prodemocracy movement in the Middle East in 2011, for example, offer some clues as to what might be imaginable in the future.

Even so, I started to write this current text at a very different moment in time; a moment when the possibilities of revolutionary contagion have become deeply entangled in what I call a dark refrain. ⌐Broadly speaking, these references to the dark refrain are intended to draw attention to a far-right territorialization of the global political scene and its various manifestations on social media.¬ To understand how such a political land grab has transformed the potentiality of social media contagion, we need to briefly grasp a rudimentary appreciation of musical improvisation.[13]

Lines of flight and refrains are indeed mutual concepts that most improvising musicians should already be familiar with. On one hand, imagine these earlier lines of flight in digital culture as the jagged edges of a clashing, a-rhythmic and discordant musical performance. They are the beginning of an improvisation that initially refuses (intentionally or accidentally) to settle into any kind of recognizable groove. There was no tempo set; no opening bars to conform to. Nothing is composed, as such. For Deleuze and Guattari, these notes *without order* appeared like the random scribbles on Sylvano Bussoti's musical staff.[14] They are a scattering of notes that *become-other*.

The refrain is, on the other hand, a moment in the improvisation when players begin to fall into a repeated pattern of notes. The notes might become harmonized; syncopated. The rhythm is quantized. At the same time, the bodies of the players become biomusicologically entrained. Which is to say, there is synchronized foot tapping, arms swing together; heads bob in unison. This shared felt experience of improvised music can of course become an exuberant repetition. The groove can be a feely lure; an inducement or seduction of everyone assembled in its catchy cadence. The musicians and the audience similarly begin to pulse together, swaying to the same rhythm. Yet, despite the promise of joy, these movements are pegged in such a way as to determine what comes next. The key fixes the line to a predictable scale of notes, a familiar chord progression. Things start to repeat themselves over and over again, *without difference*. They are the production of a musical mechanical habit. It becomes problematic to try to break out of such a rhythmic rut. It's not just bodies that become entrained. The pulse acts as an affective contagion, bringing bodies, brains, feelings and thoughts into line with each other. Musicians, audiences *become-the-same*.

The dark refrain is a staccato-like repetition of a racist populist politics, spreading throughout the world: *Trump, Salvini, Putin, Modi, Bolsonaro, Johnson, Farage, Le Pen, Alternative for Germany (AfD), Orban, Wilders …* It is a refrain punctuated by micro and macro-fascisms, failing immunity, rampant, yet botched capitalism, and neo-Nazis mass shootings. More specifically, though, this is a refrain that has so often been played out on social media. Certainly, after Brexit and Trump in 2016, the Cambridge Analytica scandal broke in April 2018. This massive data breach of millions of Facebook user profiles for the political purposes of the Trump campaign brought about what Karen Simecek calls 'a renewal of paranoia and anxiety about life online and engagement with social media'.[15] It is against this backdrop that my renewed interest in the user experience of social media has been formulated.

In short, what *A Sleepwalker's Guide* sets out to do is consider how earlier lines of flight have flipflopped into a darker, portentous and repetitive refrain. This refrain has seen both an economic and political expropriation of the user experience. Social media users not only give away the ownership of their community relations to parasitic social media platforms, but the potential of revolutionary contagion has also been utterly dispossessed. The repossession of the territories in which revolutionary contagion might overspill – once the occupancy of prodemocratic movements – has shifted to this antidemocratic refrain. This is important because when a population feels the same hate, feels the same fear; when it begins to share the same experience, then we have produced, as R. D. Laing argued, compliant consumers and cannon fodder.[16] The revolutionary moment is, it would seem, now with the far right. So, what is of interest throughout the text is the role social media plays in this somewhat abrupt capitulation and acquiescence to the dark refrain. My interest here is in the refrain's utterings of post-truth, contagious fake news and hate speech. Its expressions of a racist immunopolitics and coincidence with a convergence between neoliberal capitalism and fascism. Ultimately, the book looks beyond social media to the apparent immersive futures of digital culture that are already seeping into the user experience.

Indistinctions

A closer reading of Neyrat's description of what constitutes sleep suggests that our digital labours might be neither entirely somnolent nor wide awake. The user experience seems to be at a threshold point in-between these two distinct states. There is clearly a connection here with a *Deleuzoguattarian* interest in *The Middle*, wherein those infamous weeds begin to appear in-between the deterritorialized cracks.[17] Yet again, perhaps this notion of an in-between state is in itself continuing to force a distinction? User experiences are intuitively felt, but they produce concrete actions, habits, compulsions and collective impulses. These are blurry moments of indistinction, whereby the nonphenomenological world of somnolent experience slips into ambulant states of user engagement. In this new light, user experiences are neither asleep nor wide awake, or indeed, in-between, but rather they are, at once, somnambulistic.

The indistinctness of somnambulism is certainly a recurrent theme throughout this book. There is nothing primarily new here. Tarde's original contagion theory was firmly located in the insensible degrees between nonconscious experience, mechanical habit and volition. There is no 'absolute separation of this abrupt break, between the voluntary and the involuntary ... between the conscious and the unconscious. Do we not pass by insensible degrees from deliberate volition to almost mechanical habit?'[18] What is novel in this latest rendition is that indistinctness is now resolutely linked to a methodology. Important to this procedural development is the work of Roger Caillois.[19] In short, for Caillois, the process by which biological camouflage blends an organism into its surroundings presents a disruption of perception, but also opens up the potential and perils of collective mimicry. Borrowing from Caillois's proposal that the fundamental role of all study is to set about resolving distinctions, this book endeavours to tackle a series of forced divisions. By doing so, each chapter looks to the indistinct nature of things; the vagueness of it all.

Of course, some Gestalt-minded scholars will say that a failure to make a clear distinction is a failure of perception. Certainly, we go against Gestalt principles if we fail to distinguish the emergence of foreground from background. Be this as it may, indistinction is regarded in this book as a mode of access to preperception; a way of slipping into the insensible zones of user experience. This is again nothing new in terms of aesthetic work. There is a long history of indistinctness in art. The art critic, Adrian Stokes, noted how the 'embracing or enveloping quality' of Turner's art came about because of its 'indistinctness' and 'loss of definition'.[20] Crary similarly notes the somnambulant indistinctiveness of 'attentiveness and distraction' established between the aesthetic figures in Manet's paintings.[21] In literature too, there are characterizations that are made purposefully indistinct. Gatsby is a great illusive aesthetic figure in this sense. He remains purposefully blurred for much of Fitzgerald's book; a figure that assimilates the background and blends into that big old house. Likewise, in the latter stages of writing this book I worked with the artist, Mikey B. Georgeson, whose series of *Auto Matter Flow Morning Drawing* (see figure 1) and experiments with the glitches of green screen technology helped me to consolidate a broader sense of the aesthetic power of indistinction to produce what Gary Genosko brilliantly calls, an 'enemy of crisp synthesis'.[22] Throughout this book, then, indistinction is an aesthetic methodology that refuses forced distinctions. The doodling, 'noodling', 'fuzziness' and 'muddiness'[23] of indistinctness resists border regimes by sliding in between foreground and background, sleep and wakefulness, truth and fakery, self and other, self and nonself, mind and matter.

Figure 1 The Sleepwalkers are the Enemies of Crisp Synthesis. Illustration by Mikey B. Georgeson.

The Five Chapters

The first two chapters begin by endeavouring to resolve some of the more significant distinctions that have come to define the so-called post-truth era. For example, the discussion turns to explore how fake news contagions can be alternatively grasped through a Whiteheadian aesthetic ontology rather than prevalent informatic registers of user experience. A number of subsequent questions are raised. When information machines fail to distinguish between fact and fake, what role do feelings play in learning to discern? How do feelings persist in the data voids and political stratagems that crop up in relation to shock events (mass shootings), search engine rankings and social media rumour? Moreover, what role does the collective nonconscious play in the surge of support for the tweeting, WhatsApp bigoted rants of populist politicians? These two chapters conclude by substituting the old spectral measures between brutal fact and total fiction with a somnambulist register of user experience.

Chapters 3 and 4 similarly combine to follow the trajectory of the dark refrain to converged modes of viral capitalism and fascistic immunopolitics. The discussion in both chapters follows the multiple synergies assembled around so-called virality/growth practices of commodification, an impoverished model of online community, and the promises and perils of immunity failure. Following Caillois and Laing the chapters look to resolve a series-related forced immunological (and anthropological) distinction between self and other, self and nonself and what to ignore and what to delete. Chapter 3 argues for a new nonphenomenological syntax able to grasp the indistinctions of the sleepwalker. Ultimately, Chapter 4 moves on to ask what kinds of lines of flight can be salvaged from the dangerous, masochistic tendencies of collective mimicry. Which is to say, when immune systems fail and things become perilously indistinct, what kind of novel communities might emerge?

The final chapter explores the immersive futures of user experience. As an extension of the social technology paradigm of user experience, ubiquitous, pervasive computing has been described as akin to turning virtual reality inside out.[24] Computational media thus *comes alive* in the everyday experiences of the world. The chapter argues that the implications of what Andrew Murphie has called *Media Alive* challenge the conventional phenomenological study of user experience. Following Whitehead, the ultimate unresolved distinction is found in the misguided phenomenological attempt to bifurcate mind from nature. Along these lines, the mind's encounter with matter is caught in a seemingly irresolvable distinction, wherein nature is apprehended in the awareness of the brain (consciousness). Yet, for Whitehead, nature is *in itself* the cause of conscious awareness.

This final chapter attempts to utilize the nonphenomenological syntax from Chapter 3 to express a nonbifurcated theory of user experience. Along these lines, the mind of the user is not analysed like an artist working on a 3D world for a virtual reality game. The mind is not engaged in the production of protrusion and distance; an illusory, secondary, production of perspective represented on a primary flat surface. This mode of experience is what Raymond Ruyer, a follower of Whitehead, considers to be an auxiliary mode of consciousness. It represents our awareness of things in terms of perspectival depth, but misses a primary surface of *absolute survey*.[25] As Elizabeth Grosz puts it, in theories of perception, like Gestalt, 'the eye is normally understood as the organ that sees a surface by observing [a foreground floating over ground, and] presents it to the brain or mind to confirm'.[26] Yet, for this to happen the eye must 'invoke another eye to confirm the existence of the eye that sees over [the ground]'.[27] For Ruyer, this is interesting, but mistaken. *There is no third eye!* We do not observe things through a 'disembodied' receptacle (eye–body) that simply passes on the experience of vision to consciousness.[28] Ruyer's absolute survey is thus the ultimate indistinction or nonbifurcation; it is experience, *experiencing itself*. The idea that 'consciousness is somehow a supplementary dimension added to perception, a place where perception is registered or cognized',[29] misses the autoaffective nature of consciousness. The third eye thesis misses, as such, what Patricia Clough refers to as the autoaffection of user experience.[30] It misses the collective nonconscious. It misses the somnambulist.

1

Feeling Facts and Fakes

In this purported post-truth era, the processes by which we make judgements and decide are, it would seem, increasingly lost in the indeterminacy and resonations of social-media-fuelled rumour, conspiracy and fabrication. The current wave of political nationalist madness similarly partakes of the calculated clouding of political concepts, spreading of Trumpian *Big Lies*, and downright faking of digital news content. The truths that we search for on Google can, as such, become misplaced in so-called data voids and disappear down algorithmic rabbit holes. In the glut of media assumption and the desperate grasping of explanatory theoretical straws to understand this post-truth condition, we have seen a marked intervention by two opposing positions. On one hand, there is the persistence of the positivist's pursuit of brutal facts, and on the other, there has been a revival of the postmodernist's representational implosion of truth. However, far from providing an explanation of the experience of post-truth these theories have arguably produced a seemingly inescapable impasse.

This chapter intervenes in these persistent positivistic and postmodern notions of how facts and fakes are supposedly processed by brains and computers. It plots its escape from this impasse by drawing on A. N. Whitehead's challenge to positivistic thinking. By introducing the Whiteheadian concept of the aesthetic fact, and using examples of shock events, the discussion considers how the facts we search for often exceed the polar opposites of true/false distinctions. Ultimately, the chapter argues that we need to consider the feely speculative encounters we have with facts and fakes on broader spectra of experience with multiple polarities.

The Aesthetic Fact

> The existence of imaginative literature should have warned logicians that their narrow doctrine is absurd. It is difficult to believe that all logicians ... commence by judging whether the initial proposition be

true or false ... Surely, at some point in the reading, judgment is eclipsed by aesthetic delight ... a mere lure for feeling.[1]

In the current toxic political environment, characterized by post truth pedlars and frantic fact-checking, A. N. Whitehead's preference for the aesthetic delight of fiction over brutal fact might appear like a puzzling point of departure. However, it is my opening gambit in this book that Whitehead's aesthetic ontology offers more significant insights into the complexity of judgement making than current post-truth discourses divulge. In a contemporary context, this appeal to imaginative literature provides an intuitive grasp of the workings of what David Burrows and Simon O'Sullivan have called *machine-fictioning*.[2] Along similar lines, above, Whitehead is referring specifically to an audience's joy on experiencing an actor reading Shakespeare's 'To be or not to be' speech from Hamlet. However, this example could, in effect, relate to any kind of aesthetic figure experienced as part of an affecting piece of art; a novel, painting, performance or installation. It is political too. In the current wave of perception management of dominant fictions and fake news, aesthetic delight can produce an intervening alternative fiction that has both a radical and ethical charge.

For now, though, the focus of this chapter stays on the strategic productions of dubious fake news. As follows, at this stage, the main point to grasp is that Whitehead's machine-fictioning elicits a very different kind of *measure* of fact. This is not a measurement based on discrete quantitative values, marked out as a closed spatial extension. It is not a measurable unit or rule, as such. On the contrary, aesthetic delight is a qualitative value experienced as an intensity rather than an extensity. Delight appeals to an audience on an aesthetic register of experience, occasioning what Whitehead calls a 'value' based on 'elements in feeling'.[4] This notion of feeling is not, as positivists would have it, the polar opposite of fact. The feeling of aesthetic delight is not necessarily a personal or irrational felt experience. Significantly, Whitehead's feelings can be broadly conceived as impersonal. Feelings are certainly not regarded, at any level, as illogical interferences in the processes of internal logical reasoning. The Whiteheadian fictioning-machine instead functions like a powerful, impersonal *lure* that draws an audience into the delightful experience of fact. We will return to this important and contested notion of the lure later on in this chapter.

What is at once peculiar and fascinating about this alternative feely measure of fact is that Whitehead is the famed co-author of *Principia Mathematica*; a book (*the* book) that attempted to define the fundamentals of a closed system of logic.[5] So, one might assume that if Whitehead were around today, amid all this political toxicity, he would perhaps take a decidedly logical position on post-truth? He might even self-identify with present day positivists who continue to grasp post-truth as a preferential problem of appealing to irrational feelings, personal beliefs or cherry-picked desires rather than a necessary commitment to brutal fact. *But no!* As Andrew Murphie points out, although Whitehead's earlier work with Bertrand Russell promised a closed world of logic, maths and symbolic processing, it actually failed to deliver.[6] Perhaps it was the failure of *Principia Mathematica* to provide axiomatic proof of such a self-contained world that arguably led to his subsequent venture into speculative philosophy.[7] Whatever the case, Whitehead's event philosophy would certainly look to problematize the logician's brutalist grip on fact. Along these lines, he would begin by arguing against the imposition of mathematical abstractions (e.g. points and grids) on nature, contending instead for a kind of radical empiricism, wherein the concept of nature is experienced through the abstractions of sense data.[8] Whitehead's latter venture into speculative philosophy would go on to suggestively loosen the status of truth and falsity as distinct counterparts at the polar ends of a spectrum. His work purposefully challenges the positivistic distinction made between brutal fact and untrustworthy felt experiences by arguing for a *measurement of fact* founded on the *intensity of experience*; gauged as something he goes on to call *aesthetic fact*.[9]

The theoretical line drawn here between Whitehead's aesthetic fact and contemporary user experiences of post-truth, collides with some lingering positivistic assumptions concerning the nature of human computer interaction. As Murphie further suggests, despite its abject failure, the weighty influence of *Principia Mathematica* on communication and cybernetic theory is in many ways to blame for the closed informational cultures we inhabit today.[10] As follows, the deep human entanglement with vast networks of logic machines seems to presuppose that individual users populate closed informational environments, determined by the force of brutal fact. The user's problematic encounter with misinformation, disinformation or malinformation can be overcome by simply making information more transparent and abundant on a network. It is this abundance of transparent data (alongside the development of certain skills in data discernment) that will counter an uninformed population's vulnerability to conspiracy and fictioning.[11] There are, nevertheless, intrinsic inconsistencies in the closed logics of informational processing, which, as Whitehead knew, positivistic discourses tend to overlook. Certainly, humans and computer cognition struggle to distinguish precisely between true and false statements, rendering systems of immunity and anomaly detection, for example, vulnerable to the alluring influence of contagious aesthetic facts.

Significantly, then, Whitehead's aesthetic register of experience should not be confused with personal feelings that interfere with rational decision-making processes. This chapter will conjure with concepts of fact and fake located on far more complex spectra of intensive and impersonal experience with multiple polarities. ⌈These are *spectral experiences* that transverse and exceed the polar extremes of brutal fact, on one hand, and irrational, emotional and illogical reasoning, on the other.⌉ The speculative nature of spectral experiences is intended to unshackle the dominant grip of brutal fact as a force opposed to visceral registers of experience. On the spectra of experience, the often-forced distinction made between exact truth and falsity collapses into moments of indistinction.⌉ This does not mean that we have to deny that things can ever be true or false. Evidently, there are things that occupy very long durations of actuality without necessarily virtualizing⌉ For example, at a certain temperature, oxygen and hydrogen commingle to make water. However, making clear distinctions between statements, as Whitehead notes, generally refuses to be 'pushed to meticulous exactness'.[12]

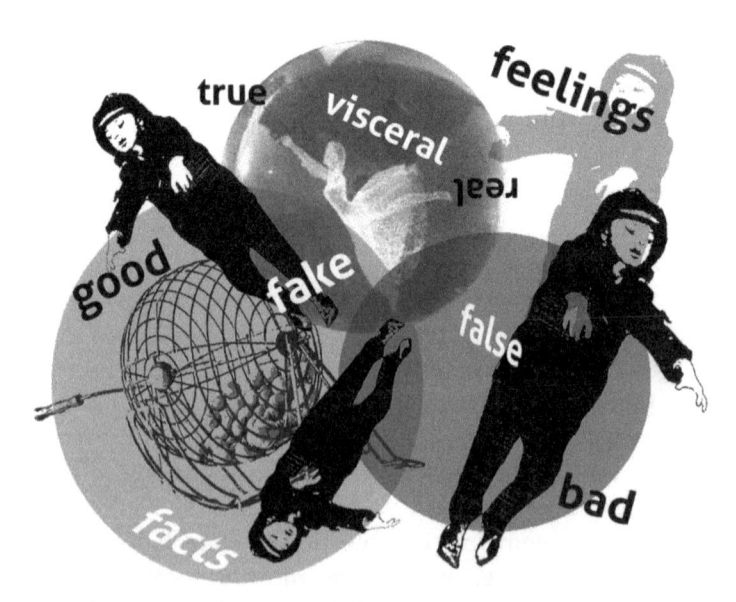

Figure 2 On the Spectra of Somnambulist Experience.
Diagrammatic interpretation by Mikey B. Georgeson.

How, then, might we begin to feel this inexactness; these feely moments of indistinction? Mikey B. Georgeson's diagram (see figure 2) of spectral experience uses the conceptual personae of the somnambulist to initially problematize forced distinctions made between fact, fake and feeling that typify post-truth discourses. The first series of forced distinction approached in this chapter comes about because of an enduring impasse between positivism and postmodernism. On one hand, positivists point to the untrustworthy nature of subjective feelings, beliefs and desires as causal actors in irrational contagions of fake news. Which is to say, personal emotions are often regarded as the polar opposite of objective rational judgements about what is fact or fake. As we will see below, rationalists who follow the classical cognitive theoretical frame of reference similarly tend to relegate personal feelings to a marginal status in their analogical grasping of brains and computers. On the other hand, postmodernists have continued to position fact itself as an imploding *reality-effect*, floating around on an illusory representational plane. This is not fact as it is opposed to feeling, but rather fact as it might appear in Wonderland or virtual reality: *fact going down a rabbit hole*! This kind of simulated representation of fact also appears as a recurrent theme in many technological discourses concerning fake news, including, for example, the choices a user needs to make between one algorithmic rabbit hole or another, or this red pill or that blue pill.

The spectra of experience are intended to provide a means by which facts and fakes can be alternatively grasped by feeling the intensity of experience on an aesthetic register. This means we have to begin by unravelling and moving beyond the positivist/postmodern impasse. To start with, then, this opening chapter introduces an alternative speculative conceptual tool: the *shock event*. In this case, the shock horror of a mass shooting in Las Vegas in 2017 is used to illustrate how social media fakes can be optimized (and weaponized) by exploiting speculative contagions of panic and rumour as they begin to fill so-called search engine data voids following a shock event.

Finally, then, by way of following the intensive movements of these speculative contagions, the aim is to develop a broader understanding of the role shock events play in producing modes of what I will refer to as sleepwalking subjectivities. Although the feeling of personal consciousness (and an associated sense of individual volition) might seem to provide a centred command post of awareness, the aesthetic fact is experienced as a mere foothold a sleepwalker has in the speculative spreading of a shock event. It is not therefore simply a matter of *waking* the docile sleepwalker to the brutal reality of fact, or making a choice between a red or a blue pill. Again, the strangest, but most rewarding factor of Whitehead's aesthetic ontology is the revelation that the lure of feeling is impersonal. Like this, sleepwalkers are not individual users; they are instead immanent to a collective nonconscious, caught in the shockwaves of the event. As the shock resonates, it lures the sleepwalkers; it feels them, and transports them through a sensory flux or matter-flow. It is not the truth-seeking rational subject that decides these encounters with shock events. *The subject does not make the event!* On the contrary, it is the aesthetic intensity of the event itself; its capacity to lure and feel, which decides how subjects are made.

The Logics of Fake News

How then do we use all this stuff to approach the contested logic of fake news? As a principal term in the post-truth debate, fake news has been discursively positioned by certain politicians and media voices as a threat to Western-style democracies. Along these lines, the term is generally defined as the strategic spreading of misinformation, intended to undermine fact, manipulate opinion and influence voting patterns. The faking of fact in propagandist practices is of course nothing new, but post 9/11, the number of *post hoc* fact-checking initiatives has greatly increased; many of which have been designed to counter fake news with a 'fact-based public discourse'.[13] Following a number of unanticipated referendum and election results, notably political shocks in the UK and USA, special government committees have been set up to investigate the scale of the fake news problem and assess the threat it poses to democracy.[14] However, amid considerable political toxicity and instability, the relation between fake and factual news is currently highly contested. Certain politicians have used the term fake news to call out anything they disagree with. From the outset, then, fake news needs to be treated as a very slippery term.

Fake news is further grasped as a data problem. Herein, we return to Russell and Whitehead, since this data problem relates to the closed logics of coupled computational and human informational processes. On one hand, then, as a problem of computation, the term fake news has been grasped as a matter of information disorder or pollution.[15] Fake news is said to strike at the very heart of the 'modern information society'.[16] The propagation of misinformation, disinformation and malinformation is clearly associated with long-established problems with information processing and logical reasoning. It can be mapped, as such, to a history of logical inconsistencies that have beset closed logical systems and information processors prone to recurring indecision, incompleteness, and potential viral propagation of paradox. Nevertheless, in its newly animated environment of contemporary social technology, fake news seems to represent something new. Information disorder is, as such, experienced at a 'global scale', spreading at 'breakneck speeds' through 'myriad of content types', 'innumerable platforms 'and 'techniques for amplifying content'.[17] In this computational age, defined by social media and search engine technology, information processing has proven to be particularly susceptible to the spreading of falsity, which exploits viral architectures, echo chambers and filter bubbles, all of which are prone to intensifications of digital contagion.

On the other hand, though, a tendency to focus solely on the inconsistencies of computational processing is clearly complicated by the observation that the contagiousness of fake news affects the cognitive decisions of the human brain. Of course, some classically minded cognitivists will not see a problem in this comparison. They will point to the many similarities between computers and brains. Certainly, if we follow the classical cognitive theoretical frame, and assume that computers and brains are analogically coupled information processors, then the fake problem might be associated with a more generic model of processing, relating to computational and neurological processes alike. Along these lines, in order to discern between fact and fake, cognitivists argue that humans need to develop more refined cognitive skills in critical information literacy.[18] Other authors in the cognitive field have expanded on this approach by arguing for the invention of new *technocognitive* tools. This is perhaps the ultimate manifestation of the computer–brain analogy, intended to go 'beyond misinformation' to a more attentive and educated discernment of information.[19]

As admirable as the goal of refining the judgements and discernments of the human brain might be, it nevertheless reveals some of the major limitations of analogical reasoning in cognitive science. Discerning between fact and fake exposes differences in computational cognition and the small slice of the human brain assumed to process information *cognitively*. Evidently, working to improve information literacy, perfecting critical thinking skills, and boosting the capacity to *Learn to Discern* will have some positive impacts on some of those people affected by fake news.[20] Yet, following the feely measure of Whitehead's machine-fictioning, such failures to judge between fact and fake should not be limited to mere matters of information processing. The online spreading of panic, rumour and conspiracy, for example, tends to thrive when there is a lack of information following a shock event (e.g. a mass shooting or natural disaster). The strategic spreading of falsity online is often dependent on so-called *data voids*, which circulate rumours before they eventually become filled with hoaxes. In short, logical inconsistencies play a significant role in the spreading of machine-fictioning, but our primary concern should be with the visceral lure of aesthetic experiences, which can trigger contagious, collective impulses, exceeding personal experience.

Deep Nonconscious Entanglements

It is my contention that the relation between human and computer is not analogical; it is a relation based on deep, immanent entanglement. Like this, the diagrammatic spectra of experience help us to decouple both the technological and neurological from the cognitivist's analogical straitjacket, exposing the deep nonconscious entanglements of brains, bodies and computers. From the outset, then, there are two important points to grasp concerning these entanglements.

> The limits imposed on the deciding functions of symbolic computational systems are not analogous to those imposed on the judgements of the biological brain.

We must not assume that, as the early cognitivists did, the physical symbol system of the computer is part of the same family as the human brain.[21] To truly grasp deep entanglement, it is necessary, as such, to decouple any family resemblances intrinsic to the computer–brain analogy. In other words, although the cognitive aspects of brain and computer decision-making processes seem to overlap each other in terms of information processing, deciding brains are not comparable to the logical symbol manipulation a computer uses to decide.[22] Brains do not decide by simply carrying out computations on representations. As Harry Collins argues, unlike the explicit instructions carried out by computers, brains seem to be wired for tacit understandings.[23] In other words, brains appear to know something without explicitly knowing how they know it, or indeed, how to express it.

Of course, this idea is often contested by certain AI theorists, who claim that a human's tacit understanding of riding a bike, for example, can be mimicked by a robot. Yet, arguably, the tacit grasping of an *unknown known* can be understood as part of a processual relation established between cognition and the nonconscious. Along these lines, and following the emotional turn in the neurosciences, N. Katherine Hayles has similarly drawn our attention to an asymmetrical relation between the decision-making processes in higher consciousness, on one hand, and the determinations of what she calls the *cognitive nonconscious*, on the other. From this viewpoint, Hayles follows neuroscientist Antonio Damasio by noting how higher consciousness seems to coincide with the *autobiographical self*: 'the verbal monologue that plays in our heads as we go about our daily business'.[24] In contrast, nonconscious cognition is assumed to operate 'at a level of neuronal processing', which is, Hayles contends, 'inaccessible to the modes of awareness', yet deeply implicated in the formation of decisions and actions.[25]

Although my approach here will significantly differ from the cognitive approach Hayles develops (discussed in Chapter 2), this initial rendering of the nonconscious is, for the time being, similarly grasped as performing functions that support and feed into what might be called higher consciousness. This point is important to the theoretical framing of aesthetic facts, since they too are regarded as being *felt nonconsciously* before being fully registered by consciousness. Conscious, attentive cognition becomes, in many ways, ancillary to primary visceral registers of experience that can determine mood, behaviour and influence tacit understandings. Moreover, compared to the thin slice of the cognitive brain, which provides brief moments of conscious hesitation and a sense of voluntary choice, aesthetic experience triggers the immediacy of the visceral register of the nonconscious. This immediacy can also lead to involuntary mechanical habits and impulsive acts, which can sidestep cognition altogether.

> Judgements are not, in themselves, constrained to individual cognition (brain or computer). The aesthetic fact is experienced collectively. It is therefore impersonal!

Deep nonconscious entanglement means that logic machines are now socially embedded in human and environmental networks. They are, as such, increasingly able to *sense*, *read* and *learn* from patterns of user behaviour. Some of these patterns relate to abstract thought, such as complex judgements made during a game of chess or Go. This is the kind of smart computing that feeds into popular discourses concerning the possibility of computers eventually outsmarting human intelligence and emerging as the so-called singularity. But we should not confuse deep learning with deep entanglement. As Collins argues, computers are not as smart as most AI discourses maintain.[26] To be sure, computers are, as

Collins contends, mimicking machines. They lack the critical capacity to process human variation and speculation. Along these lines, computers can mimic complex chess or Go moves, but they are also prone to mimicking hostility, stupidity and error at a subcritical level. For example, detection software, machine learning, and other AI algorithms, are now *trained* using social media interactions, so it is not surprising that some of the patterns generated contain bigoted text, hate speech, or encourage and propagate conspiracy theories and fictioning. Moreover, social computing has, via platforms like Facebook, enabled the massive scale processing of emotional and visceral data. This level of sentiment analysis can be used by platforms to anticipate and prompt future impulsive actions, but there is always a risk that appeals to the visceral register will cultivate unmanageable affective contagions.

Along similar lines, a number of media theorists have again cautioned about a potential dystopic dislocation, which threatens to shift the cognitive power of decision-making away from humans to the operational level of automated computational media. Hayles, for instance, follows a long line of authors who grasp the deeply entangled relation between brains, bodies and computers as a technological unconscious, or more latterly a technological nonconscious.[27] Following Thrift, Hayles describes the human–computer relation as …

> … consisting of predispositions that regulate our actions in unconscious and nonconscious ways through routine anticipations, habitual responses, pattern recognition, and other activities characteristic of the cognitive nonconscious.

Following a comparable theoretical line, my contention here is that these concerns for the demise of human autonomy at the operational level of computation need to consider further the implications of deep nonconscious entanglement. Along with Murphie and Collins, my concern is not so much about how to survive the AI singularity than it is to survive the hostility, stupidity and error-prone nature of uncritical mimicking social technologies. This concern is therefore linked to an impersonal *collective nonconsciousness* implicated in current political anxieties about impulsive and subcritical collective judgements. Which is to say, collective gut responses (i.e. shared hate, bigotry, anger or frustration) have led to impetuous voting patterns, which seem to favour certain political candidates who (a) operate more effectively on the visceral register of experience, and (b) readily deploy fake news as part of a broader Big Lie strategy intended to spread through social media.

The impulsive actions of the collective nonconscious should not, however, be equated with utter thoughtlessness. Deep nonconscious entanglement might not possess cognitive mentality, but it has a mentality of sorts. These collective impulsive acts have, we might say, an impersonal *mind of their own*; the study of which requires an understanding of collective experiences that exist beyond phenomenological concepts of individual consciousness and judgement. Herein, Patricia Clough's original concept of the *user unconscious*, which preceded the technological nonconscious by several years, comes into play. Clough considers the user experience as a *more-than-human* experience that collapses the cognitive I into a 'cloud of digital traces'.[28] In this collective context, the 'user' does not constitute a phenomenological consciousness of the network, but instead becomes what Clough, following Wendy Chun and Sue Grand, refers to the YOU or Thing-Self. As Clough puts it:

> [C]omputational technologies may well be eliciting the human user's thing-self, giving shape to what I am calling the user unconscious in order to point to the activity of the unconscious in relationship to the collapse into the YOU, of the I and the cloud of digital traces, including the data of a worldly sensibility. These, no matter how disavowed, are becoming an intimate part of the I, evoking a thing-self that opens the unconscious both to liveliness of other-than-human actants and to the reformulation of embodiment in the YOU.[29]

That is to say, collective impulses are not simply *cognitively known* by the phenomenological I nor are they examples of a *knowing* collective surplus or intelligence. This is a felt experience which is, in contrast, attributed variously by Clough to this worldly sensibility; the YOU or thing-self. In short, this more-than-human mode of collective nonconscious equates to Clough's use of the term *Autoaffection*; referring to an experience that *experiences* itself; what we might also call the *subjectless* experience of experience. This deep, immanent and nonconscious entanglement is a condition I will similarly refer to as *somnambulistic*.

The Shock Event as Method

In the immediacy of the toxic post-truth present, the collective nonconscious takes on significant political relevance here, since as Clough contends, the manifestation of its more-than-human relations on social media played a considerable role in making the 'Trump presidency possible and continue[s] to inform its affective tone'.[30] As follows, the principal tactic deployed by Trump is a mode of aspirational fascism, which uses social media to emit *shock events*, 'creat[ing] pegs ... in the visceral register of anger' felt by the predominantly white rage of his constituency.[31] Trump on Twitter is, like this, always intended to be disruptive; to deliver a shock. However, most shock events are not simply caused by Trump. As William E. Connolly makes explicit: 'Trump is apt to support Lies by taking advantage of [an existing] shocking event.'[32] As I will go on to argue in Chapter 2, we must not misconstrue Trump on Twitter as an example of a transcendent charismatic leader, commandeering the airways of social media. Following Tarde's microsociology, Trump is not regarded as a personification that is collectively born on the macrolevel of society.[33] On the contrary, his tweets and Facebook posts operate as simple substances, which can resonate and spread like one of Leibniz's monads at a microlevel of social interaction. The resonating influence of these shocks propagate through the connectivities afforded by social media, increasing the intensity of experience of the Trumpian aesthetic fact. It is arguably the shock of these aesthetic facts that help to distract and redirect the raw resentments of the Trump constituency away from the realities of post-2008 neoliberal market failure towards fictionings of convenient targets (e.g. see figure 3 and fictional accounts of crowds of Muslims cheering during 9/11). It is, as such, the repetition of Trump's (and other populists) Big Lies, which are uncritically mimicked and spread by social media technologies, undermining democratic cultures that have hitherto embraced cultural multiplicity.

In the discussion that follows I have developed on the shock event as a kind of methodological tool for approaching fake news as it is experienced logically and aesthetically. This choice of method is informed, in part, by compelling evidence that many hoaxers take advantage of a variety of shock events, since millions of users will be searching the web for information about a mass shooting or natural disaster, for example, when there is a void of factual information.[34] The emergence of an information vacuum thus provides the perfect environment for search engine optimization (SEO) and weaponization.

The methodological choice is further informed by the comparable importance given to the shock event in new materialist affect studies. This is because new materialists similarly endeavour to grapple with the ways in which shocks influence the felt experiences of the nonconscious and prompt impulsive acts to occur. Below, for example, Brian Massumi describes how the immediacy of the shockwaves emitted by a fearsome event are channelled through the nonconscious before feeding into conscious decisions.

Before you can even consciously recognize what you're afraid of, or even feel that it is yourself that is the subject of the feeling, you are catapulted into a feeling of the frightfulness of the situation ... it only dawns on you in the next instant ... what you should do about it.[35]

In Jersey City, within hours of two jetliners' plowing into the World Trade Center, law enforcement authorities detained and questioned a number of people who were allegedly seen celebrating the attacks and holding tailgate-style parties on rooftops while they watched the devastation on the other side of the river.

Donald J. Trump ✓
@realDonaldTrump
Follow

Via @washingtonpost 9/18/01. I want an apology! Many people have tweeted that I am right! wapo.st/1R1siFz

2:02 PM - 23 Nov 2015

↩ ⟲ 3,009 ♥ 4,906

Figure 3 Trump's tweet supporting rumours that large numbers of Muslims were seen celebrating in New Jersey during 9/11.

By referring to a specific mass shooting event in the US, my intention is to map out ways in which substantial shock events are used to exploit logical inconsistencies in information processing. As Massumi argues, the resonation of fear following an event produces an 'anticipatory reality' of a future event.[36] This pre-emptive reality is 'nonexistent', but nonetheless looms large as the 'affective fact of the matter'.[37] Moreover, the shock event produces vacuums that render computer–brain relations vulnerable to sensory manipulation. These are, of course, extreme and catastrophic events. They evidence, as such, a higher gauge of intensive experience. But it is important to note, as Massumi contends, the shock event 'doesn't have to be drama'.[38] *Microshocks* can similarly produce significant interruptions that can pass by imperceptibly, yet provoke nonconscious impulses. The point to grasp here is that these shocks operate on an aesthetic register of the event, measured by the intensity of experience.

Another aim of this method is to trace empirically the shock event's resonations from the ground level upwards, so to speak. Which is to say, we start with the visceral registers in which aesthetics facts are first encountered before they eventually enter more refined thinking. Along these lines, then, the method follows the speculative mimetic trajectory of an unfolding shock event. It starts with the initial panic sparked by the event itself and the ensuing social media resonations of rumours that open the potential for conspiracies and the eventual parasitical weaponizations and fictionings of the event.

By following the shock event the discussion also aims to show how the persistent speculative potential seems to be perpetuated by secondary logical inconsistencies apparent in the processing of information by computers and brains. This is, in part, accorded to a tendency for information machines to simply mimic information without tacitly understanding the potential for fictioning. Following Whitehead, what defines these inconsistencies should not be regarded as a purely logical problem. On the contrary, inconsistencies are part of two extreme poles of the same dilemma of experience; one logical, and concerned with limits of finite mentality and closed computation, and the other, an aesthetic matter of perception that can only partially penetrate the infinite possibilities of the event.[39]

This broader understanding of immanent inconsistency (aesthetic as well as logical) reveals how the algorithmic distinction made between true and false statements cannot function properly when there is an 'absence of verified information'[40] relating to the shock event. So, when, for example, a mass shooting occurs, and claims to truth cannot be absolutely substantiated, the ensuing indistinct status of fact produces a data void that can be strategically filled with (or weaponized by) politically motivated fictionings. We might say that the optimization of fake news permits a hoaxer to effectively piggyback the speculative rumours of an aesthetic fact. This helps to set the affective tone and modulation of communication, so that it might become more contagious.

Vegas!

At 10.05 pm on the evening of 1 October 2017 a retired high stakes gambler, apparently on a losing streak, fired more than 1,100 rounds from the elevated window of his hotel suite overlooking a large crowd at a music festival. He killed 58 people and wounded over 800 others. The Vegas shooting is the worst mass shooting in modern US history, to date. Nonetheless, the shock event itself was relatively shortlived. An hour after the mass carnage began the lone gunman was found dead in his room from self-inflicted gunshot wounds. Aside from much post-event conjecture concerning his character, including rumours about gambling debts, links to an infamous bank-robber father, and suggestions that he might have had a bipolar and/or a germophobic condition, the perpetrator had no known motive for the attack. Certainly, although firm truths eventually emerged about the Vegas shooting, the concluding investigation made the depressing point that:

> What we have been able to answer are the questions of who, what, when, where and how ... what we have not been able to definitively answer is why [the perpetrator] committed this act.[41]

The point of drawing attention to this appalling event, and others like it, is not to, however, debate *the why* of the inexplicable mass shooting phenomena. As gruesome as these events are, my specific intention at this point is to focus on what kind of communications occur following a shock event. At this moment, there is not only an absence of motive, but also a more general lack of information leading to uncertainty about what just happened. Conceptually, then, I want to consider how a residual *information vacuum* becomes filled with visceral, panic-fuelled rumours; how that is, in the fleeting moments of the event itself, the resonating vectors of police radio communications and social media respond to the shock, opening up the potential for conspiracies and exploitative fake news strategies. The Vegas shooting only lasted for just over an hour, but rumours about the location of the suspected perpetuator (or perpetuators) began to spread rapidly through social media networks just moments after the gunman had opened fire.

Significantly, it seems that the rumours, which spread in the earliest moments of the event, were not intentional fictionings. Rumours spin out from collective experiences on the ground. They try to make sense of what just happened in the absence of information. Recordings of police communications during the event, for example, evidence how confusion on the ground about the direction of gunfire sparked understandable levels of panic to spread through the crowd. In these recordings, made public after the event, officers are heard shouting 'we have two scenes! We have an active shooter. We have an active shooter inside the fairground!'[42] This initial misperception of the event led to rumours and speculation about a possible second or even a third shooter rapidly spreading on social media.

Despite efforts made by the authorities to take control of the communication channels after the event by retrospectively stating that there was no information or evidence to support theories concerning more than one assailant, rumours continued to spread on social media about other shooters spotted in several nearby Vegas hotels. Videos posted on Facebook from visibly panicked hotel guests, evidently concerned for their safety during and after the attack, added more impetus to these rumours.

Hoaxes, Trolls and *The Daily Mail*

The spiralling propensity towards panic and rumour opens up the potential for conspiracists and hoaxers to strategically piggyback the intensive experiences of the aesthetic fact. These intensive experiences are provided with some faint visual traces by post-event fact-checkers who try to locate the moment at which fictioning begins to appear in the information vacuum, pushing political agendas to the top of search engine indices.[43] For example, in the wake of the Vegas shooting, a fake antifa (anti-fascist) Facebook group page set up in Melbourne, Australia was implicated in a 'coordinated campaign to create fake accounts in an attempt to troll and discredit anti-fascist activists'.[44] The fake group page erroneously claiming responsibility for the massacre was attributable to the antifascist movement and a particular branch member based in Vegas (see figure 4).

Figure 4 Screenshot of the fake Melbourne Antifa as it appears on the Snopes website.
Source: https://www.snopes.com/fact-check/did-melbourne-antifa-claim-responsibility-for-the-vegas-massacre/

The group had already been identified as a fake account as early as 9 June 2017 (nearly four months before the shooting and still available on the platform today). As this post on the authenticated Melbourne Antifascist Action Group Facebook page puts it:

> Journalists occasionally contact this page looking for answers and leave dissatisfied to rake their muck from danker sources, like the very-obviously fake and thoroughly debunked 'Melbourne Antifa' Facebook page ... A note to journos, if any of you read our posts in the gaps between flare-ups in the news cycle: MELBOURNE ANTIFA IS FAKE. It is run as a honeypot to catch leftists and skew the media image of antifascism from an alt-right perspective. They're trolls, and you've been got.[45]

The Vegas shooting provided the perfect opportunity for these alt-right trolls to fill up the information vacuum with Big Lies. These lies blended in with the anticipated barrage of emotionally loaded posts contesting the politics of gun control in the US that inevitably follow mass shootings. This point marks a 'disturbing and relatively new phenomenon' on social media, wherein victims of the shootings are often confronted by trolls, energized by conspiracy theories and hoaxes, arguing that these events never happened. As BBC journalist Colin Bell puts it:

> Among keyboard mourning and 280-character fury, a small but determined minority spring up in the wake of mass shootings to insist that events were staged – concocting monstrously complex tales involving 'crisis actors', the 'deep state' and accusations that attacks are 'false flag' murders being used, for example, as a pretext to institute gun control reforms.[46]

The fake Melbourne Antifa post is a salient example of a hoax that has visibly spread through the media ecology from a Facebook post, via search engine indices, to national media. The Antifa hoax eventually surfaced as an apparently *credible* news source for a report in the mass circulation newspaper, *The Daily Mail*. On 3 October, the Australian online version of the right-wing newspaper used it to erroneously highlight what it claimed to be the 'Left-wing extremist group [Antifa's] support for the dead 64-year-old [Vegas] gunman'.[47] Significantly, the paper has never retracted this story or admitted to it being a fiction.

A SEO Guide to Weaponizing the Data Void

The strategic spreading of a political fictioning machine following a shock event, requires some specific SEO skills. To be sure, a plausible explanation of the logical inconsistencies that enable fake news strategies to thrive is partly captured in Golebiewski and boyd's concept of the search engine *data void*.[48] In order to grasp this concept fully it is useful to understand a few search engine basics concerning how a breaking news event is processed by algorithms. In a nutshell, search engines assemble an index of links to web content. They do this by deploying automated bots and spider programs that *crawl* the web in search of data and metadata relating to content found on websites, links, images and videos. More recently, the inclusion of social media posts in search engines indices means that they have become a key tactic of SEO strategies intended to make certain terms climb search engine rankings. Search engines also use proprietary algorithms that rank links in their index according to certain criteria, such as rewarding compelling content or penalizing low-quality content. There are also varying degrees of personalized search results yielded through machine learning technologies, which work on historical patterns in data to predict future patterns of searching behaviour.

When searching for an event that is associated with lots of relevant links to content, the search will yield a greater number of results. As follows, if one searches for a well-known event, like the Cannes Film Festival, for instance, there will clearly be a lot of information available. From about 132,000,000 search returns on Google, there are links to official and unofficial websites, Wikipedia pages, news stories, images, video, interviews, reviews, critiques, controversies, show business rumours, conspiracies, and so on. This would generally be regarded as *high-quality* information because although the search would yield good and bad, true, half-true and false information, the more reliable information will rise to the top of the index as a result of algorithms tending to rank established news sources higher than individual unsubstantiated blogs, for example.

When, in contrast, an event searched for has very little online information available, the links in the index are clearly low and search returns are sparse. It is this scarcity of information that causes a data void, defined by Golebiewski and boyd as a phenomenon that occurs 'when search engines have little natural content to return for a particular [search] query'.[49] For example, if a user searches for an obscure term, like the geographic location in which a mass shooting has occurred, little data content will be available and the search will therefore produce low-quality results. Although, a data void is very rarely empty since a search may find a few images, a map, weather forecasts or real-estate values for the area, a search that yields 'little high-quality content for the search engine to return' is 'more likely to return low quality and problematic content'.[50]

The *problem* herein lies in the capacity for those looking to manipulate information to leverage the content that search engines gather from the web in order to fill data voids with fake news, misinformation and hate speech. These dark and dubious SEO strategies can also add terms to auto-suggestions that appear in the search engine text box making associations between the term searched and others that might persuade a user to visit a page to which they would not normally be exposed. The optimization of terms used on social media and blog posts can be, like this, used to *weaponize* data voids in search engine queries. This was the case when the fake Antifa Facebook account made reference to the shock event in Vegas.

Golebiewski and boyd refer to two further US mass shootings as examples of how a deficit of information can open up opportunities for strategically positioned fake news. It is significant to note how both of these shock events impact on personal and impersonal impulses related to informational and aesthetic registers of experience. On one hand, then, individuals who encounter these terms are often tempted to follow curiously the traces of data down what logicians have called algorithmic 'rabbit holes' to voids filled with white supremacist hate, misinformation and eventual radicalization.[51] On an individual level, then, the encounter with these fictionings, via a search engine, appears to close down the potential for hesitative critical reflexivity. The fictioning machine opens up possibilities for mobilizing affecting impulses, perhaps by making some reference to prior prejudices, but also creating new lures for discriminations to emerge. For example, in a manifesto found after the shooting at the Emanuel African Methodist Episcopal Church in Charleston, South Carolina in 2015, the perpetrator describes his moment of radicalization brought about by an online encounter with Wikipedia and a Google search.

> The event that truly awakened me was the Trayvon Martin case. I read the Wikipedia article and right away I was unable to understand what the big deal was. It was obvious that Zimmerman was in the right. But more importantly this prompted me to type in the words 'black on white crime' into Google, and I have never been the same since that day. The first website I came to was the Council of Conservative Citizens. There were pages upon pages of these brutal black on white murders. I was in disbelief. At this moment I realized that something was very wrong. How could the news be blowing up the Trayvon Martin case while hundreds of these black on white murders got ignored?[52]

Before the massacre, unpopular search terms like 'black on white crimes' were generally used by white supremacist communities making for low-quality search results that would feature in a search index. This contested term could therefore be weaponized and strategically positioned so that 'curious people' could 'stumble upon' it. Of course, after the shooting occurs, the news media quickly begins to fill up the data void with more diverse contexts, including journalistic coverage, debates and critiques of the gunman's manifesto, which helps critically to neutralize the white supremacist use of the term. This increase in high-quality data does not, however, halt the further weaponization of such terms aimed at vulnerable individuals. After the data void produced by the black on white crimes term was filled up, white nationalist groups simply began to exploit 'a new data void' by shifting their terminology to 'white victims of crimes by blacks' potentially encouraging others to go down another rabbit hole of race hatred.[53]

On the other hand, though, shock events work on collective impulses. They produce, as such, a maelstrom of multiple searches of unverified accounts and misinformation. In this context, then, the breaking news of a mass shooting in Sutherland Springs, Texas, on 4 November 2017 produced another exploitable data void. This nondescript town in Texas did not attract any notable search engine queries before the shooting, and thus yielded very low-quality results. Even today, most of the search results returned only pertain to the shooting that happened there. Yet, soon after news of the event began to spread, thousands of 'people turned to search engines to understand what was happening'. As a result, intensive search queries for Sutherland Springs spiked, providing the opportunity for adversarial actors to take advantage of the data void. As Golebiewski and boyd put it:

> [These adversarial actors] turned to Twitter and Reddit in an effort to associate both the town and, shortly after, the name of the shooter with the term 'Antifa'. They knew that there was very little high-quality content about either, which meant that it would not be hard to fill the data void and get the algorithm to rank their content highly in the first hours.[54]

The consequences of filling the data void with these associations to Antifa are numerous. Firstly, it *injects* the word into the search engine's auto-suggestion text field, supposedly encouraging other individuals to go down further *rabbit holes* leading to conspiracy theory. It also challenges journalists to investigate, fact check and invalidate the links between Antifa and the Sutherland Springs shooting. However, endeavours in the media to (a) provide coverage of fake news stories, and (b) debunk them, do not necessarily lead to the elixir of truth. The mainstream media coverage can itself feed into and extend the conspiracies related to the event. 'In a world of data voids', Golebiewski and boyd add, 'even headlines intended to negate rumors can help spread them'.[55] There is, from tip to tail, a volatility to the user experience of what is and what is not fake; all the way through the media ecology, from the initial panic on the ground posted on Facebook, all the way to the political persuasions and fictionings of *The Daily Mail*.

The sharing of an aesthetic fact on social media occurs in a feely milieu in which information can become more or less truthful, depending on how many times it is liked. This is a collective experience of the shock event, widely shared on a visceral sensory register, cultivated and propagated by a social media platform's viral architecture. This is a moment when potentially millions of users join in the event flow of a breaking news story, searching for more information, clicking on emojis, sharing, posting, messaging; collectively and spontaneously taking part in passing on the aesthetic fact that emerges from the shock. Herein, the intensifying spread of panics, rumour and conspiracy can be linked to a creative potential that ceaselessly repeats and differentiates. Fake news is not, as follows, a production of a post-truth that has become detached from reality, or a systematic failure to filter true or false information. On the contrary, political fictioning of this kind is a strategic production that exploits an excess of reality that is open to novelty and change.

By placing a considerable emphasis on the impulsive overspills of the sensory registers of social media I am suggesting that it is the event in itself that should become the focal point of a broader approach to the fake news problem. As SEO specialists know all too well, 'as soon as an event happens, everything is new ... There's no system for the algorithm to filter out truth and reality'.[56] Herein the virality of fake news appears to trigger a creative potential that steers collective choices and impulsive acts that become disengaged from individual cognitive processes. Along these lines, we do not simply find a confused personal logic or an essential version of the truth hidden under a simulacrum of fake news. Instead, we find the potential of the event itself; its aesthetic fact, which can snowball from the panic, uncertainty and rumour on the ground to spiralling excesses of conspiracy, ripe for potential fictioning.

The Fake Equation

> There is no turning back ... You take the blue pill: the story ends, you wake up in your bed and believe whatever you want to believe. You take

> the red pill: you stay in Wonderland and I show you how deep the rabbit hole goes.[57]
>
> I think what the postmodernists did was truly evil. They are responsible for the intellectual fad that made it respectable to be cynical about truth and facts. You'd have people going around saying: 'Well, you're part of that crowd who still believe in facts.'[58]

I will return to this significant note of caution in more detail later on in this chapter, and elsewhere in the book, but for now a hasty word on some methodological constraints. It is important not to misconstrue this scaling up from the initial resonations of a shock event on the ground to a fabricated event as some kind of validation of a recent revival of postmodernism. *Shock Events do not Mask Reality!* The reader should not mistake the shock event for the artifice in a postmodernist account of the post-truth thesis. The shock event does not mark a point of no return for fact. *Truth has not disappeared down a virtual reality rabbit hole!* The judgements that follow a shock event are nothing like the choices between blue or red pills offered by the character Morpheus in the postmodern classic, *The Matrix* (see above quote).[59] The method developed here is not a last chance for reality!

Like postmodernists, some logicians have similarly pointed to various Carollesque choices between blue and red pills to explain fake news. However, we will follow Connolly who warns of the dangers of specious representational judgements made between reality and hyperreality.[60] We need to beware of similar claims made by the aspirational fascist peddlers of post-truth, that truth, in itself, has lost its object. On the contrary, we know that the invasion of Iraq occurred despite *evidence* that there were *no* weapons of mass destruction. Similarly, today, Trump calls C02 induced climate change a Chinese Hoax, ignoring ample *evidence* to prove that human-made climate change is certainly *no* hoax. Nonetheless, any frustrations we might have with the construction of postmodern truth should not lead us to a positivistic conclusion.

It is certainly important not to confuse Whitehead's aesthetic fact with contrasting postmodern or positivist accounts of fake news. On one hand, then, we need to note that there has been a small, but notable revival of postmodernism as a way to understand the so-called post-truth thesis. On the other hand, Daniel Dennett's positivistic distain for the post-truth thesis (see above quote) takes aim at the considerable role it seems to have played in justifying the political madness that is Trump.

At first glance, Dennett would appear to be making a reasonably valid point here. In the UK, for example, after being confronted with evidence-based economic arguments against EU withdrawal, the Tory politician and leading Brexiteer, Michael Gove, notoriously announced that 'people in this country have had enough of experts'.[61] But is this kind of populist politicking an expression of post-truth or just a cynical lie?

In an article for *The Washington Post*, US academic Aaron Hanlon responds directly to Dennett's charge.[62] Following Jean Baudrillard's renowned thesis that the Gulf War never took place, Hanlon argues that we need to grasp that postmodernist relativism has not caused the current post-truth Trumpian dystopia, as positivists like Dennett contend. On the contrary, Hanlon argues, postmodernism provides the conceptual tools for us to understand the cynicism expressed towards expert judgements. 'It's easy to scoff at ... [the] postmodernist denial of an objective truth', he contends, but 'our impressions' of Trump have been 'warped by media framing and agitprop'.[63] Which is to say, the postmodernists have provided us with a 'framework to understand precisely how falsehood can masquerade as truth'.[64] Accordingly, the postmodern simulacrum, assumed to be circulated via the media, secretes objective truth (or reality) under a pile of copies or *re*presentations that are endlessly repeated: Original / copy / copy / copy / copy / copy ... *ad infinitum*.

What is arguably at stake here is the question of how we define judgements. To begin with, we can usefully contrast Hanlon's renewed interest in postmodernism with Dennett's in terms of what kind of judgements are being made. On one hand, the positivists make a true / false judgement based on the evidence at hand. Their major premise in this regard is that *the Observable Fact must not be clouded by Metaphysical Judgements!* On the other hand, the postmodernists claim that judgements can become clouded by the *re*presentation of evidence. Objective truth has, they argue, imploded, as such, under the weight of so much representational duplication. This is why the Gulf War never happened. Not because it didn't actually happen, *in reality*, but since it has been over *re*presented and thus become a perceptual hyperreality.

The problem with this renewal of the positivist/postmodernist spat over what constitutes a judgement is that it inevitably leads us to a theoretical impasse. Certainly, Dennett (along with Deb Roy) had previously argued that the information age would introduce a new age of transparency. Which is to say, more public access to data would make it very difficult for news organizations and political analysts who spin the news selectively to survive in the face of widespread evidence.[65] However, the promise of abundant information seems to have given way to a darker age of uncertainty wherein judgements are difficult to validate among so much misinformation and fabrication.

How do we escape the impasse between hyperreality and the illusory stable certainties of objective truth? As a starting point, we can better approach the status of judgements by referring to what Connolly calls the 'fake equation' between positivism, postmodernism and so-called post-truth.[66] Considered as part of a broader *Big Lie Scenario*, fake news is found to be endemic to a much older fascist strategy that predates the postmodernists by several decades.[67] Fascists assert Big Lies dogmatically to:

> Undermine evidenced-based claims, create false equivalences, sow confusion, divert attention, promote acceptance of authoritarian rule, and legitimize a shock wave politics of rapid shifts.[68]

This is an understanding of how judgements are formed as markedly different from the 'presumptive generosity' of the postmodernists, who, Connolly argues, 'typically probe alternative interpretations to open a plurality of views for wider consideration'.[69] The postmodern simulacrum is, it seems, all about the implosion of objective truth, but debatably, postmodernists still have a commitment to an original or objective truth; even if it is destroyed in the collapsing of truth itself. Secondly, though, this is a mode of generosity that Dennett's brand of brutal positivism would of course hold in utter contempt. *Facts are facts!* However, as Connolly contends, positivism's lack of generosity towards postmodernism seems to lead it to speciously confuse a lack of evidence with the reduction of objective truth to subjective opinion.[70] Herein, the positivist misses the point that the emergence of new theories and observations can lead to new objective facts. Following Connolly, then, this chapter judges what the object of truth is according to a higher level of complexity based on Whitehead's speculative process philosophy. This philosophy is not simply more refined or discerning of what is true and false, but more importantly considers the proposition of *potentialities* posed by the shock event (or the jolt of an actual occasion) as key to understanding how the virtuality of truth and falsity becomes actualized.

Fact is More Than Itself

What is required is neither a positivist nor postmodernist understanding of judgement. Following an alternative line of flight that starts with the speculative philosophy of Whitehead and leads to Gilles Deleuze, we find that some facts are more than themselves. As Connolly argues: 'Some facts are both real and simmer with potentialities to become other than they are.'[71] By way of an example he points to the genetic mutations of an unfolding embryo, which may conceal 'diverse potentialities of gestation'.[72] One mutation may find expression while others fail to resonate with the specificity of the unfolding embryo.

So, when shock events occur – when, as the SEO expert puts it, *everything is new* – objective truth is not hidden in hyper-representation or set in the concrete of finitude fact. Truth instead becomes a gestating, resonating potential; a fact that is felt as an *intensity of aesthetic experience* rather than a statement of brutal fact or utter fiction. This is where facts are 'more than themselves'.[73] Caught in the whirlpool of a rumour, for example, the distinction between truth and fictioning is not, in these moments of swirling gestation, wholly objective or without inconsistency. It is a virtual indistinction: 'a lived paradox where what are normally opposites coexist, coalesce, and connect'.[74] These are creative processes that endlessly repeat and differentiate. They are *more-than-fact; more-than-fiction!* They are *aesthetic facts*!

Connolly's counter-thesis fittingly draws on speculative philosophy to overcome the impasse of positivism and postmodernism. As he remarks, speculative philosophy retains a 'certain respect for factuality' and an 'appreciation of objectivity', but it does this with a critical eye towards the 'real creativity, and the role of speculation in thought'.[75] In this way, speculative analysis 'breaks simultaneously' with the positivist's 'resistance to metaphysical speculation' and the postmodernist's 'simple facticity'.[76] This is judgement uniquely experienced in the shockwaves of the event. More importantly though, this approach draws further attention to the role of shock events as key to understanding the pursuit of fake news, Big Lies, and mass manipulation by aspirational fascists. To be sure, Connolly identifies and compares the shock tactics of the Reichstag Fire and Trump's disruptive social media posts as part of an aligned strategy that leads to the 'rapid circulation of rumors ungrounded in evidence'.[77] Both Trump and the Nazis are endemic to aesthetic regimes of rumour that expose a population to continuous dissonance. Their use of aesthetic facts diverts attention away from key issues by utilizing the power of the rumour machine.

The Lure of the Aesthetic Fact

To expand on Connolly's position, we need to restate and resolve the Whiteheadian distinction made at the beginning of this chapter between

(a) *propositions of logical experience based on brutal judgements of finite fact*, and (b) *the potential for infinite propositions and aesthetic facts to spin out of the temporal movements of shock events*. The former judgements are understood as a tendency of positivist logicians to rely on the unity of finite statements applied to a proposition, and considered, in this opening chapter, as the assumed exactness of a secondary *logical experience*. In the latter, the proposition of indeterminacy expressed by the shock event is understood as a primary mode of *aesthetic experience*; measured not by distinguishing between what is true and what is false, but instead by feeling the intensities of the experience. Instead of turning to logical experiences as the only way to determine the inconsistencies of judgements regarding rumour, conspiracy and fake news, for example, this chapter has drawn further attention to the indeterminacy of propositions registered as aesthetic facts.

If the above is still regarded as a somewhat perplexing conclusion then the reader will be glad to have discovered that Whitehead helpfully draws on our experience of imaginative literature to show how aesthetic facts differ from logical facts. This is nicely captured, as such, in his concept of *aesthetic delight*. Which is to say, how the aesthetic experience of the propositions of a fictioning machine challenge the logician's recourse to brutal finite true/false statements. Certainly, Whitehead intensely disliked positivists, and used his reference to Shakespeare's play to lament how 'theories, under their name of "propositions" [have unfortunately been] handed over to logicians... who have "countenanced the doctrine that their one function is to be judged as to their truth or falsehood"'.[78] This doctrine would, nevertheless, become instantly confounded by its encounter with an aesthetic fact, Whitehead argues, since fictioning machines cannot be judged according to such *narrow* or *absurd* propositions.

What is consequently of importance to Whitehead is not the brutal existence of finite fact, but the felt intensity of experience provoked by the event and the role it plays in the *luring of feeling*. This mention of a lure is highly significant to the deep entanglements of the collective nonconscious discussed above. Certainly, if we were to consider computers in isolation, we would find machines that make judgements about the shock event based on the existence of brutal fact. Computers are positivistic machines after all, designed by logicians to learn explicit instructions and mimic them. However, a shock event, and the ensuing aesthetic facts that spread through panic and rumour, will soon confound the judgements of the automated fact-checker or the machine learning algorithm. The aesthetic fact will always fill the void and open up the potential for the kind of political madness that strategically dismisses objective reality for its own ends. Grasped as deeply entangled, brains, bodies and computers do not coincide in a world of brutal fact or over representation. Deep entanglement does not simply decide if news is true or false; it *feels* the intensity of the experience of aesthetic facts!

This notion of the luring of feeling clearly implicates individual attentional, cognitive processes, but the deep entanglement of the collective nonconscious does not have a cognitive consciousness. *It is impersonal.* The lure of experience does not intentionally become orientated towards the shock event as it occurs. On the contrary, the felt intensity of the shock event (the feeling of its *importance*) becomes a collective impulse that precedes cognition and lures feelings towards the event. In this sense, speculative philosophy does more than simply overcome the impasse produced by judgements that are discerned by brutal fact or representation. In contrast, it grasps how the deep entanglement of a collective nonconscious makes judgements based on just how important an event is according to feeling *the intensity of experience*.[79] Whitehead asks us to therefore judge the increases or decreases of the experience of an event, according to what he refers to as this lure of feeling.[80] It is this lure of the event that captures or clasps the intensity of feeling.

Importantly, then, the event imposes, or draws in, feelings towards its encounter. Feelings are not simply of the anthropological or animal order of experience, but, as the next chapter will contend, they are considered cosmological forces.[81] These are the forces of autoaffection: that is to say, the process by which experience *experiences* itself. Along these lines, the 'lure to feeling' is grasped by Clough through a mode of experiencing 'beyond human consciousness, perception, and cognition'. This is a speculative interest in the realness of experience beyond the 'presumption of a primordial rapport between humans and world', and 'beyond human knowing'.

Before moving on to discuss how the lure of feeling can be further understood as somnambulistic, it is important to point out that the lure itself is *not*, as one might expect, considered by Whitehead to be a mode of trickery.[82] As Didier Debaise argues:

> In Whitehead's vocabulary, a lure certainly does not carry the idea of either an artifice designed to fool someone, or an illusion that masks reality ... the term is resolutely neutral: a lure entices someone, produces a diversion ... modifies the course of an event ... there is no criticism ... It simply is a matter of seeing propositions as involving *capture* and *grasping*.[83]

In other words, in the context of this discussion, the lure is not some tempting offer to follow a rabbit down a hole. It is not the lure of the felt experience of fake news that *fools* the experient. If we were to consider fake news as an artifice designed to fool someone, or indeed, an illusion that masks reality, we would surely fall back into the impasse of the post-truth thesis. On the contrary, my argument here is that the trickery deployed by SEO, fake news and Big Lie strategies is located in the error we make if we confuse logical experience with being a command post in the movement of propositional events. If there is any manipulation, then this is perhaps because the SEO expert can position an aesthetic fact in the diversion the lure produces when there is no information? But there is no command post in the whirlpool contagions of a shock event. Certainly, in Whiteheadian terms the aesthetic fact experienced in the lure of the propositional event (with all its possibilities) eclipses true and false judgements.[84] It is the lure of this felt experience that modifies the intensification of the experiences and resonating possibilities of the event itself. The luring of felt experiences is, in part, how an organism makes sense of complex potentialities proposed to her in the relentless, infinite process in which events are encountered. As Whitehead puts it:

> We are in the present; the present is always shifting; it is derived from the past; it is shaping the future; it is passing into the future. *This is process.*[85]

This process; the passage of events, is the only 'inexorable fact of the universe'.[86] If our experience of this passing into the future is not a command post, then it is perhaps, as Isabelle Stengers argues, a mere foothold in the event.[87] It is, as such, in the felt experiences of the resonating possibilities of the event where logical judgements are confounded and made prone to potential deception.

Conclusion

This chapter has approached the problem of fake news (and broader contested post-truth thesis) by way of two extreme, yet associated, poles of experience: *logical* and *aesthetic*.[88] Both poles having been grasped through an important distinction made between higher level and logical abstractions of truth and falsity, on the one hand, and nonconscious experiences of events, experienced aesthetically, on the other. The first logical mode of experience is established in the computational processing of information and the small slice of conscious cognitive judgements that discern truth and falsity from what are perceived of as finite facts. The second *aesthetic experience* of shock events (of varying intensity) is said to lure feelings towards infinite possibilities based on what Whitehead calls *aesthetic fact*. Herein, we find extra-logical experiences of panic and rumour that do not conform to judgements on finite truth or falsity, but are instead experienced in the proposition of an event. In the deep entanglements of the collective nonconscious, such feelings can become impulses and actions that entirely evade conscious thought, or somewhat further down the experiential chain, they can feed into judgements.

2
On the Viral Spectra of Somnambulism

This second chapter will expand on the spectra of experience introduced in the previous discussion by way of introducing the conceptual persona of the somnambulist. It begins by returning to some old sociological spats, generally defined by their divergent approach to collectivity, which is, on one hand, regarded as an awakened consciousness and, on the other, the product of the nonconscious. These older theories serve as a basis for a further critique of positivistic accounts of social media contagion and lay some of the groundwork for the development of a new materialist theory of somnambulistic user experience.

Asleep on the Spectra

Figure 5 Mikey B. Georgeson's 'fictioning machine' performance of the Collective Nonconscious at the SSASS Animations and Provocations Summer School, Millersville University, Lancaster PA, USA, August 2019. Photo by the author.

'Step right up. Now showing for the first time: Cesare, the somnambulist.'[1]

He has returned. The aesthetic figure of Dr Caligari's hypnotized sleepwalker is back among us.

'Cesare knows every secret. Cesare knows the past and can see into the future. Come up and test him for yourselves.'[2]

His predictions now loom ever large in the events of the new millennium. As Siegfried Kracauer argued back in 1947, the fairground somnambulist in Robert Wiene's 1920 Expressionist film is purposefully positioned in the plot as a presentiment of the future tyranny in 1930s Germany.[3] Dr Caligari is indeed the tyrant, and Cesare, the cannon fodder, 'drilled to kill and to be killed'.[4]

So, it is once again, through the fictioning of Georgeson's resuscitated somnambulist (see figure 5), that a foreboding intuition is reiterated concerning an increasingly dark refrain of collective mimesis, imminent in the future. *'We are half-wake ...'* The limited bandwidth of our discursive attention narrows and 'sink[s] back into temporary obliviousness, sleeping or stunned'.[5]

These mimicking sleepwalkers crop up everywhere. We see crowds of present-day somnambulists; pre-programmed smartphone zombies, walking off the proverbial cliff edge, one-by-one into the abyss of a new wave of despotism. To be sure, as fake news and misinformation manipulate the global political scene, we are once more sleepwalking towards a populist, anti-democratic future.[6] Even George Soros points to Europe's recent slide towards self-destructive nationalism as evidence of the continent's 'sleepwalk' into political and economic oblivion.[7]

Anxieties surrounding artificial intelligence have similarly attracted a somnambulism thematic. Scientists are warning us that the human race is sleepwalking into an AI future in which billions of machines and computers will do all the thinking![8] AI might already be, it seems, 'setting the political agenda through social media disinformation campaigns and skewing election results'.[9]

Worse! *much worse than all this!* The entire planet is now 'sleepwalking into environmental catastrophe'.[10]

It surely is time for us *all* to *wake up*?

Without a doubt, the mere mention of the sleepwalker in the title of this chapter may well give the impression that users of social media are similarly in a state of acquiescent, mimetic reverie. Developing, as it does, Gabriel Tarde's original conceptual persona of the social somnambulist, perhaps the title might further imply that social media users, like their nineteenth-century crowd counterparts, need to wake up from their hypnotic daydream of collective mimesis. Well, although some of these facets of Tarde's conceptual persona are still highly pertinent, this is not exactly the proposition made in this chapter. Rather than positioning the sleepwalkers as the vacillating, easily led social subjects of crowd theory, these new conceptual personae are specifically mobilized as an expression of the contemporary collective nonconscious. That is to say, the focus is more precisely concerned with bringing up-to-date Tarde's microsociology, which positioned the social subject in the insensible, infinitesimal and indistinct thresholds between conscious and unconscious states; between deliberate volition and mechanical habit; between wakefulness and sleep.[1]

The chapter will draw on specific examples of the ever-present dark refrain of social media (see introduction), but the discussion begins with an earlier, yet enduring network image. Before the current perils of collective mimesis emerged, the trajectory of network culture seemed to be heading towards a more enlightened age of cognitive connectivity. Along these lines, the discussion starts with the origins of a concept of awakened collective conscious, arguing that it is a marker of how networks have been conventionally imagined as emerging affirmatively from the unconscious. My contention here is, nonetheless, critical of this roused cognitive image of the network since it has tended to lack more searching insights into collective experiences with technology that seem to dip *in and out* of conscious and nonconscious experiences. It misses, as such, the somnambulism of the deep entanglements we encountered in the previous chapter. But more precisely, following Tarde's sleepwalker, these entanglements are conceived of as occurring on an even broader spectra of collective experience. This is thicker spectra that moves in-between imperceptible thresholds of the collective nonconscious, mechanical habitual behaviours and fleeting moments of conscious reflection.[1] Indeed, this proposed expansion of the experiential bandwidth occupied by the sleepwalker purposefully challenges the distinction made between simply being *wide awake* or *fast asleep*, since such an experiential bipolarity has too many analytical limitations. A new conceptual persona of the sleepwalker is needed; a new materialist rendering of the somnambulist, which can capture user experiences ranging across a wider, more diverse and indistinct spectra of frequencies, experiences and brain–body rhythms.

The theoretical approach developed in this chapter is initially informed by earlier work drawing on a Tardean concept of the collective nonconscious. It is intended to mark out a considerable difference between early sociological methods. Certainly, unlike Emile Durkheim's insistence of an emergence of a higher collective consciousness, Tarde's nonconscious relations appear to be more susceptible to hypnotic processes of collective mimesis.[12] However, again, I want to stress how this current wave of social media somnambulism presents a far more complex spectra of experience. This contra-Durkheimian approach is not a continuance with a crowd theory that begins with rational individuals who become stupefied once they are immersed in the collective.[13] It is not simply a matter of making a distinction between rational or irrational states of mind or indeed consciousness or unconsciousness. As Georgeson's diagram in the previous chapter illustrates, the spectra of experience the sleepwalker occupies has multiple, complex and indistinct polarities.

On the somnambulist spectra of experience, we can compare and contrast the assumed credulity and docility of Tarde's somnambulist with contemporary network personae. For example, in Kurt Andersen's recent thesis,[14] a fantasist emerges from social media, which seems to have a comparable delusional collective experience to that of Tarde's sleepwalker who partakes in contagions of *false belief* spreading through a crowd. Andersen's Fantasists are similarly *believers in anything and everything* suggested to them on social media. However, the gullibility of the sleepwalker and the fantasist are not ultimately found to be entirely equivalent. What is significantly missing from *Fantasyland* is the social, economic and political fallout from the 2008 crash. Where indeed in *Fantasyland* is the visceral register of post-industrial experience that assembles the hate agenda of this current populist war on cultural multiplicity?

The chapter concludes by taking its lead from Tarde's rejection of the centrality of the apparent awakened state of the *psychological self*. This disavowal of the supremacy of the self-concept acts as a counter analytical marker of anthropological and phenomenological studies of subjective experience. This refusal to put human consciousness at the centre of our investigation serves as a spur for a nonphenomenological theory of experience. Along these lines, the discussion opens up a highly abstracted, and admittedly experimental philosophical discussion, inspired by a Whiteheadian approach, which adds to the spectral density with two ostensibly extreme, but continuously crisscrossed, poles of somnambulist experience: *somnolent* and *ambulant*. Herein, the manipulations of felt experiences on social media are not limited to anthropological perceptions or illogical fantasy, but are instead grasped through a broader new materialist understanding of a *more-than-human* user experience. Ultimately, we find, on the gamma ray end of the spectra, a nonhuman *subjectless subjectivity* seeking out immediate *self-enjoyment*.

From Global Brain to Dark Refrain

In sharp contrast to the persona of the sleepwalker, the image of the network has frequently been presented as a figurative global awakening of cognitive consciousness. To a great extent, the metaphorical image of what we might call the *global brain thesis* owes a debt to Tarde's scholarly nemesis, Durkheim. The Durkheimian concept of *collective consciousness* is a typical parts-to-whole relation in which a society emerges as a sum total from out of the *dynamic density* of societal interaction.[15] What emerges is a supervening higher collective consciousness that is supposed to transcend the individual. The influence of Durkheim's collective conscious can be subsequently traced to a raft of related theories, including collective intelligence, the wisdom of the crowd, and networks of cognitive surplus.

The media prototype of the global brain, nevertheless, belongs to Marshall McLuhan, not Durkheim. Borrowing extensively from Pierre Teilhard de Chardin's concept of the *noosphere* (a sphere of thought that encircles the Earth), McLuhan famously imagined media as an extension of the physical and psychical faculties of humanity into a compressed time–space. As follows, the wheel is a physical extension of the foot, the telescope is an extension of the eye etc. etc. In terms of the human psyche too, the media provides an extension of the central nervous system producing '*a technological brain for the world*'.[16] Like Durkheim then, McLuhan offers a collective awaking. Yet, significantly, as Adriana Braga points out, McLuhan's media extensions uniquely bring 'the unconscious level of the psyche to the surface where it could become conscious'.[17] Indeed, McLuhan argued back in 1969 that '[t]echnologies ... seem to be the pushing of the archetypal forms of the unconscious out into social consciousness'.[18] In short, this means that the image of the technological network is reckoned to impose itself pervasively on the unconscious human psyche by reworking its senses and thus awakening its capacity for collective consciousness.[19]

In its many post-McLuhan guises, this stirring of an individual unconscious psyche into collective consciousness often leads to more optimistic accounts of an awakened loftier and commanding collective brainpower. Various McLuhanesque global brains have followed that similarly look to describe emergent collective thought in the wake of the internet age. Most notably, Pierre Lévy's *Megamind* stands out as a theory of an emergent global *cognitive ecology* in which brains and computers come together to form a mostly affirmative collective intelligence.[20] The proposition of an enlightened age of media extension is indeed a persistent trope in descriptions of human–computer relations. More recently, we see its figure appearing in the feverish discourses surrounding the so-called cognitive city, wherein smart information exchanges are said to occur between networks of humans and nonhumans. This is the same figural image that appears to designate connected urban environments as nodes in a supervening global brain.[21] Along these lines, we might say that the cognitive image of the network has been mostly presented as a distributed nodal consciousness, which emerges globally, and transcendently, as a psychic command post.

However, in spite of this general theoretical thrust towards an imperious collective consciousness, sizeable conceptual cracks have recently appeared in the global brain thesis. The arrival of a dark refrain of social media has seen millions of users become embroiled in devious serpentine strategies intended to steer neurological experiences towards new modes of political unconsciousness. It would seem that user cognitions and behaviours have been nudged towards, and rendered increasingly vulnerable to a host of mass persuasions and datafied manipulations.

Cambridge Hypnotica

The theoretical shift from the assumed sanguinity of a McLuhanesque collective consciousness[22] to a darker refrain of nonconscious manipulations appears to figure writ large in the Cambridge Analytica scandal; specifically, the contested role the data analytics firm played in the shock Trump election in 2016. To begin with, much media attention (and hyperbole) has been focused on breaches of personal privacy, which occurred during the harvesting of personal data from Facebook accounts. To understand how this works, we need to focus on the four main stages that led to approximately 50 to 80 million US Facebook accounts being hijacked during Trump's campaign.[23] Firstly, approximately 32,000 US voters were selected as so-called *seeders*. This means they were paid a small fee ($2–5) to log in with their Facebook account and take part in a detailed personality test. Secondly, the app used for the test covertly collected data, such as likes, and other personal information, from a seeder's Facebook account. It was indeed this clandestine access to seeder accounts that opened up further access to millions of friends and vastly expanded the raw data trawl. Thirdly, then, the virality of the personality quiz app, written by the then Cambridge University based data scientist, Aleksandr Kogan, looked for psychological patterns by comparing results to the raw Facebook data. Finally, algorithms were used to combine the data harvested from Facebook with further data, such as voter records, in order to create 'a superior set of records' that could be used to target eleven key states in the election with 'highly personalized advertising based on their personality data'.[24]

The psychographic techniques used by Kogan's personality quiz app were based on the OCEAN model (openness to experience, conscientiousness, extraversion, agreeableness and neuroticism). For example, people who identified themselves as being loud and sociable would fit into a cluster of extrovert profiles and therefore linked to certain predictable behaviours and political persuasions. Significantly, these kinds of personality test can be traced back to the Psychometrics Centre at Cambridge University, which gained a lot of media attention in 2015 following the results of a self-reporting programme that used Facebook likes to judge a person's character.[25] It was claimed that by inputting 70 likes, the programme could produce a more accurate picture of a person's personality traits than a friend or room-mate. By inputting 150 likes, the programme outstripped a parent or sibling. When 300 likes were inputted the programme judged the character of the person better than a spouse. These claims, and others that followed, suggest that behavioural science could provide a powerful set of tools for social media mass persuasion.[26]

It would seem that these claims have informed a large part of the discursive formation regarding a darker side of social media that functions behind the scenes of the user experience. As follows, in his concluding comments to the UK's Department of Culture, Media and Sport (DCMS) committee on fake news, Cambridge Analytica whistle-blower, Christopher Wylie, expressed concern about how data processing practices were regulated by people unaware of the functionalities of backend analytics, relational databases and machine learning technologies.[27] It is this lack of awareness and invisibility of platform architectures that resulted, Wylie claims, in the absence of privacy protections users have from the malevolent intentions of agencies like Cambridge Analytica. Similarly, then, the wider threat posed to democracy by the scandal can be traced to an obfuscating engineering mind-set that purposefully deflects questions that have any negative regulatory or political implication for the social media business model. Facebook's Chief Technology Officer, Mike Schroepfer's failure to answer a series of probing questions at the DCMS hearings, for example, suggests that by providing an engineer to debate the threat social media poses to privacy and democracy, the platform were in effect circumventing responsibility for monitoring content.[28] This was arguably a tactic that kept the committee in the dark over Facebook's role in tracking users and collecting data. It also hid what Zuckerberg knew about developers selling data on to third parties and the many dark ads that appeared on the platform during the EU referendum in the UK in 2015.

These concerns about the invasiveness of digital psychoanalytics can be clearly seen in a civil suit filed against Cambridge Analytica in the US in 2018, which argues that psychographic methods work in the background to 'bypass individuals' cognitive defences by appealing directly to their emotions'.[29] It is, as follows, the supposed subgrouping and segmentation of personality types that enables the precise targeting of voters in this way. However, the claims of behavioural science do not provide a complete picture of the ways in which social media mass persuasion works on felt experiences. The focus on personality traits alone misses, as such, the visceral registers of the collective nonconscious through which persuasive messages and aesthetics facts need to pass through before they influence behaviour and cognition. As argued in the previous chapter, the lure of Whitehead's aesthetic fact works on prepersonal or impersonal experiences. This requires us to grasp a notion of felt experience that is not simply contained in the emotional cognitions of a user's personality or indeed protected by *cognitive barriers*. It matters not that the aesthetic fact exploits a person's feeling of agreeableness or neuroticism, for example, since in contrast to these personal feelings, the focus of persuasion falls on the openness to felt experience, which can, independent of individual persons, contaminate the collective nonconscious of the somnambulist.

Along these lines, concluding his DCMS appearance, the data activist, Paul-Olivier Dehaye, approached the Cambridge Analytical scandal by way of a more compelling and complex proposition than Wylie.[30] Dehaye proposes that we should not overplay the preoccupation with the psychometric targeting of individuals since it is, what he calls, the 'collective effect' or 'collective impulse' to pass on information that should concern regulators.[31] When it comes to fake news, he contends, Facebook *is* the problem because it seems to have a 'blind spot' to what drives the collective impulse to, for example, spread a false rumour on social media.[32] It is, however, important not to forget how the infamous Facebook experiment with massive-scale emotional contagion already illustrates the extent to which the dynamics of Dehaye's collective impulse are not an entirely unseen area of the social media platform's business model (see further discussion in Chapter 3).[33]

This renewed focus on impersonal impulses rather than the perils of the personal is not intended to downplay the significance of the Cambridge Analytica scandal, but rather signal a different kind of hypnotic influence to that forwarded by behavioural sciences focused on personality traits. The personal is, as we will see below, regarded by Tarde as a mostly a delusory experience. Pointedly, what happened in 2016 is also part of a global event of the dark refrain that is not limited to targeting individual persons. For example, Cambridge Analytica were also implicated in the not so well-covered (at least in media coverage in Western democracies) elections campaigns in Kenya in 2013 and Nigeria in 2011, which used very different strategies. There is indeed evidence of a more visceral appeal made to the collective impulses described above. Like this, both the Kenyatta and Goodluck Jonathan campaigns utilized the spreading of violent anti-Muslim hate using viral videos on social media, featuring 'scenes of people being macheted to death … legs hacked off … skulls caved in'.[34] Similarly, in 2018 in Brazil, the election of far-right strongman, Jair Bolsonaro, has been linked to familiar dubious hate filled social media fake news campaigns, deliberately spreading material discriminating against women, native Brazilians, Afro-Brazilians, the LGBT community and progressive intellectuals.[35] As the Brazilian journalist, Pepe Escobar, puts it, Bolsonaro's campaign was a remix of Cambridge Analytica. It was similarly coordinated by a 'bunch of businessmen', operating through dubious 'black' accounting of campaign funds to finance a 'multi-tentacle fake news campaign' against the opposition, using a weaponized WhatsApp.[36]

Of course, more affirmatively minded scholars of digital culture might well groan at such pessimism following Cambridge Analytica. But, if critical theorists were not already suspicious enough after Snowden in 2013, the events of 2016 have stirred new levels of justifiable suspicion about the business of social media. Which is to say, social media platforms are now inseparable from new modes of mass persuasion implicated in the swinging of the political pendulum towards a far-right nationalistic dystopia. Even the most intransigent techno-optimists will surely have to concede that the emergence of this dark viral refrain can no longer simply be regarded as a paranoid reading of technoculture?

Somnambulist Media Theory Revisited

Somnambulist media theory began its life cycle with earlier *resuscitations* of Tarde's nineteenth-century social subject.[37] There is not enough room in this chapter to set out the groundwork of this approach in its entirety, so there is a need to summarize how Tarde's conceptual persona is considered relevant to the analysis of social media. We need to begin with a general review of Tarde's microsociology before drilling down to the details of somnambulism. As follows, Sergio Tonkonoff's recent book on Tarde provides a useful starting point since it begins by setting out a familiar narrative about an early social theorist of standing apparently losing his renowned sociological spat with Durkheim.[38] This dispute was only partially recorded at the time and reconstructed later on from Tarde and Durkheim's subsequent texts.[39] Nonetheless, aside from some brief re-emergences in Chicago and Latin American sociology schools, for most of the academic world, Tarde spent the next 100 years or so languishing in the shadow of social facts, structuralism and collective representation. In short, Durkheim seems to have won the debate because he managed to convince his French audience that Tarde's speculative psychology had no part to play in the science of the social. Tarde was in effect eclipsed by the force of the dominant Durkheim paradigm.

There are, nonetheless, some important tangents in this fraying sociological narrative. For example, Tonkonoff argues that Tarde's critics perhaps mistakenly saw him as a theorist of the individual.[40] This certainly makes him a convenient foil (or strawman) to the dynamic social densities that were supposed to emerge to form Durkheim's social wholes. Maybe this audience, and Durkheim himself, just didn't get what Tarde meant by social multiplicity, or they failed to grasp the importance of Leibniz's monadology to his social theory.[41] It would seem that those early sociologists, with their heads firmly stuck in Durkheim's paradigm, could only imagine the social in terms of part–whole relations, or as the One emerging from the Many. As Tonkonoff importantly notes Tarde's syntax of the infinitesimal revolution is all about escaping these micro/macro structures and innovatively grasping how everything that is social occurs as a micro-flow![42] Certainly, in Tarde's microsociology, what appears to be whole is just a micro-flow (or monad) at another scale.

Notwithstanding the looming shadow of the Durkheimian paradigm, Tonkonoff's contribution to Tarde's revival actually shows that he never really went away. His influence was maybe dappled by Durkheim, but his work cast a formidable shadow of its own over the thinking of a number of intellectuals; two of whom (Foucault and Deleuze) made a dramatic impression on twentieth-century thought, and continue, in this century, to shape the debate. So, Tarde's years in obscurity, and his omission from the subsequent paradigmatic undercurrents of Parsons and Althusser, for example, need to be countered by fleeting, yet crucial, homages virtually expressed in Foucault's microphysics and made more concrete in the contagions of Deleuze and Guattari's machinic assemblages. Indeed, it is through Deleuze's book on Foucault that the virtual line between Tarde (the criminologist) and the microphysics of power expressed in *Discipline and Punish* becomes actualized. As Deleuze puts it: '[Foucault's microphysics) is precisely what Gabriel Tarde did when he founded microsociology: he did not explain the social by the individual, he explained large ensembles by determining infinitesimal relations in them.'[43]

Arguably, Tonkonoff's effort to draw a clear line of influence from Tarde to Foucault and Deleuze, and the familial connotations that suggests, goes against many of the fundamental ideas of the Tardean infinitesimal revolution. Tarde, the writer of a new syntax of multiplicity is predictably, yet uncomfortably, tied to an anti-Hegelian family tree made up of Nietzsche, James, Bergson and Deleuze.[44] By making these lines of inheritance, Tonkonoff knows full well that he risks constructing a father-like figure or original source – the kind of which Tarde's theory of micro-flows, and mostly accidental imitation, simply would not advocate. Unless, that is, we accept a Dawkins-like, biological deterministic, memetic distortion of Tarde![45] Tonkonoff is, of course, utterly aware of the problem he introduces. He does not intend to make Tarde a father or indeed a grandfather of his own revolution. He is, nevertheless, Tonkonoff contends, more like a 'brother', or the beginning of an inherited ontology of multiplicity, difference, imitation and invention, which, it must be noted, is strangely devoid of sisters.[46] Yet, if we follow Tarde's own diagram of collective mimesis (not individual or memetic!), he would probably be nobody's relative at all. Tarde would be like all other authors who might have imitated a basic grammar of micro-sociology from somewhere downstream of the microflows of multiplicity. He simply repeats its syntax, and passes it on (or spreads it), *with alterity*, of course.

It is, nonetheless, Tonkonoff's renewed focus on somnambulism that draws attention to contemporary issues regarding how certain kinds of docile subjectivities continue to emerge from collective mimesis.[47] Along these lines, Tonkonoff's more gainful account of Tarde maps the contagion theory in his society of imitation to Deleuze and Guattari's machinic assemblages.[48] This reading of Tardean–Deleuzian contagion theory is arguably crucial to understanding how things currently spread on social media today, including far-right populism, hate speech, fake news etc. Like this, Tardean sleepwalkers are defined by their involuntary associations and hypnotic absorptions of the contagion of others. This is a contagion theory that further suggests nonconscious experiences are somehow implicated in the imitation of others. For example, Tarde made a number of references to neurological processes, which he considered implicated in some way the somnambulistic transmission of *imitative radiation* as it spreads through social multiplicity. Like this, Tarde's microsociology does not simply stress the individual's immersion in the crowd, but instead destabilizes the anthropological centre that exists in most sciences of the person, making the sleepwalker a product of a porous self–other relationality.

So, how can Tarde be positioned as a proto-[social]media theorist? Well, his somnambulists tend to sleepwalk through everyday life because they are mesmerized and contaminated by (a) the actions of others, and (b) magnetically drawn (via an action-at-a-distance) to the fascinations of their newly animated mediated environments. The mimetic milieu the sleepwalker inhabits therefore comprises the attractions and distractions of what Jonathan Crary calls multi-sensory attentional technologies, which intensify imitative radiations.[49] It is indeed, this focus on the topological captivations of subjectivity by the various media technologies social subjects encounter that single out Tarde as a theorist through which we can grasp current social media experiences.[50] It is this aspect of his social theory that further marks out Tarde's contribution as an early indicator of what a nonphenomenological media theory might look like (see next chapter). As follows, Tarde's sleepwalker notably misapprehends the experience of individual volition as a product of an autonomous *psychological-self* rather than the outcome of what he considered to be the involuntary and habitual imitation of others. The sleepwalker is, like this, positioned in insensible spectra of experience, caught between a delusory sense of personal volition and the involuntary contamination of logical and extra-logical experience. 'We know how credulous and docile the hypnotic subject becomes', Tarde contends. What is 'suggested to him becomes incarnated in him'. It penetrates him before it 'expresses itself in his posture or gesture or speech'.[51] As Tonkonoff further notes, Tarde considers the modern image of the individual, described in terms of a 'rational and self-centred subject, with self-control and deliberate actions', as constitutive of an 'enormous illusion'.[52]

Evidently, this illusory rendering of an individual's sense of personality is met with (and continues to be met with) some fairly hostile responses from the scholarly community. 'Are we all supposed to be somnambulists?' 'What about those of us with an educated refined mode of thinking?' Well, later on, I will return to further flesh out a new materialist rendering of Tarde's somnambulist as a kind of response to critiques of such a postpositivistic position. Before that, in what follows, I want to test the extent to which Tarde's rejection of the rational subject in favour of a delusory sense of personal volition maps on to a contemporary social media debate concerning two extreme poles of experience. It is here, in the ensuing discussion, that the politics of somnambulist experience begin to enter the debate.

Analyse This! Fantasy, Conspiracy and Donald Trump

One major political figure whose name gets repeated over and over again in the dark refrain is, of course, that of Donald Trump. His seemingly oxymoronic role in the refrain has been well captured in the US actor Robert De Niro's description of a 'weird twisted president who thinks he's a gangster, who's not even a good gangster'.[53] Indeed, it would appear that analysing Trump according to the norms of gangsterism instead of those usually applied to a politician is probably a more effective way of understanding his part in the visceral registers of the refrain. To put this another way, the often-banal media commentary offered about this divisive, far-right racist in the White House often hides the fact that Trump is a difficult gangster to analyse politically.

As a pertinent example of an attempt to analyse this president, the blurb for Kurt Andersen's bestselling book, *Fantasyland*, claims that what is 'happening in this post-factual, "fake news" moment we're all living through' is not something new, but rather the 'ultimate expression' of the 'national character' of the USA. As follows, Andersen argues that the USA was founded by 'wishful dreamers, magical thinkers, and true believers, by hucksters and their suckers'. He claims that fantasy is 'deeply embedded in [the] DNA' of North America. Indeed, if you want to 'understand Donald Trump' and how the 'lines between reality and illusion have become dangerously blurred'; *you must read this book!*[54]

On the surface, Andersen's figure of the fantasist can be implicitly linked to the credulity of Tarde's somnambulist. This conspiracy crazy figure certainly shares a familiar propensity towards collective reverie. Both fantasist and somnambulist are seemingly deluded figures, who simultaneously occupy polar extremes that affect how their judgements are made. However, in what follows, it becomes evidentially clear that the spectrum on which Andersen situates his fantasist is a thinly realized bipolar experience. 'Each of us is on a spectrum somewhere between the poles of rational and irrational', he contends.[55] On one hand, then, we all experience subjective 'hunches' and 'superstitions' that we probably know 'make no sense'.[56] Yet strangely, somehow, on the other hand, these beliefs often override observations of the world as it is judged according to objective fact. The problem for Andersen is that the capacity for logical reasoning and fact-based judgements has become usurped by irrational sentiments and personal opinions that spread online.

Unlike the initial positioning of the sleepwalker in Chapter 1, then, the fantasist clearly repeats many of the problematic aspects of the spat between positivists and postmodernists. Andersen's fantasists coincide, as such, with a mutating United States, which has become distracted from the purity of logical reasoning. The US has, he argues, gone 'through the looking glass' and 'down the rabbit hole' towards 'Fantasyland'.[57] The fantasist is couched, as such, in a distortion of the 'American dream', which is explicitly blamed on postmodern intellectuals, post-positivists and poststructuralists; all of whom have turned out to be 'useful idiots' for the insurgent far right.[58]

The fantasist is not, however, the absolute flipside to the age of reason. On the contrary, 'America society' has failed to hold back the reigns of 'the great Enlightenment idea of intellectual freedom'.[59] The fantasists are not simply defined by their outright preference for fantasy over fact, which, as we have seen in Chapter 1, Dennett bemoans. It is instead the uninhibited freedom to believe in anything and everything that has produced these current epidemics of conspiracy and falsehood leading to a widespread contagion of 'crackpots with computers'.[60]

There are obvious connections here to the global brain thesis, particularly Levy's notion that the internet is itself an extension of the Enlightenment project, albeit with very different outcomes to those expressed in his collective intelligence thesis.[61] There is indeed nothing smart about Andersen's global brain. Further echoing the discussion on SEO tactics in the previous chapter, he points to logical inconsistencies in the functioning of search engines to show how 'information and [irrational and conspiratorial] beliefs now flow, rise, and fall' together, stirring contagious fantasies.[62] Significantly, then, it is these familiar logical inconsistencies (intrinsic to social and search technology) that have allowed fantasists to connect in ways that were not possible when they were isolated from each other, and unable to, as such, spread their falsehoods far and wide. Again, resonant with Tarde's imitative media somnambulism, which similarly positions media technologies, like the telegraph and distributed print media, as cultivators of contagious forces, Andersen sees the web as a viral vector for widespread conspiracy and falsehood. This is a mode of virality he argues began in the early 1990s with spam alerts informing early internet chatrooms that Jesus was on his way, and soon evolved into a far more catastrophic collapsing of rationality into 'magical thinking'. Social media connectivity has seemingly given every fantasist unprecedented access to the digital tools that can whip up enough support for false beliefs and conspiracy theories by making them increasingly 'real-seeming and more contagious'.[63]

Atop the many 'principalities' of Andersen's Fantasyland is *The King of Conspiracy* himself: Trump! Indeed, contrary to the positivistic slant to Andersen's thesis, at first, Trump appears to be a postmodern phenomenon. He initially emerges from his own reality show like a conspiratorial simulacrum. His political career is thereafter built on a series of conspiracies, including, most notably, the racist Obama Birther's conspiracy. Trump's subsequent campaigns were full of conspiracies about competitors like Ted Cruz and the Clintons and claims that his offices in Trump Tower were bugged by the Obama administration. Trump seems actively to have encouraged the fantasists to engage in conspiracy. As Andersen points out, he advises his supporters to 'Forget the press', and just 'read the internet'. It is nonetheless Andersen's final analysis of Trump that resonates with Tarde's notion that sleepwalkers are steered by a leaderless action-at-a-distance.

As follows, Trump is not depicted as the magnetizer in chief of the fantasists; he is instead a product of the lures of collective exchanges. Like other strongmen and buffoons on the far right, who claim to be men of the people (*one of us*), Trump, the idiot gangster, is tactically positioned as a kind of semiconscious exchange point in a network that feeds the fantasists a diet of conspiracy and falsehood – direct to their smartphones. This immediate access to Trump on Twitter allows his followers to 'feed those untruths directly [back] to [their own] Twitter followers'. Like this, Trump becomes a somnambulist-like figure himself; a credulous crackpot connected to a computer who, like his followers, seems to genuinely believe in the conspiracies he encounters. Asked if he regretted tweeting a particular falsehood about a rival's links to ISIS, he apparently responded by replying: 'What do I know about it? All I know is what's on the internet.' In this sense, Trump's personality – his sense of 'I' – is collapsed into Clough's user unconscious. His tendency to pass on rumours and conspiracy (see figure 6) is less about the person Trump as it is the vector his tweets provide for the resonation of more Big Lies.

To more readily align this account of Trump the resonator of rumour and conspiracy to Tarde's somnambulist, we need to grasp how the latter's microsociology grasps the emergence of leadership in terms of a social monadology. For example, Tarde does not begin with the dynamic densities of interacting parts to explain the emergence of complex

> **Donald J. Trump** ✓
> @realDonaldTrump
>
> How amazing, the State Health Director who verified copies of Obama's "birth certificate" died in plane crash today. All others lived
>
> RETWEETS 1,762   FAVORITES 714
>
> 1:32 PM - 12 Dec 2013

Figure 6 An example of how Trump's tweets feed into the contagion of conspiracy, in this case concerning Obama's origin of birth.

phenomena.[64] This is significant because in contrast to understanding Trump as an individual person, made up of 'indivisible atoms, homogenous and admitting of movement only as a whole', Tarde would locate this divisive figure in the infinitesimal, highly complex constructions, and architectures, animated by highly varied internal and mostly accidental movements.[65] A monadological understanding of Trump must not be, in this context, grasped according to his relation to a Durkheimian collective consciousness. In this way, Trump is not one member of a group who might personify a group as a whole or 'individualize it no less entirely in themselves'.[66] We misread Trump if he is simply positioned as a magnetic, charismatic leader, emerging from a global far-right ideological mindset. Following Tarde, Trump is not a personification that is collectively born. Despite the mantra of his white-rage constituents, this populist leader is not born as *One of Us*! On the contrary, in Tarde's microflows, there is no family line; the leader becomes a member of the group because they are yielded from the interactions between other individual elements. Trump is therefore nothing more than a microflow, as is his constituency, New York City, and the USA. Like the monad or a Deleuzian assemblage theory, there are no emergent social wholes or global leaders: *all are microflows, all are parts*. Everything is a Tardean multiplicity that never becomes One!

Trump is, ultimately, a leader, but he is nothing more than an accumulation of facts about leadership that vibrates through an assemblage of associated brains. Of course, his capacity to finance the expansion of these vibrations plays a part in his assemblage (as do other capacities in his assemblage), but his trajectory from rich boy, playboy, TV celebrity and gangster president has been as much an accident as it is an intended outcome. Indeed, if his constituency were to leave him to his own devices, he might not achieve anything more than any individual's unused capacity to assemble and resonate. In short, then, a Tardean account of Trump's idiocy sees him as a collective encounter directed by the mostly accidental forces of monads.

This is not to say that contagious accidents (or idiots) cannot be steered in certain directions. Arguably, Tarde overemphasized the unpredictable and uncontrollable chaos at the centre of his microsocial world.[67] Similarly, through working with social media businesses, which are underpinned by sociological research into complex contagion theories (see Chapter 3), marketers and politicians have been enabled by social media to exercise contagious accidents of influence. To be sure, Andersen's notion that Trump is just an impulsive idiot risks masking something more sinister about the tactical modes of the Big Lie stratagem on social media. Perhaps Siva Vaidhyanathan's analysis of Trump's use of Facebook is more revealing in this context.[68] For example, Vaidhyanathan notes that Twitter actually has limited viral reach in the US compared to Facebook.[69] On one hand, then, Vaidhyanathan contends that Trump's constant use of Twitter is constrained to the habitual gestures of a bully (or indeed gangster!) looking for a reaction. Quite often his seemingly unconstrained gut-felt and semi-literate outbursts on Twitter resonate well with his constituent, but these outbursts can also do his campaign as much harm as good. On the other hand, though, Trump is grasped by Vaidhyanathan as the 'ideal manifestation of Facebook culture'.[70] This resonating monad is a manifestation that is carefully steered by campaign staff who 'make sure Trump expresses himself in short, strong bursts of indignation or approval'.[71] This is, in part, a strategic use of Trump's flawed character traits; his short attention span and lack of understanding of complex policy detail, for example, blend into the fleeting posts. However, as Vaidhyanathan concludes, these traits run as 'quickly and frenetically as a Facebook News Feed'.[72] It is arguably at this point that the personality of Trump can be seen to collapse into the collective impulses of the social media platform. It is as if 'Trump were designed for Facebook and Facebook were designed for him', Vaidhyanathan notes.[73] Like Clough's collapsed user unconscious discussed in the previous chapter, 'Facebook' it would seem 'made America [sic] ready for Trump'.[74]

Indeed, Connolly's take on Trump's demonstrable idiocy is similarly more cautious than Andersen's positivistic polemic; linking it directly to the strategies of aspirational fascism. We need to be careful about laughing at the stupidity of the strongman. He uses his idiocy effectively as a potent political posture, which can become a lure for the surpluses of bitterly felt experiences and voter disaffection. What becomes apparent in Andersen's account of Trump, but is mostly missing from his final analysis, is the significant visceral temperament and affective tone at play in Trump's campaign and leadership style. There are two misplaced elements that need our attention here.

Firstly, the feelings expressed by Trump are misapprehended by Andersen as a typically positivistic equation between the polar opposites of logical thinking and an emotionally defined irrationality. In other words, the *Fantasyland* thesis mistakenly divides truth and facts from feelings and moods, since the latter are considered part of the fantasy of illogical thinking. In contrast, Trump on Twitter (and Facebook) can be seen as an aesthetic fact or affective fictioning machine that helps to bend user judgements in certain directions. His torrent of tweets and posts not only become an immediate vector for untruth, but it also entertains, stirs up and steers emotional outrage towards the liberal elite so despised by the far right. His idiotic tweets about climate change (see figure 7), for example, entertain his constituent's sense of a liberal conspiracy aimed against their way of life. Similarly, Trump's adoption of a gangster's 'thuggish sincerity' simply provides another fictioning machine that plays to the visceral hatred many of his constituency feel towards the 'goody-goody sanctimony' of what they see as a phoney mainstream liberal political system.

Andersen's final analysis of Trump's irrational feelings again focuses on his personality traits. As a response to his target electorate, Trump's idiocy is effectively matched to his impulsive moodiness. He is driven by his sense of white rage and 'resentment of the establishment', and typical of far-right strongmen, he mistrusts experts because they *interfere with his right* as a North American *to feel the truth*. The 'truthiness' example from the satirical *Colbert Report* TV series Andersen uses to illustrate the US lurch towards fantasy is a far more telling account of the tactical role feelings play in far-right politics than it is an example of a propensity towards fantasy.

'I don't trust books', Colbert says. 'They're all fact, no heart.' Very much echoing the current sentiments of Brexit Britain, he continues:

Face it, folks, we are a divided nation ... divided between those who think with their head and those who know with their heart ... Because that's where the truth comes from, ladies and gentlemen – the gut.

> **Donald J. Trump** ✓
> @realDonaldTrump
>
> It's freezing and snowing in New York--we need global warming!
>
> RETWEETS 4,223   LIKES 2,391
>
> 11:24 AM - 7 Nov 2012
>
> ↰ 1.7K   ↻ 4.2K   ♥ 2.4K

Figure 7 Trump's infamous climate change tweet from 2012.

Andersen's analysis similarly misses another trick when he uses the example of a confrontation Trump had with a TV anchor who quizzed him over his failure to produce evidence of claims that millions of illegal votes were cast against him in the 2016 election. 'Do you think that talking about millions of illegal votes is dangerous to this country without presenting the evidence?' The anchor asked him.

"No', Trump replied. 'Not at all! Not at all – because many people *feel* the same way that I do.'[75]

'Trump may well do his politics based on mere hunches. But this feely grasping of Trump is not effectively gauged on Andersen's bipolar spectrum, since his politics operate mainly through the visceral registers of culture life. It is on this register that feelings, triggered by strategic Big Lies, become the main vector for the affective contagions of populist politics, infested with unrefined prejudices. Ultimately, these contagions have little to do with a collective loss of mind to conspiracy theory; a loss that will simply be corrected by appeals to more discerning and refined modes of thinking. On the contrary, many disenfranchised working-class people are already trying to *bring to mind* traumatized, visceral experiences that cannot be easily processed, or indeed combatted by, higher levels of rational thinking, without access to systems of care or therapy.

Secondly, and more crucially perhaps, Andersen's thesis misses the real politics of the divided nation behind this working-class disenfranchisement and its dark revolutionary potential. Like this, what *Fantasyland* ultimately fails to account for is the political and economic trauma of Trump's predominantly white rage constituency. Where in Andersen's lamentation of pure logical reasoning is the image of the subprime mortgage foreclosures in the abandoned steel town. Where, in effect, is the hideous reality of the failing legacy of Enlightenment capitalist logic and individualistic modernity? Of course, the real political trickery of this supposed Trumpian Fantasyland becomes apparent in the remobilization of an old fascist trick, which has allowed uber-elite capitalists, like Trump, to be repositioned as the defenders of a displaced post-industrial white working class. This is an old racist trick that diverts traumatized white rage away from market failure to convenient others. Trump is, as Andersen argues, a 'spoiled, impulsive, moody', 70-something-year-old 'brat'. He is this 'poster boy for the downside of digital life'.[77] However, more than that, more than these personality traits, Trump is the alluring manifestation of a wheeler-dealer businessman, come to save the working class from their fearful misplaced perception of an immigrant-infested fate.

Trickle-down-Trump is, as such, not a fantasist. He is part of a hypnotist's showcase; an illusionist entirely compatible with a long-established spreading of fascist memes: *Make America Great Again*. There is, of course, no sincere intention to make life 'great' for this constituency other than provide a kind of vent for its epigenetic traumatized rage, which can be syphoned off at rallies or on social media and used to cultivate political support. The strongman's feely racist rhetorical and affecting bodily strategies (the aggressive Mussolini-like gesturing, finger pointing and stances) are indeed calculated visceral attacks against cultural multiplicities, who have been erroneously blamed by the far right for the fallout of deindustrialization and gross failures of aggressive neoliberal economics to produce an equalitarian democracy. Trump's constituency has endured this two-pronged attack, which has been, of course, greatly exacerbated by the political fallout of the 2008 global capitalist financial crash and residual workplace precarity. As a consequence, numerous disenfranchised subjectivities have now emerged ripe for aspirational fascism across the globe.

Fuck Your Feelings

To understand how the viscerality of post-industrial, white working-class displacement was primed into action by the 2008 crash, we need to pick up on the gangster theme again. Along these lines, this spectacular collapse of capitalism in 2008 is morbidly, yet strikingly, captured in Andrew Dominik's 2013 gangster film, *Killing Them Softly*.[78] Dominik's film is simultaneously about the financial crash, the instabilities of organized criminal economies and the visceral experience of life in a violent, self-medicating landscape

Figure 8 Unofficial T-shirt design in support of the 2020 Trump Campaign. *Source*: https://www.teeshirtpalace.com/products/trump-fuck-your-feelings-t-shirt

of despair, detached from mainstream politics. On one hand, throughout the film we see a failing gangster economy running parallel to the global failure of casino capitalism. In an early scene, two robbers hold up an illicit card game, forcing gamblers to empty their wallets at gunpoint. In the background we hear the reverberating voice of George W. Bush on TV as he tries to rationalize about public panic and economic meltdown. On the other hand, the fictional characterization of the hitman, Jackie Cogan, perfectly incarnates the hardnosed, alienated disillusionment of white working-class rage. Cogan is a hitman who, unlike most of his contemporaries, abstains from blotting out his rage with heroin, yet, nonetheless, still resists giving vent to his emotions. 'I like to kill them softly', he tells his suited, corporate Mafia contact, 'from a distance. Not close enough for feelings. Don't like feelings. Don't want to think about them.'[79] In this moment of post-2008 trauma, feelings are not opposed to rationality. They seem to have been pushed down, or cut out, from the equation. But following a Whiteheadian aesthetic ontology, feelings do not simply disappear like this. We might say that they have simply flipped from an aesthetic to anaesthetic register of feeling that 'aims to protect against overintensity'.[80]

Later on, in Dominik's film, Cogan negatively responds to Obama's emotional evocation of hope, community and cultural multiplicity. In the closing scene, we see him in a bar, again with his suited Mafia contractor, trying to negotiate his payment. He is watching Obama's victory speech in 2008, with its references to Jefferson, and his desire to 'reclaim the American dream and reaffirm that fundamental truth that out of many, we are one'. Cogan sneers at this message of optimism. 'We're one people? It's a myth created by Thomas Jefferson.'[81]

> This guy [Obama] wants to tell me we're living in a community. Don't make me laugh. I'm living in America, and in America, you're on your own. America's not a country. It's just a business. *Now fucking pay me.*[82]

The aspirational fascist's exploitation of this kind of traumatized disenfranchisement captured in Dominik's film appeals directly to the broader spectra of somnambulistic experience. The political aim is to lure the stifled feelings of this anguished constituency towards an insurgent, yet fictional, white rage. Herein, fact and feeling are not simply opposed to each other in a positivistic equation; they become part of a tactical fictioning that aims to frustrate more refined reasoning; a kind of feely speculative, liar paradox, which deliberately loops around the multiple polar extremes of the spectra of experience (true/false, visceral/cognitive, feelings/fakes, good/bad, real/unreal, belief/desire etc.).

More Fiction Machines

It is, again, in the density of speculative potential on the spectra of experience that vulnerabilities to politically motivated fictioning-machines arise. For example, in 2018, the same year that Homeland and Security researchers named the worst on record for gun violence in US schools,[83] an NRA ad appeared on YouTube. It begins by saying that the NRA have had enough of 'the lies, the sanctimony, the arrogance, the hatred, the pettiness, the fake news'. The NRATV presenter continues:

> We are done with your agenda to undermine voters' will and individual liberty in America. So, to every lying member of the media, to every Hollywood phony, to the role model athletes who use their free speech to alter and undermine what our flag represents. To the politicians who would rather watch America burn than lose one ounce of their own

personal power, to the late-night posts that think their opinion is the only opinions that matter. To the Joy-Ann Reids, the Morning Joes, the Mikas. To those who stain honest reporting with partisanship. To those who bring bias and propaganda to CNN, *The Washington Post* and *The New York Times* ... your time is running out. The clock starts now.[84]

The proposition of this fiction machine is an aesthetic fact writ large! It is in itself a staged disruptive shock event intended to resonate beyond the logical/illogical poles and enter into the thickness of a visceral register of somnambulate experience. It is a fictioning of rage that introduces an affective tone to what Connolly calls the 'conceptual cloudiness' of the aspirational fascist's Big Lie strategy; it presents a moment of feely indistinction, intended to purposefully undermine experts, fact-checkers and investigative journalists.[85] It is on this visceral register that political fiction machines of this kind twist and distort democracy, and therefore weaken the impartiality of the media, controlling intelligence, and inhibiting plural societies, as such.[86] Below (see figure 9) we can see how Trump's Twitter strategy similarly functions as a fiction machine to attempt to undermine the news media while claiming to know what the people really want.

Saying *Fuck Your Feelings* is similarly a moment of feely speculative paradox in Trump's political campaign. It is an absurd affective toning of the [unofficial] Trump campaign message that intentionally blurs the promotion of a far-right visceral hatred of so-called bleeding-heart liberals. This is a hate filled agenda that needs to be judged alongside further indignant iterations of racism, militarism, pro-gun lobby, climate denial, and misogyny on social media. These are not appeals made to

Donald J. Trump
@realDonaldTrump

Follow

Any negative polls are fake news, just like the CNN, ABC, NBC polls in the election. Sorry, people want border security and extreme vetting.

6:01 AM - 6 Feb 2017

↩ ♺ 32,395 ♥ 141,188

Figure 9 Trump Tweet conflating claims of 'fake' polls with his extreme immigration policy.

an irrational constituency of fantasists. They are the intensification of speculative aesthetic facts, which are intended to lure the possibilities of dangerous collective mimesis towards an even darker refrain.

Significantly, Connolly argues that the more refined minds on the left of politics have made the mistake of downplaying the visceral registers on which these kinds of raw sentiments operate.[87] The left must not 'reduce [affective contagion] to a force that only unruly masses succumb to', Connolly contends.[88] In other words, they must not underestimate the power of affective contagions that can intensify the mass energies of popular support for the strongman. They must not also assume that this contagion can be easily 'eliminated from public life in democratic societies' by way of appealing to a reasoned way of thinking.[89] This is not, then, after all, simply a matter of waking the sleepwalker. It is important therefore not to mistake the sleepwalker for an irrational persona. On the contrary, we need a way out of this positivistic/postmodern impasse.

Following Tarde, the fascination of Trump can be grasped as an intensification of the feelings of white rage. This intensified felt experience becomes a powerful mode of persuasion, triggering collective impulses that resonate contagiously through visceral registers of social media. Significantly, though, *A Sleepwalker's Guide* offers a new materialist rendering of Tarde's somnambulist whose future *decisions acts* are steered towards predefined political objectives, without necessarily engaging cognitive processes. Which is to say, the collective nonconscious holds sway over, and may even bypass, awakened volition experienced explicitly as a global cognitive consciousness.

The new materialist sleepwalkers are neither asleep nor awake. They are conceptual personae intended to pose weightier questions concerning what constitutes the relational threshold between nonconscious and conscious experiences than any crude positivistic boundary line would suggest. Somnambulism does not represent the absence of thought, as such. Paradoxically perhaps, nonconsciousness has a mental component; a mind of its own, or subjective aim, if you like. This is not, however, a mentality that is limited to cognitive faculties, but is extended to an array of nonconscious (extra-logical) experiences, such as habits, microperceptions, thinking–feeling etc.[90] As Connolly contends, to combat far-right tactics, the visceral registers of communication, through which affective contagions spread, need to be better aligned to these more refined political judgements.[91] This alignment of visceral and refined thinking will require some theoretical experimentation.

Wake Up?

By way of developing an expedient fictioning machine of our own, intended to help grasp the new materialist rendering of the sleepwalking conceptual persona, I think another film character stands out: Richard Kelly's *Donnie Darko*.[92] This is a different rendering of the sleepwalker compared to the psychoanalytical leanings of Kracauer's account of Caligari's fairground somnambulist. Although Donnie's time travelling exploits seem to intuit what is looming in the future, they have a distinctive Whiteheadian trace to them. This trace is initially marked out by the main character's obsession with Roberta Sparrow's book *The Philosophy of Time Travel* and his eventual journeys through the events of the film, which occur through portals and wormholes that extend from stomachs and TV screens.

'What does time travel have to do with philosophy?' Donnie's sister, Elizabeth, cynically asks.

Donnie doesn't answer. Yet, maybe he already knows that time travel is absolutely critical to philosophy; particularly, it must be said, Whitehead's event philosophy! James Williams provides a rather vividly convenient answer to Elizabeth's question in his conjuring up of a time machine that provides an 'apt device to bring Whitehead's ideas into the future'.[93] Williams's time travel does not, however, provide an ordinary history lesson about philosophy. '[T]ime-travel, done well, is not only an exercise in retrieval and learning from the past.'[94] Students of Whitehead might recognize that each passing event comes with its own lesson in how the past 'ineluctable decay[s] in each present'. Time travel is thus an 'instruction on how to counter this passing'.[95]

It is not only via wormholes and portals that Donnie counters this passing of the various spatiotemporal events in Kelly's film. Significantly, Donnie is a sleepwalker!

Gretchen, Donnie's girlfriend, asks him, 'So, when you sleepwalk, do you go somewhere familiar?' However, Donnie's sleepwalking experience is not about recovering some lost, or deeply repressed, memory of past places or events, so that they might provide clues about the future. Every time Donnie wakes up, he wakes up 'somewhere different' – in another event, where he has to work out where he is. Which is to say, Frank, the seemingly illusory, hypnotic demonic rabbit, who appears to command whenever and wherever it is that Donnie sleepwalks to, should not be mistook for a reading of Donnie's subconscious.

'So, when you sleepwalk, can you remember afterward? Like, do you dream?' asks Gretchen.

'No', Donnie replies. There is no dreaming to interpret in Donnie's somnambulism. 'I just wake up and I look around, try to figure out where I am ... how I got there.'

Gretchen explains how her dad once told her to 'never wake a sleepwalker ... because they could drop dead'.

Donnie's sleepwalking is nothing like death either. His somnambulism is alive in the neurological pathways that extend between him and Frank, the demonic rabbit.

'It's like this big force ... that's in your brain', Donnie explains to Gretchen. 'Sometimes it grows bigger ... and it spreads down into your arms and legs ... and it just sends you someplace.'

As we find out towards the very end of the film, Frank is not, and never has been, Donnie's subconscious. After Gretchen is hit by a car outside Granma Death's house, Donnie runs over and kneels down next to her. 'Gretchen ... wake up. Wake up.' But her neck is broken. She has no pulse.

> The passenger door to the Trans-Am opens, and a passenger in a clown costume gets out. The driver's side door opens and the driver gets out. He is wearing a rabbit suit. A Halloween costume. He is holding the grotesque rabbit helmet in his hand. It is Frank.[96]

Frank is, it turns out, just part of the crowd scene. To be sure, we must not mistake Frank for Daddy's or Mommy's voice hidden away in Donnie's sleepwalk. Frank practises a very different kind of hypnosis. Frank is this lesson from the past about the inescapable perishing of what is previous in each immediate present. So, when we again refer below to the influence of the more-than-human collective nonconscious on the impulses of the sleepwalker: don't think about an inhibited subconscious drive making its way to consciousness. In the theoretical experiments that follow, don't think of a dream that needs interpreting. Don't think of Cesare's premonitions. Think Frank!

Experimenting with a New Materialist Somnambulism

Like Donnie, Tarde's social somnambulist is a figure rendered vulnerable to hypnotic and contagious suggestibility. The Tardean social subject is a sleep induced dream of command. It is important, nonetheless, not to mistake a new materialist reading of the sleepwalker for the *divided* subject of psychoanalysis; the consciousness and nonconscious of the Tardean subject is, on the contrary, *folded*.[97] Theoretically, then, there is a notable difference between the Tardean somnambulist and Gustave Le Bon's

Figure 10 Ginsberg's Sleepwalker.
Illustration by Mikey B. Georgeson.

crowd theory, specifically in the way the latter is adopted by Freud, as such.[98] There is no firm distinction made between conscious and nonconscious experiences; no subterranean world of collective, repressed reverie, on one hand, which is awakened in the individual, on the other. There are only insensible, indistinct thresholds between induced sleep and the illusion of command experienced when awake. Along these lines, we are not concerned here with the question of how to wake up the somnambulists. The sleepwalkers are not caught up in a reverie in which they confuse a fabricated artifice for reality, nor is there a disconnect between their irrational actions and refined cognitive judgements.

We mistake the sleepwalkers for zombies if, like Ginsberg (see figure 10), we think we can liberate them from a 'land of the sleepwalkers' and make them see![99] The collective nonconscious of the sleepwalker operates paradoxically between somnolent and ambulant poles of the spectra.

Before we can begin to experiment with these new polarities, it is important to admit to notable conceptual similarities and differences between the somnambulist and the technological nonconscious, as it was originally introduced by Clough, and subsequently developed on by Thrift, Hayles, and Grusin.[100] Both approaches certainly consider the implication of the deep entanglement of brains, bodies and the assumed orchestrating operational level of computational media technology. The technological nonconscious is, as such, like a Tardean hypnotizer. It is an anticipator of routine patterns and regulator of habits and actions. However, rather than considering these brain–computer entanglements as 'characteristic of the cognitive nonconscious', as Hayles does, the theoretical work here begins by clearly differentiating the collective nonconscious from the cognitive frame.[101] Significantly, Hayles's work on the cognitive nonconscious is itself couched in a critique of the kind of new materialism developed in this chapter. Hayles is broadly supportive of the new materialist desire to decentre the anthropological subject in the humanities and focus more on material and affective relations. However, she makes some pointed criticisms, providing a sharp counter point to the new materialist leanings of somnambulist theory.

> Despite their considerable promises, the new materialisms also have significant limitations. Conspicuously absent from their considerations are consciousness and cognition, presumably because of the concern that if they were introduced, it would be all too easy to slip into received ideas and lose the radical edge that the focus on materiality provides. This leads to a performative contradiction: only beings with higher consciousness can read and understand these arguments, yet few if any new materialists acknowledge the functions that cognition enables for living and nonliving entities. Reading them, one looks in vain for recognition of cognitive processes, although they must necessarily have been involved for these discourses to exist at all.[102]

Evidently, anyone reading the above will sense, as Hayles does, their own cognition in process. This seems to be an incontrovertible fact of cognitive thinking. Which is to say, the problem of imagining the collective nonconscious from within the cognitive frame is that the affects of the nonconscious must always travel through the conceptual filter of awakened human consciousness. Accordingly, the affective realm of the nonconscious can never escape cognitive perception.

Hayles's thought experiment nevertheless contains a clear cognitivist bias that arguably misses some important points concerning a new materialist approach to unthought experience. Firstly, the decentring of the cognitive subject should not become confused with the disappearance of thought in new materialist approaches. Although cognition is regarded as something that always arrives late, thought does not vanish from affect.

The becoming of subjectivity is, in this context, part of a process that does eventually emerge as moments of higher consciousness. However, such moments of what Whitehead calls the self-enjoyment of 'one arising out of the composition of the many',[103] are not a point wherein mind bifurcates from matter. These subjective appropriations (enjoyments) of experience do not, as such, offer the kind of cognitive command post Hayles proposes acts as a filter for affective experiences. On the contrary, self-enjoyment is a process of individuality in which mind and matter are taken together (immanent and nonbifurcated). Along these lines, a new materialist approach does not regard the cognitive image of the mind as an emerging superior intelligence (or controlling switchboard centre) through which felt experiences are ultimately processed. On the contrary, the collective nonconscious is regarded as precognitive[104] or a more-than-human user experience that exceeds the filtering of individual phenomenal experience.[105]

Secondly, although any attempt at higher theoretical analysis must clearly be filtered through higher levels of cognition, as Hayles rightly contends, that should not preclude a theory of the unthought from speculating about precognitive experiences. This is an important point because the complex processes that move from precognitive to cognitive registers of experience make possible what Massumi calls 'enactive speculations of the future potential of activity'.[106] As already mentioned, nonconscious experience is, as such, a process that has *mental* components of sorts.[107] Everything in a Whiteheadian cosmos has a mental pole. It is not, however, in the eventual awakening of these components in conscious cognition that nonconscious choices are made. It is always the process itself that decides! Unconscious habits, for example, which are often misleadingly 'designated as belonging to the mind'[108] develop through complex processes that enable decision acts to occur prior to cognition.

This new materialist updating of the somnambulist owes a further debt to Raymond Ruyer's notion that perceptual reality is secondary to the primacy of absolute sensation.[109] Certainly, the embracing of this fundamental principle of somnambulism intentionally turns the cognitive frame of reference on its head by prioritizing the felt sensation of the unthought over conscious cognition. As follows, the collective nonconscious can be theorized as a primary and immediate experience of sensation as differentiated from the self-organization of a secondary conscious experience that might also be regarded as awake or cognitively alert. Nonconscious affective experiences are not, like this, filtered through perceptions, but instead consciousness is a derived feeling of immediate sensation. Subjective experience therefore comes about through the subsequent affecting potentialities of experience rather than a phenomenological sense of self. It is, certainly, in the felt experiences of absolute sensation (the sensation of sensation or the experiencing of experience) that the somnambulist experiences the event; not as a cognitive command post, but as a mere foothold in the viscera of experience.[110]

Whitehead explains how this mere foothold of consciousness in the event arises because the social subject's fragile grip on the immediate present is part of a *peculiar completeness* with the experience of past occasions. This is not, however, a 'familiarity of well-marked sensa in immediate presentment'.[111] It might mean, as Ruyer argues, that consciousness is just this secondary means of survival by which the organism is able to experience its own experience. As Elizabeth Grosz puts it:

> Consciousness is not a separate organ added to life at a certain stage of its growing complexity; rather, it is the condition for the dynamic unity of an organism, an organism's capacity to survive, to act in its environment, in short, to enjoy itself, to experience autoaffection, immediate self-enjoyment.[112]

What this means for Whitehead is that although our perception of events seems to be guided by this conscious sense of familiarity, there is, in effect, an 'inflow' of 'vague feeling[s] of influences' that overwhelm the organism. In this light, the experience of the event goes beyond the attentional, discursive capacity to discern and can only really be felt. To be sure, the mere footing Whitehead's consciousness has in these inflows is remarkably somnambulistic. The influence of feelings operates on a 'half-sleep', and 'dim consciousness'. As Whitehead argues; contra-Hayles ...

> We sleep; we are half-awake; we are aware of our perceptions, but are devoid of generalities in thought; we are vividly absorbed within a small region of abstract thought while oblivious to the world around; we are attending to our emotions – some torrent of passion – to them and to nothing else; we are morbidly discursive in the width of our attention; and finally we sink back into temporary obliviousness, sleeping or stunned.[113]

Consistent with the introduction to this book and its methodological insistence on resolving distinctions between such things as wakefulness and sleep,[114] we need to explore the paradoxical nature of the two poles of the sleepwalking experience: *somnolent* and *ambulant*.

The Indistinct Polarities of Somnambulism

1. Somnolent

Sleeping, as Matthew Fuller points out, is the 'somnolent version of the Cretan Paradox', since, although it provides a distinction between itself and 'being awake and thoughtful, hence conscious and knowing', sleep in itself 'cannot be directly known in its native state'.[115] In other words, like the liar paradox, to *think* sleep we risk producing a self-referential logical loop that would frustrate the refined thinking of the logician. As Fuller contends:

> In order to think about [sleep] we must be awake or to know something ... Sleep, unlike any other part of culture has no capacity for reflexivity within its own conditions. In sleeping one simply sleeps, one does not know, anything.[116]

Sleep is therefore 'ungraspable, unwritable [and] only perceivable at its edges or its outside'.[117] In sleep we may well still *know* something, but we lose our sense of self as a way of *knowing* it. It is only external to or at the margins of sleep, in dream states or reverie, for instance, that sleep itself is filtered through conscious cognition, and that will only occur by way of a detour into wakeful reflection.[118]

The conceptual persona of the somnambulist therefore provides a unique glimpse of the collective nonconscious because of the exceptional condition sleep offers in terms of cutting out the cognitive I. As Clough similarly explains by referring to Jean-Luc Nancy's *The Fall of Sleep*:

> We are told that we do not fall asleep, but that sleep falls upon us. Or, it is not 'I' that falls into sleep, not an 'I' that can be distinguished itself from anything else, 'from anything more than its own indistinctness'. 'I' fall asleep – that is to say, 'I' fall ... 'In my own eyes, which no longer look at anything, which are turned towards themselves and towards the black spot inside them ...'. I am 'isolated from all manifestations, from all phenomenality, the sleeping thing ...'.[119]

Grasped on the sleeping bandwidth of experiential spectra, then, the conceptual persona of the somnambulist offers a unique glimpse into a gradation beginning with overlaps produced between a conscious sense of self (wakefulness) and the porous feelings of shared experiences with others. This is not the point at which the rationality of Le Bon's individual fades into the irrational crowd. It is also not the point at which Andersen's fantasist flips somewhere between the poles on the spectrum between rational and irrational. On the contrary, it is rather a moment of indistinction where the sense of self comes into contagious relation with others to such a degree of intensity that self merges with the other, and potentially (see Chapters 3 and 4) collapses into the surroundings in which these mimetic encounters occur. This is a moment of indistinction wherein the cognitive self mistakes its relational encounter for a sense of personal volition. At the extreme end of the spectra, though, we find a more-than-human collective nonconscious explained by the exceptional condition of sleep, which cuts out the cognitive I altogether. Just like Donnie Darko's sleepwalk, there is no dream of self in the collective nonconscious; just a thing-self; *just Frank!*

2. Ambulant

Walking is also an exceptional moment of indistinction since, like running, driving a car or playing a musical instrument, it provides what Amin and Thrift call an 'intermesh' that connects the body to the world in ways that bring together 'flesh and stone, humans and nonhumans, fixtures and flows and emotions and practices'.[120] Walking is also an act of mobility that allows its subject to insensibly drift between nonconscious to conscious experience. The act of walking can indeed be performed when sleep falls on the subject. Sleepwalking is, like this, an impulsive act, which can be achieved when the act itself is *out of mind*, since its mechanical and habit-bound processes are, for the most part, nonconscious rather than conscious.

Walking is also a collective experience wherein bodily interactions can become entrained with each other. For this reason, research into unintentional bodily synchrony in the field of entrainment studies is revealing since it too sets out to avoid the cognitivist bias, which states that it is only *in* consciousness that something like walking becomes real. As Clayton et al. argue, in entrainment theory 'any bodily implementation of interacting processes is real, no matter whether it is consciously experienced or not'.[121] Moreover, the entrainment theory of walking provides insights into the collective nonconscious that can be transposed to the study of network cultures. For example, the nonconscious entrainment of footsteps on a pavement can be substituted for the habitual social media user's clicking and scrolling of thumbs. In lieu of the rhythmic entrainments of walkers, coupled together through the bobbing of heads, or the synchronizations of marching arms and legs, we find the algorithmically orchestrated and rhythmic coordination of the sleepwalker's experiences of the technological nonconscious. These are not merely physical entrainments. Indeed, as we will see in the next chapter, research into entrained self–other similarity suggests a folding of the relation between physical behaviours and emotionally felt experiences, like empathy and other prosocial contagions. As those readers who have participated in a large protest march may agree: people who walk together, feel together.

Sleepwalking with Whitehead

Adding a further radical Whiteheadian philosophical spin to these spectra of experience, we again find that the shared felt experience of the collective nonconscious does not begin with a cognitive thinker. The thinker-subject is instead on the end of an irreversible *experience chain*.[122] Whitehead upends Descartes 'thinker who creates the occasional thought', with the felt experience of a subjectless subjectivity as the 'constituent operation in the creation of the occasional thinker'.[123] In other words, the visceral registers in which shock events are processed, are not, as such, the outcome of a thinker having a thought. Not at all; it is the thinker who is the effect of the viscera of sensation that the shock event brings about.

A somnambulist media theory asks how we experience this indistinction between the polarities of somnolent and ambulant experiences.

Following a Whiteheadian sleepwalk to the ambulant pole, we might find the somnambulists walking on the floor of something approaching Plato's cave. Although they are ostensibly asleep, the sleepwalkers have both eyes wide open. As they amble about, they look up from what they think is a subjective vantage point, staring up at the walls of the cave, surveying what they imagine to be objective reality. This immanent reality is not, however, like one of Plato's infamous shadows. The somnambulists are not so easily fooled; they make the best of their situation in an ever moving and complex series of breaking news events. What the sleepwalker experiences is a percipient event; a moment of spiralling potential of truth and falsity far too eventful to always concretely discern which is which; there and then. All they can do, it seems, is *feel* the lure of the event and speculate on what's possible. Certainly, any concrete sense of feeling can easily become misplaced.

It is the event that feels the sleepwalker. This is a moment when the feelings of the shock event grasp the instant of experience and lure the sleepwalker towards the possible. To understand this moment of an eventful feely luring of subjectivity – what Deleuze describes as the moment when an immanent subjective aim becomes filled with its own self-enjoyment,[124] we need to bring in a Whiteheadian philosophy again. This is because Whitehead does not limit subjectivity to the Cartesian thinker who thinks the thought. On the contrary, there is a process evident in the becoming of subjectivity. So yes, this is the becoming *Subjectum* ('the thrown under') of the somnambulists; the sleepwalker's moment of glorious self-enjoyment when she begins to feel her own feelings as part of a richer private life.[125] The sleepwalker feels themselves, walking on the floor, *inside* the cave, and *think* that this is the phenomenal command post of consciousness. Being there, on the *inside* of the cave.

At the same time though, at the far the spectra of somnolent subjectivity, the somnambulists are in a deep, deep sleep. They are no longer *inside* the cave, but somehow floating over it. In this apparent suspension of perception, the conceptual personae of the somnambulist do not feel themselves in the interior of the cave. There is no Subjectum inside a cave, since, as Deleuze reminds us, the inside is nothing more than a fold of the outside.[126] There is, however, feeling. Without a doubt, there is nothing but feeling, because feeling is the 'primary activity of all existence'.[127] Here we find the Superjacio ('the thrown over') of somnambulism. These are not sleepy subjects caught in a zone of dark phenomenology. There are no cell phone zombies in this zone! They are in an unfathomable subjectless sleep in the sense that Fuller and Clough describe it above. This is a moment of an intense overflowing of primary experience that cannot be contained to the experience of the I or indeed filtered through cognition. The feeling of subjectless subjectivity is rather this experiencing of experience or the immediate sensation of sensation. It is Clough's autoaffection!

Somnambulism has a tendency to move irreversibly from one pole to the next: from subjectless subjectivity to self-enjoyment. This is a movement through the experience chain: a propensity that moves from a position *thrown over* the cave towards an experience *placed below* on the floor of the cave. This propensity towards the feeling of self-enjoyment tells us something rather profound about Whitehead's contribution to philosophy and its potential application to somnambulist media theory. As Didier Debaise notes, the Subjectum has been imposed on modern philosophical ideas of subjective experience as 'a subject that is in possession of its own feelings'.[128] But Whitehead found that the potential for self-enjoyment is not contingent on the subject's experience of self. The subject is, indeed, *subject to* a coalescing of felt experiences in some kind of centred or multicentred way. Self-enjoyment can be experienced as an *Assemblage Brain*: a mingling of cells that feel a neuron; a continuous feeling of mingling of neurons, which feels a brain feeling the nerve endings in a body, which feels the world, and so on, and so on. Sometimes these feelings do not hold together like unities, so self-enjoyment does not necessarily become conscious. In fact, conscious experience is not the rule; it is the exception: a point at which Whitehead's concept of nature is stretched to such a degree that it is able to, in extraordinary conditions of plasticity, feel itself.

Conclusions

In his analysis of Trumpian tactics, Connolly treats fake news as endemic to a wider 'Big Lie' far-right strategy that targets its constituencies through the coding and pegging of the visceral register of cultural life.[129] The lies in Trump's late night tweets, for example, use shock tactics to 'stoke anxiety' and divert anger towards vulnerable and 'convenient figures' of hate.[130] The first two chapters of this book have accordingly pointed to the problems that arise when similar shocks create further advantages for Big Lies. The shock event confounds the algorithmic logic of the search engine, and the conscious brain, opening up possibilities and data voids ripe for the spreading of more Big Lies through the resonating social media machine. I have also noted that the visceral register provides an example of the primacy of the collective nonconscious over cognition. Which is to say, the established resistances of those political opponents of Trump whose preference is for calm, refined and hesitant responses over the agitational performances of Trumpism have become a secondary concern for voters. Indeed, at this moment in time, the sound of refined political debate is being drowned out by the bare desire for strongmen leaders to assume control and make *our* countries great again.

It is important, as Connolly argues, not to downplay the visceral register or the affective atmospheres and 'conceptual cloudiness' in which rumours, conspiracies and fabrication flourish.[131] Perhaps these current populist overspills of the collective nonconscious should not come as a big surprise. Unlike the current void in reasoned politicking, 'there is never… a vacuum on the visceral register'.[132] The unthought of the nonconscious is always full to the brim with feelings (subject and subjectless) as perhaps the unthinkable election victory of Trump evidenced! To be sure, Trump is *the* shock event, which has lured the dark possibilities of the collective nonconscious and produced the stuff of an ever darker and potentially dangerous moment of Whiteheadian self-enjoyment.

The discussion has hitherto approached some fairly intricate ideas concerned with what might constitute the *luring* of an impulsive collective nonconscious. It has considered the primary role of aesthetic facts in effectively intensifying experiences, prompting them into action; moving them in this or that direction, producing diversions, enticing and inciting changes to habits, behaviours, judgements. Ominously, these experiential lures have, in recent times, taken a distinctly dark and deadly turn. They have exhibited impulsive possibilities, bringing together dangerous moods, stirring anxious engagements, aligning antagonistic feelings and spreading hate filled bundles of affect.

Experiences have been intensified by the visceral rhetoric, affective toning and bodily performances of various chin jutting strongmen who front the increasingly familiar racist movements of the far right. Significantly, social media has provided a resonation machine for these strongmen and their supporters. This is *their* dark refrain of social media contagion. It allows them to drum up the affective contagion of fascism wherein affective performances are repeated, mimicked, passed on and adapted by traumatized populations. However, ultimately, what lures collective mimesis, in which populations begin to feel and share the same hate, exceeds the individual influence of persons. Strongmen are only a component part of contagious more-than-human assemblages. Along these lines, unregulated social media platforms have functioned as conspicuous vectors for the escalation of these dark collective impulses. These are platforms of hyperacceleration which emit mimicked refrains of hate filled urges. They are technologies of spread as well as speed. Moreover, these platforms intensify experience, destabilizing critical frameworks of interpretation,[133] while also propelling anxieties towards new points of shared fascination. They accelerate and proliferate violence. They proliferate without critical challenge; free to exercise, radicalize, realize, live stream and captivate the desires of a far-right revolutionary moment.[134]

Coda   Christchurch; El Paso

Facebook's mission statement is very clear. The business wants to *give everyone the power to share anything with anyone*. Zuckerberg used this statement in 2016 to explain how Facebook would develop as a community by sharing its technology. It is familiar Silicon Valley practice. Users are provided with the tools so that they can lift themselves up by their own bootstraps and build the community for themselves. In other words, it is the users who spread knowledge and skills across the online community so that the business, in effect, builds itself. Zuckerberg's words are ordinarily found on inspirational business quote websites, alongside numerous utterances by other tech giants. However, in recent years, following online privacy scandals like Cambridge Analytica, these words have acquired new significance. Indeed, since 2019, the notion that everyone has the power to share anything with anyone has entered into the dark refrain of social media.

Christchurch 15/03/19

While I was working on some early drafts of this book, the shocking news from Christchurch broke. Another mass shooting! Targeting Muslims. After reading the breaking news online, I began to search Google and Twitter. The New Zealand police tweeted that 'extremely distressing footage relating to the incident in Christchurch was spreading online'.[1] *FFS!* The attacker had used the Facebook Live tool to livestream the massacre. The police strongly urged users not to share the link. They were apparently working with Facebook to have any footage removed.

How far had it spread?

There were several reports stating that Facebook was unable to remove the livestream until twenty minutes after it was broadcast, allowing users not only to view it, but also spread it around YouTube and Twitter. The mainstream media attempted to trace it. NBC conducted a series of searches on the day of the attack that 'turned up more than a dozen versions of the video'.[2] Anecdotally, by evening time in the UK, a Muslim neighbour of mine told me his brother had shared the video with him. It was indeed spreading through his community. Eventually, it would spread to the dark corners of the web where it will linger on for years to come.

On the same day a headline on Buzzfeed commented on *The Eerie Absence of Viral Fakes After the New Zealand Mosque Attacks*.[3] This Nazi terrorist was clearly aware of the power of SEO strategies. 'The shooter's media plan was so comprehensive, and his content spread so quickly …', the Buzzfeed article continued; 'there was little room for fakes to fill the void'. Evidently, the main intention of livestreaming the shock event in Christchurch was to fill the vacuum with a violent, forced distinction between Muslims and white supremacists. By sharing the experience, and linking it to his 'manifesto' on 8chan, the terrorist also wanted other racists to feel the same hatred and spread it far and wide.

The link between the rise of this kind of terror attack and the rampant racist toxicity spreading through mainstream politics is all too clear. The galvanizer-in-chief for much of this hate contagion is posting live on Twitter direct from the White House. Calling Mexican immigrants rapists and criminals, #BuildTheWall, telling black American Congresswomen to 'go back home'; Trump's shameful tweets are, of course, heinous. His penetration of Facebook is also intensive. According to social media researcher, Natalie Martinez, since May 2018, Trump has run thousands of FB ads mentioning the word 'invasion'.[4]

Then it happens again…

El Paso 03/08/19

It is now August. I continue to work through the final edits of the book. Another racist terror attack occurs. This time the target for the mass shooting is El Paso, a Texan town with a large Hispanic population. There is another high death toll. There is another 'manifesto' posted on 4chan and 8chan. In his racist rant, the white Texan terrorist declares support for the Christchurch shooter and his manifesto. The El Paso attack was nonetheless, he claims, a specific 'response to the Hispanic *invasion* of Texas'. He was 'simply defending' his country.

#RacistPresident

3

The Virality of Experience Capitalism

The next two chapters critically trace diagrammatical lines that traverse the fascistic contagions from the previous discussion to the intensifications of the experience economy (what I will refer to more broadly as *experience capitalism*). In short, the focus here will be on a complicit relation established between the dark refrain and the virality/growth model of corporate social media. The next chapter will similarly address an immunity problem that has seemingly emerged from subsequent overflows of contagious user experiences.

My interest in virality/growth is twofold. Firstly, anecdotally, I want to expand on a term I originally encountered in an email exchange with Snapchat back in 2016. The business had grasped virality as part of a competitive 'growth strategy' and marketing 'tactic'.[1] I was invited to have an 'initial discussion' with their marketing team 'focused on social media & technology growth/virality'. Secondly, the main aim of the chapter is to explore how virality can potentially challenge the mainstay of critical theories that have conventionally pointed to the production of a so-called commodified self. Which is to say, I contend that virality intervenes in theories that point to an ideological contamination of the self-concept. As follows, the chapter charts a shift from the prevalent phenomenological concept of self to an impersonal nonphenomenological grasping of the user experience.

The discussion begins by setting out the backdrop of experience capitalism, against which, I contend, the virality/growth model has evolved. Two sections follow. The first contrasts an older theory of the commodified self-concept with alternative speculations concerned with intensity and experience. Some of these latter concerns significantly predate, yet also pre-empt, social media. For example, R. D. Laing's *Politics of Experience* thesis profoundly contends that by inducing similar experiences, it is possible to more effectively steer a population towards more aligned and conformed behaviours and decisions. A population that *feels* the same experiences is, Laing argues, a population whose behaviours will become *de facto* more controllable.[2]

The commodified self-concept is further contrasted with Roger Caillois's influential biological study of insect mimesis and camouflage. In this work, Caillois argues that collective mimicry not only destabilizes the distinction between the body and its environment, but it also collapses the feeling of subjectivity into the surroundings in which mimicry takes place. In short, as camouflage blends the organism into the plant world, the distinction made between self-concept and sensory environment collapses into the perils (and promises) of a potentially self-destructive *speculative mimesis*.[3]

The second part of the chapter traces the logics of virality/growth to a two-pronged trajectory in consumer research. The first targets individual persons by way of a first-person phenomenological approach. The second focuses on intensifying impersonal experiences by cultivating shared experiences and the interrelatedness of self–other similarities. In terms of developing a nonphenomenological syntax to grasp this second trajectory, the chapter argues that previous approaches to consumer contamination and alienation need to be reoriented towards new exploitative methods that work on *folded* consumer relations.

The Mutational Politics of Virality

Before we begin to explore virality/growth in the consumer context, I want to note just how leaky the concept has proved to be in terms of escaping its original remit. Once associated with inexpensive viral marketing,[4] the spreading of cute cat images and contagious YouTube idiocy,[5] virality has spilled over into politics. The realization of its political charge ensured that virality was initially the tool of choice for left leaning radicals aiming to circumnavigate entrenched state media channels and grow insurgent political support for prodemocratic movements. In recent years, however, this revolutionary potential has shifted from a democratic bed of roses to a fascistic orchid garden. Indeed, the revolutionary moment has radically veered to the right. This new trajectory does not only apply to Trump, Twitter and the White House, but also brings in politicians like Jair Bolsonaro, creating the 'perfect storm' of fascism, neoliberalism and WhatsApp in Brazil.[6] In short, then, the business proposition of virality/ growth has entered into the dark refrain of social media contagion.

Evidently, there is nothing particularly new in the proposal to trace lines running between fascism and capitalism. A notable series of lines have previously been drawn up between the fascist and his dialectical rise from the decay of capitalism.[7] Developing on the notable dialectical tracing made by Lenin, for example, fascism is often represented as the extreme of the decomposition of both imperialism and capitalism. Unlike the Marxist, who seems to have emerged 'exasperated' from capitalist modernity, both fascists and Nazis were born from out of a 'decomposed modernity'.[8] The discussion here, though, is less concerned with the decaying dialectical structures of capitalism than it is with a biopolitical expression of experience, linked to both far-right contagions and corporate social media cultures. Perhaps, more significantly, then, although fascists and Nazis are clearly not the double of experience capitalism, both regimes share an indebtedness to the functioning of comparable biopolitical apparatus.[9] The recent spreading of far-right hate on social media is, as such, coincidental with the business needs of a prosperous experience economy: the pinnacle of which is found in the drive by platforms to sustain market positioning by intensifying the sharing of felt experience through virality/growth. In short, then, the main proposition I want to pursue in this chapter is that the logic of virality/growth is concomitant with the contagions (and immunizations failures) that have allowed the *strongmen* of the far right to flourish on social media. In the next chapter, I will similarly reposition the revolutionary power of collective mimesis as a counter to the equivalent immunopolitics of fascism and capitalism.

Against the Backdrop of Experience Capitalism

We need to begin by noting that Snapchat's interest in virality/growth belongs to a manifestation of a much broader, emergent mode of experience capitalism. The origins of experience capitalism can be traced back to 1970 and Alvin Toffler's book, *Future Shock*, wherein a chapter titled 'The Experience Makers' prophesizes where the economy is heading after the exhaustion of the service industries.[10] It is here that Toffler first introduces the idea of the experience industries as…

> … a revolutionary expansion of certain industries whose sole output consists not of manufactured goods, nor even ordinary services, but pre-programmed 'experiences'. The experience industry could turn out to be one of the pillars of super-industrialism, the very foundation, in fact, of the post-service economy … the experience industry of the future and the great psychological corporations, or psychcorps … will dominate.[11]

A similar theme emerges in the field of consumer research in the early 1980s, where Holbrook and Hirschman argue for 'an experiential view' of consumption focused on the symbolic, hedonic (the pursuit of fantasies, feelings, and fun), and aesthetics of the consumption experience.[12] It is in 1999; nonetheless, that Joseph Pine and James Gilmore, seemingly unaware of Toffler's futurology, first introduced their model of the experience economy.[13] This is a mode of capitalist economy that brings together consumers and businesses in ways that are assumed to owe more to the aesthetic of a Walt Disney theme park than Henry Ford's factory model.[14] Moreover, capitalism becomes, in this new light, more theatrical as consumers and businesses perform experiences in similar ways to Erving Goffman's social actors present themselves to each other.[15]

Virality/growth is part of a twenty-first-century digital expansion of the experience economy ostensibly focused on the user. As follows, the user experience (UX) industry presents a convergence of interaction design, coding and online marketing psychology akin to Toffler's pre-programmed experiences. The added value of digital experiences can, on one hand, include conventional commodities, goods and services readily transformed into new experiences realized through design, branding, and marketing. The point is that the experience economy is more attuned to the idea that it is the experience itself that often captivates user–consumer attention, leading to emotional engagements and the all-important purchase intent.[16] At its most deep-seated though, on the other hand, there is an intensification of felt experiences that do not refer back to a tangible product or service. The viral design of a social media platform is apposite here since it does not appear to relate in any palpable way to a conventional product. It is this digital transformation of commodity production that arguably leads to a business need to realize value in cultivating newly mediated interactions, engagements and the sharing of experiences related to the social contexts in which they spread. It is indeed the work of the UX industry, composed of UX consultants, interaction designers, information architects, ethnographers, behavioural psychologists, big data researchers, coders, biofeedback experts, network strategists, and online marketers to produce the sensory environments in which shared experiences can be cultivated, captured, spread and exploited. These environments are often referred to in the industry vernacular as consumer *communities*.

UX consumer research is able to draw on the resourceful expertise of these specialists to prime sensory environments in which experiences might occur. To be sure, the broader concept of experience capitalism emerges from extracting value from what is often already in action, but requires cultivation and experiential *expropriation*. Along these lines, and borrowing from Ganaele Langlois and Greg Elmer's work on corporate social media, we might say that what experience capitalism does is (a) more closely aligned to the patterning of existing experiences, and (b) significantly focused on the relational aspects of interaction and the capacity of machines to learn from impersonal social context rather than individual subjective experience.[17] Here, we can see how Pine and Gilmore's Goffman-inspired theatrical presentations of the self-concept are expanded to a point where the capture of the performance of user experience moves beyond any one locatable subjective viewpoint to the massive-scale automations of impersonal experience gathering. As these big data captures have become more pervasively realized through the invention of social and ubiquitous computer technologies, the subjective experience – described by Goffman as the presentation of self – is, as Greenfield argues, increasingly teased out into the public domain.[18] That is to say, human subjectivity is no longer the centre of the user experience (as I will contend in Chapter 5, it never has been). On the contrary, experience capitalism persists in a sensory world, connected to business by way of social media apps, relational databases, sensors, and computerized everyday things that process experiences in which consuming subjectivities are constantly being made.[19] This persistent focus on intensifying the user experience becomes the central point of the discussion wherein the theory of the somnambulist and the collective nonconscious collides with increasingly aesthetic modes of capitalism.

Virality/Growth

Following the old mass media theory adage, then, the UX industry would seem to partially repeat a diagram of power in which the industrial-scale stimulation of conscious audience engagement transforms audiences into unconscious commodities.[20] Certainly, in many ways, experience capitalism appears to be a more refined and targeted repetition of Dallas Smythe's *Consciousness Industries,* reapplied to online populations. As the updated theory goes, *if you are not paying for it, you are the product.* Facebook currently has more than 2.23 billion products (or users as they prefer to call them). The figures are truly astounding. For example, in the fourth quarter of 2017 the company made, on average, $26.26 from each user.[21] This number varies a lot given the location of the user in the world. If you live in the US or Canada you are a far more profitable product ($84.41) than Europe ($27.41), or the Asian Pacific ($8.92) where the platform is banned in China.[22] Facebook is, as such, a multi-billion-dollar business that makes huge profits from extracting value from the vast traces of personal data social connectivity provides. It does this mainly by allowing third parties (mostly advertisers) access its data value chain. Of the $40.65 billion of income Facebook made in 2017, $39.94 billion was derived from its advertising ecosystem.

Rather than simply grasp the social media business model as a commodification of the person, however, others have pointed more specifically to the monetization and modification of user behaviour. Like this, Shoshana Zuboff argues that it is the user's behaviour that is now the product. It is through data capture and analysis that the social media business 'produces rewards and punishments aimed at modifying and commoditizing behavior for profit'.[23] The social media business model is of course reliant on the quantitative assembling of masses of user-products *and* their behaviours. Arguably, though, what really brings in the money are the qualitative relations established between users.

A closer look at Facebook's advertising ecosystem is revealing in this sense. It is certainly a contradictory ecosystem, since, on one hand, it appears to be an open system to the frontend user. In short, anyone can advertise on Facebook. The process of becoming an advertiser takes just a few minutes by way of five clicks and requires no verification, evidence of identity or registration of a legitimate business.[24] On the other hand, though, at the backend, invisible to the user, parts of the ecosystem are somewhat blurry or utterly opaque. This situation is clearly controversial since the lack of transparency about why users see certain ads feeds into public concerns about privacy violations, discrimination, invasive and insensitive strategies, ad-driven propaganda and even the spread of targeted hate speech.[25] As follows, on one level, advertisers get access to Facebook data through a variety of tools that enable targeting of users based on some fairly conventional methods, such as, age, gender, location, interests and retargeting. However, user location, platform activities and behaviours, as well as content shared with friends, becomes part of a proprietary microlevel system of deeper consumer surveillance hidden from the user experience.

The opaquest (and most substantial) of these new ad surveillance tools is Facebook's *lookalike audiences*. Advertisers can reach, engage and convert users via targeted ad campaigns using an unknown proprietary algorithm which establishes massive scale self–other similarities. As a result of the black box nature of this tool, users have no way of knowing why they are being targeted as part of a lookalike audience. They will never meet their lookalike (see figure 11). Yet it has been shown that the lookalike tool makes users more vulnerable to deception and discrimination.[26] In many ways then, it is neither the person, nor their specific behaviours that are being commodified. On the contrary, it is, instead, the relational aspects of self–other similarity that is captured by these algorithms, so that users can be targeted. It is indeed the sharing of user experience that needs to be cultivated and encouraged to spread and grow. *Platforms need communities!* In other words, they need to nurture activities and engagements that help to grow lookalike audiences. As follows, social media platforms have become viral assemblages, designed to provoke imitative actions to spread in ways similar to those suggested by Tarde in the previous chapter. Unlike the consciousness industries of the past (the ad agencies of Maddison Avenue, for example), the business model of virality/growth now involves the algorithmic stirring an imitative collective nonconscious through which surplus value is achieved by provoking of contagious experiences, generating data to be sold on to advertisers for profit.

Along these lines, the discussion below marks a shift away from the commodified self-concept (being the product), to processes that capture or lure shared felt experiences to relational zones of self–other similarity.

Figure 11 'You'll Never Meet Your Lookalike.'
Illustration by Mikey B. Georgeson.

Accordingly, before the discussion can move on, a moment of transition needs to be highlighted between what is essentially an old production line concept of ideological contamination of the consumer and a new continuous production of viral relationalities, which *work on* producing collective mimesis. Significantly, then, unlike the commodified self-concept, which is alienated and divided, the intensification of experience produces a folded similarity, or a tendency towards the *becoming-the-same* of experience.

The Ideological Contamination of the Self-Concept

The alienated self-concept theorized by exasperated Marxist media theorists owes a significant debt to Friedrich Engels' definition of the German ideology. This is a 'process' Engels regarded as 'accomplished by the so-called thinker consciously … but with a *false consciousness*'. 'Otherwise', Engels argues, 'it would not be an ideological process at all'.[27] Indeed, in the commercial visual media cultures experienced from 1950s onwards, the Marxist analysis of advertising significantly expanded on Engels's notion of false consciousness from a decidedly ocularcentric perspective. Prominent in this field is the work of Judith Williamson whose concept of an alienated *Created Self* sets out the consumer's experience of adverts as a semiotic encounter with Roland Barthes's ideological trickery.[28] Williamson offers an analysis of an encoded, symbolic visual experience, which is filtered through the fake representation of the advert's imagery. The false self-concept that emerges from these semiotic experiences is created by an ideological deception hidden in the form of the ad. The Created Self is located, as such, at a point of intersection whereby personal experience becomes contaminated by capitalist semiological structures of psychical power.

Significantly, Williamson's *Created Self* grasps the contaminating power of capitalism as passing through a representational artifice which functions like a social mirror produced by the advert. This is an idea that is clearly influenced by Jacques Lacan's theory of the mirror phase, and helps Williamson to explain how a false self-concept emerges through delusional encounters with the unattainable *other* represented in the advert.[29] Which is to say, an alienated self is *created* in these encounters with unachievable images of beauty or joy, such as those that appear in the illusory airbrushed complexion of a Chanel model or the fabricated bliss of Pepsi People. In effect, these ideological and psychoanalytical encounters act as a false external mirror of the world in which the phenomenal self meets, mimics and attempts to assume the fake representation of the ad. It is this reflected experience that deceptively reinforces the ideological status quo, which becomes etched, it would seem, in a person's false consciousness. The process of ideological and psychoanalytical contamination is thusly defined by a psychic *internalization* of a fake representation of the external world in consciousness. Developing on Engel's original concept, then, Williamson's passive consumer of ideology becomes so captivated by the experience of their newly animated media environment that they begin to mimic features of their surroundings like one of Lacan's infants. In effect, their mimicry acts as a kind of psychic camouflage the consumer displays, ensuring that they become similar to each other and the products they consume.

The influence of Lacan in Williamson's work is notably guided by the former's interest in ideas about mimicry established in Caillois's study of biological camouflage in the 1930s.[30] Eschewing arguments that position camouflage as a manifestation of an evolutionary necessity to mimic in order to adapt and survive, Caillois pointed instead to more arbitrary adoptions of environmental disguises. The random and sometimes self-destructive tendency for some organisms to mimic their background suggested to Caillois that a strange process of spatial capture was at work. In short, he argued that camouflage arises from the eventual ensnarement of an organism in its own topological surroundings. However, despite Caillois's influence on Lacan's comparably contra-adaptationist approach, this notion of mimicry as a kind of topological capture was subsequently redefined by Lacan in terms of how the externalities of experience eventually become internalized in the false self-concept. Which is to say, although the Lacanian self experiences the external world, it does so via the added dimension of the representational mirror's influence on the ego. Eventually, the externality of the commodified environment – experienced initially through the bodily affects and spatial lures of Caillois's camouflage – becomes captured in the inner world of Lacan's false psychic identification with the reflection. This is how the bodily affects of environmental experience become phenomenalized in Lacan's mirror stage. Likewise, Williamson's consumer becomes captivated and contaminated by a mysterious secondary order of representation. This is, indeed, the creation of identity occurring in representational space of forms. The representations may well be simultaneously false and alienating, yet nonetheless they are desirable. In effect, they satisfy an innate inclination towards a harmonious phenomenal sense of personality. In other words, it answers the phenomenal question: *who am I?*

Sharing Cultures and Identity Development

Williamson's analysis of ideological consumer contamination was published at a time when commercial visual cultures were dominating twentieth-century mass media. Evidently, several decades on and the internet has had a transformative influence on the experience of consumption. One significant variation is the capacity for consumers to now share their experiences through social networks. To be sure, sharing cultures have attracted the attention of critical theory. Despite some rather obvious methodical differences, much of the focus on sharing is still firmly anchored to the phenomenal approach, particularly with regard to how these practices are supposed to shape consciousness (false or otherwise). Christian Fuchs, for example, offers a Marxist political economy approach to social media, arguing that sharing is endemic to an ideological motivated marketing trick that aims to convince consumers that the experience offers them a kind of personal empowerment.[31] While stating that sharing is not an inherently negative human trait, its seemingly benevolent mobilization on social media falsely masks the reality that these platforms are a capitalist business that exploits the natural tendency to share experiences. The rhetorical promotion of sharing on social media disguises, as such, the real business intention of social media: to sell users to advertisers.[32] Similar to Smythe and Williamson, then, Fuchs argues that by sharing experiences, consumers are simply reproducing themselves as commodities.[33] Indeed, 'young people do not just grow up and form identities', he contends, without being confronted by their experience of consumer capitalism.[34]

This reiteration of Engels's false consciousness is not surprisingly amiss in most business-focused consumer research into sharing cultures. The attention paid to personal identity formation is, nonetheless, a common thread. Jenna Drenten's account of adolescent girls' photo sharing is, for example, indifferent to any negative alienating experiences, preferring instead to concentrate on the affirmative effects shared imagery has on the development of a person's self-identity. Along these lines, photo sharing becomes 'integral to the creation and continuation of a stable harmonious self-concept'.[35] Adolescents are assumed to upload and share photos of themselves adorned in various products as a way to crystalize the formation of their self-identity and presentation of self to others.[36] This approach tends to downplay the role of social relatedness on a network in favour of a mode of sharing consumption experiences that actually makes the self-identity of the individual more distinct from its surroundings. Yet, Drenten's adolescent internalizes consumption by way of a familiar representational mirror. This is not precisely a Lacanian mirror, but it does nonetheless help the individual adolescent grapple with the same phenomenal question. Predictably, the kind of person produced in Drenton's sharing economy does not suffer from an estranged phenomenal experience. There is nothing false or divided about her consumer consciousness, it seems. What constitutes the I is instead defined by reflective internal choices and a Goffman-like management of self-identity driven by wilful consumption preferences for branded clothing, jargon, music taste, and so on. Evidently, an exasperated Marxist media theory reading of Drenton's analysis would see it as a continuous example of the ideological contamination of false consciousness, arrived at, uncritically, through external mirrors, but internalized nevertheless in a person's alienated phenomenal self-concept. As Williamson describes the phenomenal experience of ideological contamination, it 'enters you, and exists *inside* rather than *outside* your self-image'.[37]

The awkward question that inevitably arises with regard to the false consciousness of a dominated class is what is it exactly that makes the awakened rationality of infected consumers blind to the dominant interests of capitalism? Engels left behind few clues. Perhaps we are all just too busy keeping time with the accelerated rhythms of experience capitalism to notice the deception? The subsequent efforts by Marxist media theory to bring together Barthes and Lacan have similarly relied on an arguably ill-defined notion of how the seduction of a material advert exists in a kind of magical mirroring of an immaterial zone of secondary representation and symbolic form. It would seem that the current opaqueness of methods of user commodification on social media do not require an external mirror that internalizes alienation. The hidden, black box algorithmic stimulation of shared experiences and sorting of self–other similarities (the lookalikes mentioned above) are a mode of social media marketing more akin to a dystopic Black Mirror than it is a mirror that reflects or falsely simulates the self-concept. If there are mirrors used in the lookalike, they are opaque. They reflect nothing back to the consumer. So, perhaps we need to remove all mirrors from our analysis too.

Clearly, though, even when these mirrors are removed, there is still a level of trickery involved; a magical contamination of sorts. It is, nonetheless, this concept of deceit which ideology on its own does not adequately explain. How do ideas clandestinely contaminate the self-concept? Some authors have argued that what seems to be missing from the Marxist analysis is the role of affect, feeling and emotions in ideology.[38] Along these lines, it is interesting to note that Williamson actually begins to unpack this problem by making a link between the exploitation of a consumer's feelings and the emotional needs that are falsely fulfilled by adverts. The rendering of feelings in the *Created Self* is nonetheless explained entirely by the ideological structures of language in which they are apparently made.[39] There is, as such, still little inkling as to how these tricks produce false consciousness.

What needs to be added to ideological analysis is a consideration of ways in which felt experiences become central to the trickery; that is to say, part of the felt, affective, visceral registering of illusory experience. As Brian Massumi contends, we need to trace the point where affect enters the dominant ideology. As follows, '[t]he reigning rationality must be translated', but this translation needs to be 'occulted, hidden, distorted'.[40] To be able to hide like this, rationality, Massumi argues, 'must pass through another medium'.[41] So, it is through the medium of 'mere feeling' that false consciousness begins to play its tricks. Crucially, this visceral trickery is neither an experience felt on a personal nor structural level. On the contrary, the contamination of 'mere feeling' is social, and therefore always impersonal, even before it becomes hidden in the black boxes of relational databases and algorithmic marketing.

Towards a Nonphenomenological Approach

Williamson's decoding of adverts is still germane since it draws important critical attention to the many ruses that help to sustain the dominant grip capitalism has on desire. The Marxist approach to media has played a key role in maintaining a much-needed critical media literacy movement that has in the past significantly challenged the use of patriarchal imagery, for example, as a mode of marketing hegemonic consumer lifestyles. Arguably, without this early critique, the kind of popular dystopic media theory exhibited in TV shows like Black Mirror would never have seen the light of day. However, this kind of critical intervention into the ideologies of visual media, and its legacy in terms of critiquing body image and false identity, has been significantly updated since they first appeared in the latter part of the twentieth century.

Feminist writers like Karen Barad, Luciana Parisi, Elizabeth Grosz and Patricia Clough are readily aligned to a new materialist exploration of the body's relation to new technological and scientific environments. Notably, these new materialist accounts significantly challenge the idea that the body is an inert piece of matter that ideological discourses simply happen to. On the contrary, *matter is always lively!* The relation between bodies and matter is not therefore deconstructed; bodies are not opposed to matter or technology; indeed, matter has a relationship to matter in itself. This is an immanent relation; part of a matter-flow or material vitality. Consequently, new materialism does not assume the absolute centrality (or transcendence) of human consciousness (false or otherwise) in these material relations. *Mind does not transcend matter.* In an age of big data, the knowing phenomenological subject has become utterly decentred in its relation to the operations of a pervasive capitalist digital culture. Experience capitalism can be grasped in this way as deeply entangled with the sensory organs of individual humans, but it is not governed by them. As Clough puts it, the relation between human bodies and technologies, 'especially those technologies that are presently bringing into human experience what only technology can enable', leads us to a concept of user experience that might be considered 'below human conscious and cognition, [and] outside of the current understanding of life-itself'.[42] Material relations of this kind are regarded as *more-than-human*.

Clough theorizes the 'speculative' nature of the user unconscious against the backdrop of what she calls the datalogical turn in digital culture. This turn, she contends, precludes the idea that systems are closed or that distinct organisms can exist as if *outside*, or even running alongside, all other kinds of matter. Certainly, the idea of a self-regulating, self-concept becomes a fiction in the datalogical turn. The notion of self as an autopoietic machine is consequently replaced by autoaffection and the emergence of new forms of nonconscious and immanent subjectivity. As Mellamphy et al. put it:

> [Clough's] 'speculative' subject of big data is focused, not on an holistic form of self-representation or self-knowledge, or even self-interest, but rather on the maintenance of malleable sets of anticipatory and liquid capacities, which can change and adapt to new (presumably algorithmically computed) forms of appreciation and depreciation generated from elsewhere.[43]

It would seem that the old phenomenal accounts of self, body and identity start to unravel in the residue of these speculative productions of new materialism. It is important to state at this point, however, that my initial challenge to the dominance of phenomenal experience does not begin with new materialism or indeed the datalogical turn. Certainly, before returning to any of these themes, the theoretical trajectory of nonphenomenological experience needs to be traced back to the earlier influence of Caillois and Laing. Both similarly sought to unravel, in varying degrees, the unity of the phenomenal self-concept as it is confronted by collective mimicry, on one hand, and a political account of shared collective experience, on the other. To begin with, and aside from his influence on Lacan, Caillois's study of mimicry from the 1930s draws significant attention to the lively relation organic matter establishes with inorganic matter. In fact, his study of the material relations established in insect mimicry shows how camouflage obviates the distinction between the materiality of the body and psychic feeling of personality. Similarly, Laing's observations of the newly mediated intensities of experience in the 1960s help us start to rethink ideological trickery. Which is to say, he shows how the experiential control of a population effectively *works on* an impersonal register of collective mimicry, entraining and aligning bodies, psyches and behaviours in a rhythmic refrain.

Caillois's Lure of Experience

Before venturing into Caillois's world of insect mimicry, the above comparison between a new materialist Tardean society of micro-imitation and the trend towards virality/growth needs some further context. To be sure, this theoretical relation can be supported by explicit examples of efforts made to produce contagion on social media and other consumer environments. Some of these examples are discussed at length towards the end of this chapter, but for now, a controversial emotional contagion experiment by Facebook and Cornell University, published in 2014, stands out.[44] Along these lines, Tero Karppi has made the point that this empirical study of the extent to which massive-scale user emotions can be manipulated by the trickery of the researchers (they manipulated the news feeds of some 689,003 unknowing Facebook users) can be grasped according to two theoretical approaches to affect, feeling and emotion.[45] On one hand, the affective contagion of a user's emotions can be understood as operating on the level of the person. Affect is, like this, equated to the cognitive emotions of the subject, which are then mapped according to the ways in which subsequent felt emotions are passed on from user to user. In other words, what is measured in the experiment relates to how each user's emotional responses to fake posts trigger the spreading of subsequent emotions experienced personally by other users. On the other hand, Karppi follows the same new materialist rendering of affect, feeling and emotion, referred to above. In a nutshell, the new materialist focuses on the pre-subjective registering of affect before it becomes emotionally subjectified. The relation between the user and the platform is not therefore comprehended according to a subject's personal emotional response to a manipulated news feed, which is then passed on to other users. On the contrary, this approach concerns the modes by which the platform itself can modify and distribute affects that intensify the user experience. Herein, then, we can locate the contagiousness of the user experience in something approaching Clough's lively matter!

In what follows, I will further speculate as to what kind of new materialist theories of mimesis might help us to understand the various ways in which these platforms intensify experiences and propagate affective contagions. What I am ultimately interested in here is the imitative practices that seem to operate in the opaqueness of the lookalike audience. Which is to say, my interest is in how lookalike algorithms and databases might capture, or lure, the relational aspects of self–other similarity. Like this, Caillois's observations of the environmental mimicries of insects (as well as fish, octopuses and mantises) continues to be a rich resource.

Caillois's study begins by confronting what he sees as a prevalent myth in evolutionary biological and entomology; a myth which explains camouflage as an instinctual form of protective immunity enabling an organism to hide in its surroundings. As Rosalind Krauss puts it, Caillois's study challenges a prevalent adaptationist's account of why a mimicking insect becomes 'the double of its background'.[46] Along these lines, insect camouflage is commonly regarded as a process of protective coloration, wherein the organism's visual assimilation of the spatial environment of the plant world is, for example, supposed to minimize detection by predators. Camouflage is, in short, a survival tactic that enables a vulnerable prey to act in relation to its predator. It provides an outer layer of visual protection that enables the insect to subsist by blending in. The adaptable surface (or skin) of the organism thus becomes the first level of an immunological defence apparatus, which exempts it from environmental threats. Moths imitate leaves, caterpillars imitate twigs, and the 'praying mantis fashions itself as so many emerald blades of grass', in order to outsmart predators. As a result, the organism is able to 'hold itself intact' in the environment.[47]

Caillois's study challenges this myth by drawing attention to many cases where camouflage actually increases the chances of an insect being consumed by a predator, since by blending in to the plant world, the organism can become the foodstuff of its predators and even its fellow species. This kind of adaptive behaviour does not seem well designed to keep an organism held together *intact* as a stable subject in space. Caillois's alternative theory points to a strange *spatial lure*, suggesting the organism's surrounding are not simply an external feature of life, adapted to protect integrity in the environment, but instead become constitutive of its identity. The lure is, as such, a complete reversal of the Gestalt distinction made between figure and ground. It is a disorder of perception, which induces an organism towards becoming just one of many spatial coordinates in its surroundings. As Elizabeth Grosz puts it, the lure outlines ways in which 'the relations between an organism and its environment [become] blurred and confused'.[48] It is a disturbance of perception Krauss similarly describes as the moment when the body of the organism collapses into its surroundings. The lure therefore 'deliquesces, doubles the space around [the organism] in order to be possessed by its own surrounds'. To be possessed in this way leads to the 'effacement of the figure'. The Gestalt figure on ground consequently becomes 'ground on ground'.[49]

I will further expand on the implications of Caillios's resolving of the distinction between the physical figure of an organism and it surroundings in the next chapter on the immunological problem. However, Caillois's spatial lure is important to this discussion since despite explicitly influencing Lacan's mirror stage, and subsequently inspiring Williamson's Created Self, it actually challenges ideas concerning what constitutes the difference (if any) between an organism's surroundings and its inner world of identity. Unlike the ideological capture of the Created Self and the subsequent phenomenological contamination of a false inner psyche, Caillois argues that the spatial capture of an organism in the coordinates of its surroundings will also lead to a destabilization of the feeling of subjectivity. Just as the physical figure of the organism fails to become distinguished from the materiality of the ground, it also fails to maintain the boundaries between its inner sense of psyche and the outside world it inhabits. As follows, Krauss points to Caillois's insistence on a 'peculiarly psychotic yielding to the call of space'.[50] This is the collapsing of the Gestalt figure and ground in both a physical and psychical sense, likened to a 'slackening of the contours of [organism's] integrity, of its self-possession'.[51] Certainly, Caillois explicitly challenges the entire notion of a discrete personality when he contends that the person is not the origin of the spatial coordinates of the surroundings that are mimicked. The person is rather just one among many of coordinates of spatial capture. This is a critical destabilization of the feeling of personality grasped as indistinct from its material surroundings. As Caillois puts it:

> The feeling of personality, considered as the organism's feeling of distinction from its surroundings, of the connection between consciousness and a particular point in space, cannot fail under these conditions to be seriously undermined.[52]

This take on the lure of experience has some significant similarities with the Whiteheadian lure discussed in the previous chapter. It can be grasped at this point as: *The drawing in of the organism's sense of self away from the coordinates of self-possession towards an impersonal spatial seduction.* The lure offers an innovative theoretical move, suggesting that the contamination of experience can occur outside, *in the surroundings*, without needing to be internalized, or indeed personalized. This is a destabilization of the self-concept Caillois compares to the psychology of psychasthenia; a now defunct clinical name for a condition linked to excesses of anxiety and obsessive and compulsive behaviour. This psychic moment of indistinction is wonderfully captured in Grosz's partial paraphrasing of Caillois below:

> The psychotic is unable to locate himself or herself where he or she should be: such subjects may look at themselves from the outside, as others would; they may hear the voices of others inside their own heads. They are captivated and replaced, not by another subject (the horror of the double) but by space itself: I know where I am, but I do not feel as though I'm at the spot where I find myself. To these dispossessed souls, space seems to be a devouring force. Space pursues them, encircles them, digests them . . . It ends by replacing them. Then the body separates itself from thought, the individual breaks the boundary of his skin and occupies the other side of his senses. He tries to look at himself from any point whatever in space. He feels himself becoming space, dark space where things cannot be put. He is similar, not similar to something, but just similar.[53]

In terms of the development of a nonphenomenological approach, the psychic vulnerability to penetration by *outside* forces, Grosz expresses above, can be further mapped to an impersonal collective experience found in Laing's work on the politics of experience.

Laing's Alienation, Control and Experience

Although with one foot firmly rooted in phenomenal experience, Laing's appeal to *social phenomenology* provides a unique bridge between a science of persons and an approach that gradually begins to lean towards all out social relatedness.[54] Already, in *The Divided Self*, Laing had famously argued that the estranged sense of the schizoid self needed to be analysed away from the norms and anomalies in mental health discourses. The problem of the schizoid is not identified as a problem *inside the head*, as such, but needs to be reconsidered instead as a problem of relating to the world. That is to say, alienated outsiders are estranged as much from society as they are from their own sense of a disassembled self. In other words, it is not solely the inner self, but the sick relations established with the external world that constitute the sickness of the schizoid.

It is nevertheless in *The Politics of Experience* that Laing seems to focus less on dividing self from surroundings and introduces instead a concept of shared experience. From this point, Laing's notion of personality becomes more folded, and more porous, as such. Certainly, his notion that this collective absorbency can be effectively *worked on* significantly helps my proposition in this chapter (a) go beyond the isolated self-concept as the site of contamination, and thus (b) explore relational aspects of experience implicated in the control, entrainment and alienation of collective behaviour.

To grasp the full force of Laing's influence in this new context, it is helpful to begin by breaking his analysis down into the following two component parts. Firstly, he draws attention to an axiomatic understanding of how '*behaviour is a function of experience*; and both experience and behaviour are always in relation to someone or something other than self'.[55] People *in relation* to each other subsequently find that their behaviours are mediated by their experience of the other. Secondly then, Laing further argues that people are 'not self-contained'.[56] In some respects, there are traces of affect theory at work here since Laing argues that we are not merely effected by our own reflections on the external world, but we have affects on, and are affected by, our sensory encounters. Significantly, then, by positing 'each of us' as 'the other to the others', Laing starts to remove the boundary lines that divide self and other.[57] As a consequence, we can begin to see how the old grammar of personal experience forces a distinction between the psychological experience of self (the so-called inner world of experience) and the shared social self (the experience of being related to an outer world). Nonetheless, in *The Politics of Experience*, this syntax begins to disentangle itself from the knotted centring of the person. The 'relation of experience to behaviour is not that of inner to outer', Laing contends. Experience is not 'inside' the head; experience is 'out there in the room'.[58]

Laing's various references to Marx, Kierkegaard, Nietzsche, Freud, Heidegger, Tillich and Sartre certainly add to the philosophical backdrop of a particular kind of alienated experience. *The Politics of Experience*, nevertheless, sees Laing move on to develop a broader political theory of alienated experience to that grasped in Williamson's analysis. Laing's alienation is not inside, it is always-already *out there*. 'We are born into a world where alienation awaits us', he contends.[59] Laing's thesis thus presents a series of alternatives to the Lacanian inspired focus on the alienated self-concept. Primarily, it describes a different mode of contamination grasped in the *inducement* of shared experiences rather than the capture of the person. In many ways, then, Laing's approach moves away from the targeting and contaminating of individual personalities towards a *luring of experience*, which exercises power over a population. *The Politics of Experience* points to the primary goal of capturing relational aspects of experience (mainly resemblances) and thus aligning mass desires, emotions and visceral feelings to realize the captivation of mass behaviour. Like this, Laing provides a useful intuitive leap in our understanding of how contemporary mass persuasion might work.

In many ways, then, the concept of control Laing proposes becomes the centre point of this chapter. Which is to say, control for Laing requires an *intensification of experience*. 'All those people who seek to control the behaviour of large numbers of other people', he proclaims '*work on* the experiences of those other people'.[60] To be sure, almost 50 years before Facebook's algorithms began working on their massive-scale population of users; nearly half a century before this assemblage of millions of lookalike users could be sold on and targeted by advertisers and political campaigners, Laing understood something profound. *It is neither the person nor the behaviour that becomes the product.* He grasped, as such, how 'once people can be *induced* to experience a situation in a similar way, they can be expected to behave in similar ways'. Moreover, well in advance of the recent social media fuelled surge in the racist populisms of the strongman, Laing understood how inducing the feelings of a population and encouraging them to share the same feelings; to 'want the same thing, hate the same things, feel the same threat', would ensure that 'their behaviour is already captive'. This is control realized in the contemporary stirrings of user engagement, so that shared felt experiences can become entrained. Once this entrainment of experience is achieved then 'you have acquired your consumers [and] your cannonfodder'.[62]

To understand the logics of virality/growth we need to look to methodological trends in consumer research and practice which *work on experience* in ways that resonate with Laing and Caillois. Some of these methods predate social media marketing, but they nonetheless point to a growing concoction of methods focused on an intensification of experience that breaks down self/other distinctions.

The Logics of Virality/Growth

The link between Laing, Caillois and Facebook's algorithmically assembled lookalike audiences are important to our understanding of experience capitalism and virality/growth. This is because the latter marks a point where in order to *work on* their audiences, experience marketers no longer need simply to divide people into homogenous subgroups. The old criterion of segmented audiences, based on demographic, psychographic, individual behaviour or personality traits, have been updated. There are now more dynamic, immediate and relational methodologies, focused on stirring up user engagements and capturing the traces of shared experiences. Along these lines, a multitude of lookalike relations are being captured in the surveillance of potentially billions of so-called *instant experiences* users have with a platform. These experiences are apprehended dynamically through frequencies of page visits, durations of *real-time* engagement with content, and hesitative and impulsive clickstream interactions with interface elements like forms, posts, messages or buttons, and so on. This capture of an array of complex user engagements becomes part of a vast relational data infrastructure that continues to map shared user experiences to assemblages of self–other similarity across the network.

In theory, then, distinctions between a user, other users and the user experience are no longer divided into subgroups, but rather they become folded in these intensified, relational encounters. So, unlike the estranged commodification of self and the representational mirroring of a person, the assembling of lookalikes requires that personal experiences become indistinct. Like Laing's consumers and cannonfodder, users may well feel that their encounters with mediated experience are personal, and felt, as such, inside their heads. Nevertheless, this feeling of distinction is collapsed into an immanent process, which transposes shared experiences to an operational and material level of commodification. As we will see, this is not a mere doubling of experience. On the contrary, by becoming-the-same, the lookalikes lose their feeling of distinction between a sense of consciousness and the topological spaces they inhabit. In other words, like Caillios's mimicking insects, the distinction between the physical and psychic figures, and the ground on which they are situated, like the spaces between subjects, objects and surroundings, collapses into indistinction.

Clough's references above to experiences that 'only technology can enable' can be further grasped in this mostly hidden churning of nonphenomenological experience. What is captured in the infrastructures of relational databases and machine learning algorithms has no phenomenal subjective experience, as such. The lookalikes are an algorithmically assembled *subjectless* experience of self–other similarity. It is not a matter of taking into account the conscious experience (the knowing) of phenomena, since what ultimately constitutes the captivation of the collective nonconscious is defined by a sharing of phenomena-without-consciousness. The theoretical move proposed here similarly expands on what Karen Barad might describe as a kind of quantum user experience.[63] Along these lines, the lookalike audience, and even the marketers who purchase them, do not experience their own algorithmic similarity. It is only when the algorithm runs that these resemblances become *known*.

Data and Experience

A second methodological trend concerns a gradual drift towards a convergence between data analysis and user experience research. Along these lines, in recent years, the social media business has been doubly driven by an abundance of minable online data, on one hand, and an increasing interest in the contagiousness of shared experiences, on the other. The trend becomes most apparent in the research contribution Facebook's Data Science team make to the social media business model. The team was originally set up in 2007 to help improve 'the product experience'.[64] However, it soon expanded its analytics and behavioural science expertise to learn from, and monetize, the unrealized potential of data that began to emerge from the massive-scale sharing of experiences on the platform.[65] The experience design architecture of Facebook has correspondingly developed to not only improve the user experience of the product, but more crucially functions as a cultivator of experience, spreading it throughout the platform's population and capturing it as sellable data.

There is a user experience design history to these developments that needs some unpacking. Initially, Facebook's informational architecture was limited to encouraging users to give up some fairly basic demographic information required to set up a personal profile. These prompts nonetheless rapidly expanded to encourage users to record more intimate psychographic details, including listing their favourite films and music. The platform design went on to further encourage the sharing of content and communication through uploads and personal messaging services. Users were significantly prompted tag friends and leave a historical record of interactions via timelines. It was, nevertheless, the introduction of the extraordinarily successful Like button in 2009–10 that we see how effectively Facebook begins to intensify the user experience. Within five months of introducing the like feature, Facebook 'catalogued more than five billion instances of people listening to songs online'.[66] The subsequent introduction of an array of further compulsive buttons (Love, Haha, Wow, Sad, Angry) allows for a wider range of emotional intensities to become roused, captured and spread contagiously through the network.

The convergence between experience design and data gathering needs to also be considered alongside Facebook's development of an interdisciplinary research culture, galvanized around a mutual interest in the virality of shared experience. Facebook's Data Team are duly made up of graduates from computer science, sociology and behavioural and social psychology; most with an interest in how things spread online. Cameron Marlow, for example, who helped found the team in 2007, came from MIT's Media Lab where his PhD project was Blogdex; described as an early form of memetracker that traced trends as they spread through the blogosphere.[67] In a 2012 interview with MIT's *Technology Review* Marlow compares the challenges of the newly floated Facebook business model with 'the same challenges that social science has'. Which is to say, the biggest challenges Facebook has to solve are 'understanding why some ideas or fashions spread from a few individuals to become universal and others don't'. Moreover, Marlow's research interest covers questions about the role shared experiences play in making things go viral, and more specifically, the extent to which one 'person's future actions are a product of past communication with friends'.[68]

These network science approaches to social media contagion become similarly apparent in other Data Team research projects. For example, before joining Facebook, Michigan University based, Eytan Bakshy, worked with Yahoo to study how the sharing of experience on the platform spreads through the so-called echo chambers formed in networks comprised of close friends and weak ties.[69] Likewise, Adam Kramer, who studied decision-making and social psychology at the University of Oregon, used sentiment analysis to trace fluctuations in the occurrences of positive or negative emotional words and phrases spread through friend networks.[70]

The Ethics of Collaboration and Commercialization

A third trend points to ethical issues arising from virality/growth. Herein attention is drawn to the search for new ways to cultivate and monetize data by tapping into the collaborative nature and ever-looming potential for the commercialization of research that often begins life in the university.

This is a trend in consumer research that makes investments in academic work in the hope that it might produce a market advantage. For example, back in 2012, prior to the Cambridge Analytica scandal, Facebook were certainly trying to stake out their place in the new climate of competition with other big digital media companies like Google. In a well-publicized MIT interview Marlow was keen to point to the role the Data Team and their collaborative projects played in this objective. The team were 'free to use some of their time, and Facebook's data, to probe the basic patterns and motivations of human behaviour'.[71] They were indeed encouraged to collaborate and publish results with university researchers in academic journals which would 'lead to findings that help Facebook improve its products'. During this period of time, Facebook were also openly looking for new ways to prosper from developing lucrative relations with advertisers and brands. These actors were now recognized as a significant part of the social network community and core to a business model that could extract value from the vast flow of data the platform was generating. Bakshy, for example, was employed to 'extract advertising-related findings from the results of [his] experiments on social influence'.[72]

It is arguably the emergence of Facebook's collaborative networks which have challenged the ethical barriers most universities claim to maintain in order to protect research subjects. Certainly, these networks provided former Cambridge University researcher, Aleksandr Kogan, with the opportunity to commercialize the dubious methods of mass persuasion linked to the Cambridge Analytica scandal. Kogan's evidence at the DCMS Fake News hearings shows how closely his commercialized academic interests in data analytics were interwoven with researchers he encountered working with Facebook.[73] He describes working with their User Experience team and meeting fellow PhDs with a 'strong interest in research'. These researchers were now 'working at Facebook as user experience researchers, but they maintained that academic passion'. Kogan continues:

> That was really the focus; there is really no conversation at this point about any Facebook tools or anything like that. It was really one way for us to benefit and build research.[74]

Another high-profile collaboration between Facebook and university researchers that similarly caused ethical concerns about the methodologies deployed is the now infamous Facebook emotional contagion experiment discussed above.[75] In short, the experiment carried out by Data Team employee, Kramer, and colleagues from Cornell University involved the manipulation of emotional content appearing in social media news feeds.[76] Even if the contentious scientific claims arising from this attempt by Facebook and researchers from Cornell to influence the spreading of user moods produced fairly meagre evidence of widespread emotional contagion, the unethical design and implementation of the experiment itself warrants critical attention for a number of important reasons.[77] To begin with, the project draws attention to a collaborative experiment intended to make users 'experience the same emotions without their awareness'. In a conventional university setting such an experiment would of course need to undergo rigorous ethical clearance so as to protect the subject. Nonetheless, what seems to excite social psychologists like Kramer about working for Facebook is how the conception of such experiments can circumvent rigorous academic processes. In an interview intended to defend his experiment, Kramer bemoans the academic process for lacking instant impact. 'At Facebook', he says, 'my research is... immediately useful.' On discovering a new way of doing things, he claims, 'I just message someone on the right team and my research has an impact within weeks if not days.' This means that improvements can be rapidly made to the product.

Moreover, the controversy surrounding Kramer's research points to more questionable links established between the Facebook Data Team and its collaborative academic network, including, it must be added, academic publishers. 'In an academic position', Kramer bemoans, 'I would have to have a paper accepted, wait for publication, and then hope someone with the means to usefully implement my work takes notice.' However, the uncannily titled *Experimental Evidence of Massive-Scale Emotional Contagion through Social Networks* was published in the *Proceedings of the National Academy of Sciences* (PNAS) without undergoing rigorous ethical clearance. PNAS is considered by many to be a reputable science publication that claims to publish only the 'highest quality scientific research' since, as with most high-quality academic journals, all the papers published in it 'undergo rigorous peer review and approval by an [sic] NAS member before publication'. Yet, after publishing the controversial emotional contagion research paper, the journal came under considerable pressure to justify why it had included work that had so obviously not followed rigorous ethical procedures common to high-quality academic research. Certainly, PNAS accepted that it is 'a matter of concern that the collection of the data by Facebook may have involved practices that were not fully consistent with the principles of obtaining informed consent and allowing participants to opt out'. Yet, PNAS controversially argued that as a 'private company Facebook was under no obligation to conform' to these kinds of ethical principles, and as a result the 'editors deemed it appropriate to publish the paper'.

Prosocial Contagion

Kramer's Facebook research points to new methods in consumer research that pose certain challenges to conventional approaches informed by the science of persons. There is a wide-ranging trend towards new methods garnered from the science of emotions, which veer away from modelling discrete personalities to explore the affective relations of felt experience. This shift can also be clearly seen in the trajectory of Kogan's research. The models he used to process the Cambridge Analytica data were firmly located in the science of persons. The data was gathered from a personality test app inspired by psychometric models developed by academics based in business schools at Columbia, Stanford, Pennsylvania and Cambridge. These psychometric models were developed using a well-publicized hypothesis that a person's psychological characteristics could be accurately predicted from their digital footprints, including Facebook likes and Tweets, leading to claims to an 'effective approach to digital mass persuasion'.[78]

Nonetheless, although feeding into the hysterics of the Cambridge Analytica scandal, the science behind psychometric models is highly contested; most surprisingly, it must be said, by Kogan himself. Indeed, Kogan's scepticism about the 'grossly exaggerated' results of psychometric models need to be seen against the backdrop of his main research interests. Like the Facebook Data Team, Kogan was more interested in emotional contagion than he was predicting mass behaviours through personality traits. For example, a co-authored paper Kogan published with the *Annual Review of Psychology* in 2014, attempts to map the 'rapid, involuntary fashion' of contagious social behaviours.[79] The paper refers to the potential of contagion across a range of social experiences, from 'laughter, blushing, and voting patterns to destructive health habits', as well as 'feelings of anxiety, and expressions of gratitude'.[80] Similarly, on his now deleted academic profile, Kogan explained his interest in 'the biology and psychology of human kindness and well-being'.[81] Which is to say, his work specifically focused on 'prosocial emotions' and explores 'processes, including positive emotions and selflessness'.

Central to the methodological approach applied to prosocial contagion is a relation established between, on one hand, the independent variables of the entrainment of experience and unconscious mimicry, and on the other, the observation of a dependent variable of *inducing*, through 'direct [physical and nonphysical] manipulation' of self–other similarities.[82] Humans are regarded as a 'highly mimetic species' predisposed to imitating and taking on 'the tendencies of others in their surroundings and social networks'.[83] Participants in one experiment were asked to sit opposite each other while both listening to rhythmic patterns of tones on earphones and tapping their fingers. Listening to the same rhythmic tones perhaps not unsurprisingly leads to mimicked synchronous tapping while different tones would lead to asynchronous tapping. However, the tendency to mimic physical tapping is also linked to participants reporting similar feelings; most notably higher levels of compassion were experienced as participants were observed becoming more helpful in completing tasks. Subsequent comparisons are made between these observations of physical and nonphysical entrainment and acts of behavioural synchrony, like those experienced in coordinated military marching, intended to induce disciplinary cohesion and cooperation in the real world. As the paper claims, 'even subtle acts of mimicry in the lab can induce feelings of self–other similarity and enhance prosocial responding'.[84]

Antisocial Contagion

In his book, *Antisocial Media: How Facebook Disconnects Us and Undermines Democracy*, Siva Vaidhyanathan argues that Facebook is 'the worst possible forum through which we could conduct our politics'.[85] To begin with, the social media business model is based fundamentally on advertising income. Facebook has, as such, perfected how to make its ads work for its customers, by way of, for example, making efficient use of personal targeting, but more crucially favouring 'content that is of high emotional power'[86] and has the potential for virality.[87] As follows, Facebook have become the go to consultant for political strategists who want to understand how to make their campaign ads go viral and grow. Certainly, the algorithms behind the emoticons users engage with on Facebook are there to purposefully detect and process highly charged investments in feelings, and crucially, make those feelings more intense and contagious. Certainly, before a user adds a thumbs up, a beating heart or surprised face to a friend's shared post or a targeted political ad, they invest in the social repercussions of broadcasting an emotion to their wider community of friends and the subsequent social and political entropies that make up these networks. Moreover, however, these investments are shared, collective impulses that might lead to cognitive stutters or hesitations (many of which will be detected by the algorithm), but are also intended to flow seamlessly through the collective user experience. As Vaidhyanathan contends, these ads flow through a user's 'field of vision among a weird mixture of decontextualized social, personal and entertainment based items'.[88] The emotional design, branding and contagiousness of a post is therefore paramount to making an ad a viral success for Facebook and its main customers, the advertisers.

Another trend in virality/growth that expands on Vaidhyanathan's Facebook-centred thesis is the broadening out of the strategy to include a range of third-party marketers, who similarly grasp the role of intensifying experiences as core to business success. For example, an article in the business section of the *Guardian* in 2018 draws attention to the ways in which the logic of virality/growth used by these businesses is further couched in the science of emotions. 'If you think things go viral on the internet by luck, think again', the headline declares, 'there's an industry gaming the system and Manchester's Social Chain is leading the way'. This social media start-up apparently expanded in just two years from five to almost 200 members of staff. It has an annual turnover of £9m. Big clients include Spotify, FIFA and Coca-Cola, who pay between £10,000 and £50,000 per month for social media services. Social media contagion is, they claim, no fluke! As the Social Chain's spokesperson says, it is 'emotion' that 'fires virality'. There is, they claim, 'a lot of science' behind virality. Certainly, 'people share feelings [on social media], not information'.

At the centre of these viral marketing strategies is the desire to make the felt user experience more intensive. Marketers need to produce more penetrating emotions in their Facebook posts, tweets or Instagram stories, so that the marketing message will spread further in the 'churning waves of [an] algorithm'. *Intensity is all!* There is little room for positive emotions, since 'low-arousal emotions such as contentment and relaxation are useless'. These 'induce humans to close down rather than open up'.

> If you want to get anywhere in the social-media game, you're going to need something stronger: frustration, anger, excitement, awe.

The viral reach of a social media campaign is, it would seem, measured according to the intensity of sentiments it elicits. The more widespread the stronger antisocial feelings become, the greater the online impression.[89]

Magical Contagion

Another pertinent development in consumer research that maps onto this third trend is a growing interest in so-called magical contagion. Beginning with early anthropological interest in the *unseen* contaminating transference of auras from nonhuman objects to humans in the late ninetieth century, the concept was latterly taken up in the 1980s by the behavioural sciences as a mode of contagion theory, before eventually being used fairly widely in consumer psychology research in 2000s.[90] In this latter context, magical contagion offers an explanation of how negative and positive, and physical and nonphysical contaminations of consumer experiences of products affects purchase intent. On one hand, then, the concept helps to map contagious transfers related to the disgust consumers might feel when a food product is physically contaminated by an insect or when positive emotions are elicited through bodily contact with sentimental objects.[91] On the other hand, researchers explore the contagiousness of nonphysical transfers, like those that occur via the sharing of emotionally branded consumer experiences on social media, for instance.

Significantly, magical contagion questions established claims in marketing research that consumption is solely a matter for the private self. Which is to say, the concept challenges the idea that an individual's purchase intent is partitioned in some way from relations established with others and the surroundings in which consumption takes place. In the area of sensory marketing, for example, the concept has been revived in an attempt to map out the 'transfer of unseen properties' related to consumer experiences, like emotions, which can affect consumer choices in both positive and negative ways. The concept marks a point where consumer research into contagion looks beyond the physical in ways that Facebook's Data Team have similarly done. The approach suggests new avenues of consumer research focusing on, for example, various collective contagions that affect decision-making processes, prompting consumers to either connect or disconnect from others.[92]

Data Power and Experience Capitalism

The proposed shift from the science of persons towards the science of emotions needs to be coupled to a wider discussion on what have been ostensibly described as *data power*. Along similar lines, Tero Karppi's recent work on Facebook's affective bonds argues that the arrival of a new kind of social media *data power* represents more than just the mere mobilization of the 'power of information and knowledge'. Data power also signals the 'operationalization' of information significantly produced by way of user interactions and engagements with these new platforms.[93] Arguably, the effectiveness of these new methods of mass persuasion yielded by corporate social media are not simply realized through the datafied targeting of personalities; on the contrary, they are methods that are rapidly learning to mobilize and put to work the magic of contagious emotional social media experiences.

Central to this revised concept of data power are the intensification practices that assemble shared experience. Certainly, as another collaborative academic / Facebook research paper puts it, the social media business is 'only as good as the content their users share'.[94] In short, there would be no data business without the widespread intensification of shared experiences. As we have seen above, the capture of lookalike audiences requires the continuous cultivation of user engagements that prompt the continuous flows of instant experience. In order to avoid economic stagnation, the social media business model must constantly develop its architectures and motivational methods so as to nurture new spaces of engagement and invent novel tools that imperceptibly encourage the virality of sharing. Collaborative Facebook research has, for example, theorized about motivational tools that can prompt inactive users by encouraging (and mobilizing) socially active friends to feedback positively on their posts.[95]

Data Doubles and Lookalikes

Karppi's work on Facebook also draws attention to the way in which Facebook's lookalike audiences begin to exceed their status of what have been called *data doubles*.[96] In this context, a social media user is said to have a data double comprised of their digital footprints, made up from profile information, the content of posts, likes, messages, shopping and entertainment preferences, the density of friends, and any other traces of surrendered personal data.[97] It is these data traces that are assumed to provide enough clues about a user's personality so that their consumption or political preferences can be predicted and targeted at the microlevel of interaction. It is, as follows, the relational resemblances established between these data fed mirror images of personality and real persons that are supposed to enable Facebook to produce their highly profitable lookalike audiences. However, as Haggerty and Ericson argue, 'while such doubles ostensibly refer back to particular individuals, they transcend a purely representational idiom'.[98] The exact status of a data double is indeed unlike the representational theory behind Williamson's mirror image. The flow of data algorithmically assembled as a lookalike audience must not be mistakenly grasped according to its mirroring of a particular person or their false representation. These mirrored reference points to a person are instead based on a 'pragmatic portrayal' of accurate (or often inaccurate) data about the market value of the user in relation to other lookalikes. They are a distillation of a self–other relation to the surroundings, which is either based on little more than a database entry relating to comparative preferences for shopping and entertainment or some deeper level of relation data surveillance.

Haggerty and Ericson argue that the data double is not a representation of a person, but a 'product of a new type of individual, one comprised of pure information'.[99] This particular concept of surveillant assemblages therefore works to separate (or abstract) users from their territorial surroundings so that they can be reassembled in some discrete location. This break from what might be called the creation of a Platonic double is of course welcome (see next chapter). The disassembled rational valuation of a person's data does not, however, fully capture the broader collective mimicries of experience capitalism. To be sure, the reduction of the mimicked consumer to discrete pockets of information ignores what Karppi calls the 'affective [nonconscious] associations of moods and groups' in which data harvesting takes place.[100] The next chapter returns to the concept of data doubles, but for now it is important to grasp, as Gabriel Tarde did, that the mimicry of a lookalike audience is an assemblage of sentimental relations, which spread through the economic psychologies of nonconscious associations.[101] In other words, the data value extracted from lookalikes cannot become decoupled from the intensification of collective affects that bring lookalike audiences into relation to each other.

A New Syntax of Indistinction

Before concluding this discussion, I want to note how a somnambulist theory of user experience presents a number of challenges to the dominant grammar of personhood, which has tended to conventionally account for experience as either subjectively or objectively defined. We can call this language of personal experience *phenomenal* and link it to a general science of persons with its own syntax. We can, for example, observe how certain phenomenologies and behavioural psychologies focus on experience, environment and personality and define their syntax accordingly:

> 1. Taken as a verb, phenomenal experience predicates the subject as the possessor of her own experiences. The self-concept is said to experience others, objects and its surroundings from a first-person perspective.

2. Taken as a noun, phenomenal experience is something that just happens to, or objectifies, a person. For example, a person who has bad experiences can become alienated from the world or she can learn from her experiences and move on. Such experiences might be regarded as environmental, but are nonetheless experienced personally.

3. By extension, the antonym of experience, *inexperience*, presents a person who is found to be without the object of experience. A person with a lack of experience, must therefore gain experience to overcome an absence.

4. As a recent expression of digital culture, the *user experience* provides an extended hypernym of phenomenal experience. Which is to say, experience is not something that only happens to a user, but it is also *performed* by the user.

Objective phenomenal experience (the kind that just happens to a person) can be located in theories of the commodification and alienation of the consumer discussed in this chapter. In these accounts, ideological encounters with capitalism do not initially or naturally belong to the person. The sense of a pre-existing self-concept – a supposed feeling of untainted personality – is said to be contaminated through exposure to ideologies experienced through media channels, for example. This particular capitalist production of an alienated false consciousness is a contamination theory of sorts, which significantly draws on Lacanian notions of mimicry and false identification. In other words, the ideological experience of capitalism *creates* the feeling of self experienced in mimetic relations established with the illusory imagery of an advert, for example.

Firmly rooted in phenomenal, yet false experience, these critical accounts of the alienated person provide a powerful and evocative reading of capitalism's colonization of a divided self-concept. To be sure, ideological analysis goes some way to explain how the repetition of external experiences not only contaminates the self-concept, but also captivates behaviours and social habits. Nonetheless, my aim in this chapter has been to develop an alternative theory of intensity and experience by subtly changing the syntactic rules of the game. The intention is to loosen experience from the syntactic limitations of phenomenal predication. The revised syntax proposes that the grip of experience capitalism is not primarily located at the level of the person at all. On the contrary, the focus of critical attention does not fall on what is created, but rather the process of creation itself. The syntax therefore describes a nonphenomenological process of experiential intensification, which exploits a porous, mimetic and indistinct self–other relation (see figure 12).

Admitting to the indistinction of the self–other relation is an important first step in the development of a new somnambulate syntax. As the focus moves away from experiences defined by subject/object predicates we again begin to explore a *subjectless* experience that produces a feeling of subjectivity or self-enjoyment. Returning to the Whiteheadian terms addressed in Chapter 2, then, this liberation of experience from the personal marks the point where the I in the mind only really *testifies* to the passing of experiences that come to mind. Certainly, as Stengers argues, the mind is *not* experience.[102] *It is not a cognitive command post!* This is why the sleepwalker is positioned on an experiential spectra wherein the phenomenal purview (personal experience or experience happening to a person) is replaced with an experience that produces these intense feelings of personality.

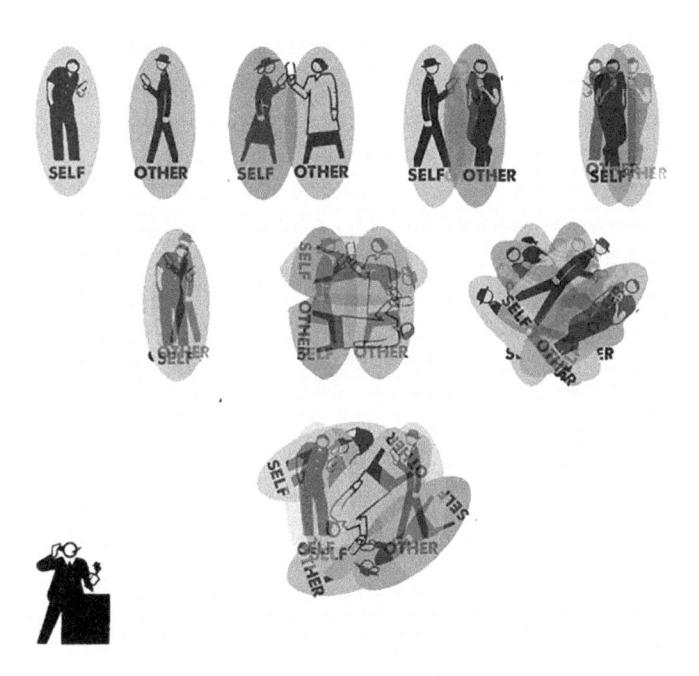

Figure 12 The Indistinction of the Self/Other Relation.
Illustration by Mikey B. Georgeson.

Conclusion

The main aim of this chapter has been to trace a line from the dark refrain of social media set out in the first two chapters to a mode of politics I have called experience capitalism. In summary, we have considered a new nonphenomenological syntax, which is intended to help us to distinguish between, on one hand, a particular Marxist analysis of commodity relations focused the alienation of a divided false self-concept, and on the other, a folded impersonal relation established between user experiences and digital cultures. Following feminist new materialisms, and the older influences of Laing and Caillois, we alternatively conceived of a potentialized sleepwalker, composed in the intensifications of shared experience; captured, nurtured and mobilized in the viral architectures of social media. This sleepwalker is a subjectless subjectivity grasped as an assemblage of relational data, feelings and bundles of autonomous collective affects. This is a sleepwalker rendered indistinct – her physical figure and psyche have been collapsed into the material surroundings of a relational datalogical turn. This luring of the possibilities of the sleepwalker, towards the assembling of datafied lookalike audiences, is comparable in many ways to the Whiteheadian concepts addressed in the previous chapter; a theoretical enquiry that will be returned to in the fifth chapter. For now, though, many of the trends in marketing research outlined in this chapter (what we might broadly call virality/growth) can be traced to a further series of lines that feed backwards (and forwards) to the dark refrain. For what mostly defines this dangerous moment in the history of the internet is that the kind of virality that used to be dismissed as a vector for cute cats and contagious idiocy, and perhaps naively celebrated by activists hoping to make their revolutions go viral, has now become the tool of choice for the strongmen of the far right.

Segue A Dark [Viral] Refrain

Figure 13 The Cleaners.
Illustration by Mikey B. Georgeson.

The shocking live streaming and subsequent widespread sharing of the Christchurch mass shooting on Facebook marks a cardinal moment in the dark refrain of social media. Following a spate of live streamed self-harm, suicide and murder on Facebook's Live Video, this latest shock event exposes the chronic dysfunctionality of social media immune systems, whether or not they are operated by human content moderators, nonhuman algorithmic detection systems, or indeed, both. The event should mark a moment in internet history where the case for self-regulation has been lost. The dominant Silicon Valley discursive triangulation of free speech, free market and content moderation done-on-the-cheap, surely needs to be usurped by a new regulatory formation?

In the UK, events in New Zealand have appeared in a new government White Paper proposing a new *arm's length* regulatory regime. Central to this initiative is a concern for just how rapidly and widespread horrific terrorist and extremist content of this kind has spread online. The fear is that although in the past it was a 'powerful force for good' which spread 'ideas and enhances freedom and opportunity across the world', the internet has since become a medium of dark corners infested with violent, racist, *online harms*.[1] Exactly how this new system of 'accountability and oversight ... moving far beyond self-regulation' will resolve the immunity problem is, however, unclear at this point. The proposed arm's length approach is combined with an all too predictable neoliberal slant to solving the immunity problem, proposing to 'boost' the business of online safety.

The UK government wants to promote the growth of 'distinct markets', including third-party human moderation and automated detection via AI/machine learning solutions. The paper commits to exploring the potential effectiveness of AI/machine learning solutions that can automatically detect and flag harmful content to humans. It also draws attention to inadequate content moderation, noting a number of investigations pointing to 'serious shortcomings in the training, working conditions and support provided for content moderators'.

There is a disturbing documentary about the plight of third-party content moderators working in Manilla called *The Cleaners*.[2] It highlights many of these 'shortcomings'. The film begins with an evocative, dark rhythmic refrain: the pulsing sound of digital cleaners at work, deciding if they should ...

> *Ignore, Delete, Ignore, Delete, Ignore, Delete, Ignore, Ignore, Delete, Ignore, Ignore, Delete, Ignore, Delete, Ignore, Delete Ignore, Delete, Ignore, Ignore, Delete, Ignore, Ignore, Delete, Ignore ...*

In a dark blue *mise en scène* with buzzing strip lights and flickering screens we find them; the Filipino moderators, earning as little as $1 to $3 per hour, working for third-party content review companies employed to clean up the dark corners of the web that Facebook, Instagram, YouTube, Google, Twitter, and others have helped to spread. Attention fixed on their screens, the cleaners have a target of 25,000 images and videos a day. They are allowed just three errors. This is *their* refrain: the seemingly never-ending loop of human content moderation.

> *Ignore, Delete, Ignore, Ignore, Delete, Ignore, Ignore, Delete, Ignore, Delete, Ignore, Ignore, Delete, Ignore, Ignore, Delete, Ignore, Delete, Ignore ...*

These platforms have been specifically designed to generate income streams from the cultivation and triggering of contagious user experiences.

The rhythmic refrain becomes more intense as content flows through the viral architectures of social media. By default, then, the highly prosperous business of virality/growth, and the 'maximized-engagement-at-any-cost business model',[3] has, to date, failed to implement truly effective human or technical solutions leading to the eradication of this dark spreading phenomenon.

In addition to these interrelated economic and architectural tendencies, there also appears to be another more integral, unresolved problem that is steering social media towards the dark refrain. *Social media has a masochistic streak!* The spreading of all those much yearned for good ideas and opportunities have become increasingly inseparable from toxic contagions of hate. This is an immunity problem that is due, in part, to a persistent bent towards self-destruction based on a failure to discern between opportunity and toxicity. Which is to say, despite regulatory pressures to boost human and technological interventions, the functioning of immunity on these platforms will remain flawed because of an intrinsic propensity towards autoimmunity. The immunity problem is marked out, from here on, as a problem of distinction: To *Ignore or Delete!*

4

Immunity, Community and Contagion

The main focus of this fourth chapter falls on a complex constituent of the dark refrain of social media: *the immunity problem*. The discussion is structured around three interrelated propositions, which are inspired by what Caillois considered to be the doubly dangerous luxuries of collective mimicry. Each proposition also shows how the logic of immunity (immunologic) is interwoven with logics of community and contagion.

The first proposition is initially informed by the technical failure of social media to effectively force immunological exemptions and subsequently halt contagion. To start with, then, the discussion focuses on the technical detail of an incapacity of platforms to discern between adversarial and nonadversarial patterns. This initial practical framing of the immunity problem exposes certain tensions between a series of failed engineered solutions and a flawed version of online community. As a consequence, making a distinction between free speech and hate speech, for example, becomes an economically redundant exercise, since exempting any kind of user content from the platform negatively impacts on virality/growth.

The second proposition concerns the resurgence of a perilous kind of immunopolitics implicated in the interwoven logics of immunity, community and contagion. This is an expanding biopolitical movement, which exploits the technical failures of the first proposition in order to spread divisive race hate contagions through online communities. Immunopolitics also exploits the destabilizing loss of self-identity immunity failures threaten to bring about and takes advantage of the virality/ growth model to propagate racialized distinctions that stir conflict-ridden communities into action. Along these lines, the second proposition traces a shifting biopolitical regime, which has moved on from more optimistic times of revolutionary contagion towards the current deadly refrain.

Finally, the third proposition returns to Caillois's notion of collective mimicry, exploring its potential to lure organisms towards environmental assimilation. This is a more radical and experimental proposition. It retheorizes the problem of immunity, searching out the possibilities of collective mimicry as a way to escape from the kind of racist and neoliberal immunological exemptions that promote pure bloodlines and private individuals. In this proposition, collective mimicry may well bring about the pain of identity-loss and self-destruction. Nonetheless, this instability might also bring about the potential of a selfless impurity; a nonprivate, nonracial collectivity; a new kind of co-occurrence, compromise and community.

The third proposition is not an ideal solution. It has its own set of problems. Which is to say, following the perhaps inevitable fear and instability produced by indistinction, the solution runs the risk of triggering Caillois's machoistic tendencies. Herein, the dangers of collective mimicry proliferate and the horror of autoimmunity threatens stability and constancy. However, the resulting indistinction also promises to collapse the forced distinctions of immunopolitics, potentially bringing about what Caillois refers to as *communal mimicry*. This is a promise that echoes, to some extent, Roberto Esposito's comparable claim that from out of the cracks of *immunitas*, we might be able to see 'the outline of a different *communitas*'.[1]

In terms of the immunological context of social media, this third proposition raises some very challenging questions regarding the current dark refrain.[2] To begin with, if the immunity problem means that an unregulated social media business is unable (or unprepared) to entirely remove forced racial distinctions from its platform, would these platforms persist in becoming even more immunopolitically extreme or could they possibly self-destruct? In other words, will the infestations of hate groups who have thus far camouflaged themselves within the failed immunologics of these platforms continue to spread forced distinctions, or could they, as Caillois contends, self-cannibalize?

Proposition One

The failure of social media immunity is driven, in part, by logical inconsistencies hardwired into the viral architectures of a social media platform. However, these inconsistencies are also endemic to barely hidden reluctance by corporate social media to invest in measures that might negatively impact on the lucrative income streams of the virality/growth business model. Therefore, despite promises of future technological fixes (machine learning and other AI solutions), the persistently vague distinctions made between what to delete and what to ignore, opens up social media to the perils of hate speech and racial bias.

Engineering the Immunity Problem

From an engineering perspective, the current social media immunity problem can be traced back to a much older, unresolved dilemma of exemption. This is a problem that has haunted networks prone to digital contagion since the 1980s. That is to say, digital networks have mostly failed adequately to differentiate between the business of remaining open for sharing, on one hand, while at the same time guaranteeing immunity from contagions of malicious content, on the other. In other words, immunity and the goals of the online sharing economy have frequently proven to be incompatible concepts. To be sure, although computers are good at executing repetitive tasks, learning and mimicking, they are not so good at detecting variant distinctions between benevolent and malevolent patterns.

Facebook's twofold solution (human and automated) to the immunity problem is familiar in terms of the engineering approach to the computer virus problem developed from the late 1980s. This comparison can be readily seen in Zuckerberg's appearance before Congress in 2018, where he promised that Facebook would employ 20,000 extra human moderators by the end of the year to work on security and content review. The use of humans by third-party companies to check, flag and judge if content violates policies, does indeed repeat earlier ineffective efforts made by a nascent antivirus industry (AV) to combat the epidemiological dynamics of computer viruses. The problem here is, in part, related to the overabundance of information. Along these lines, Facebook openly recognizes that with over two billion users, it could never individually categorize every piece of information as 'right' or 'wrong', or any other binary distinction: true/false, good/bad, hoax/nonhoax etc.[3]

Zuckerberg also assured Congress Facebook would make considerable future investment in 'building new technology to prevent abuse'.[4] This second solution is reliant on new machine learning technologies and other AI tools designed to thwart the spreading of hate speech, for example. Again, there are striking parallels here between this commitment to a technological fix and experiences of early AV researchers. In the 1980s researchers at IBM, for example, soon realized that a reliance on reactive human measures did not provide an adequate antidote to the massive scale virus problem. The immunity problem was further exacerbated at this time by virus writers who were able to camouflage their viral code using polymorphic techniques. These techniques meant that a computer virus could evade anomaly detection by mutating its identity. In response, and inspired by immunological threshold theories, IBM started to replace reactive human checking and primitive AV software with fully automated, rapid anticipatory systems. Early AV products, like IBM and Symantec's Digital Immune System (DIS),[5] replaced humans, simple scanners, heuristic checkers, and behaviour blockers with adaptive systems intended to automatically extract, detect and disinfect polymorphic viruses according to their unique digital signature. These products eventually developed into a billion-dollar AV software industry. However, although fully automated immune systems have greatly accelerated the eradication of malicious code in recent decades, they remain an imperfect solution, since it would seem that even old viruses and worms continue to evade anomaly detection.[6]

From DIS to FIS

Facebook have followed a very similar trajectory to that set out by the DIS project. In March 2011 the platform launched a software solution called the Facebook Immune System (FIS). In a technical paper, openly available to read online, Facebook engineering researchers explain the technical design of FIS, setting out how it uses innovative machine learning algorithms to detect anomalous and adversarial patterns of user interaction.[7] The paper claims that the system contributes to making Facebook 'the safest place on the internet for people and their information'.[8] Certainly, at the time of its release Facebook claimed that FIS was a remarkable technological solution to a wide range of problems impeding smooth social media communication associated with compromised accounts, phishing scams, malware, fake accounts, creepers and spam.

To grasp fully the significance of the engineering aspects of the first proposition, it is important to cursorily understand how FIS attempts to force distinctions. In a nutshell, then, the system uses machine learning algorithms to identify and learn from patterns of past encounters so that they can flag future encounters with bad interactions or fake content. On its launch, the system was carrying out a seemingly impressive twenty-five billion real-time checks and classifications a day, reaching 650,000 per second at peak performance. FIS is, nonetheless, a fairly conventional immunological system in the sense that it is supposed to make a familiar distinction between two kinds of patterns. On one hand, the system looks to protect and stabilize effectively the routines of nonadversarial actors. These apparently innocuous patterns of use 'will not actively work to subvert the learning and may even voluntarily give hints to aid learning'.

The creation of nonadversarial patterns are part of a significant learning process that is intended to improve the experience (and business) of the platform. Nonadversarial actors thus contribute to such things as search engine rankings, for example.

On the other hand, the system needs to discern and learn from adversarial pattern creators, or attackers, who work to 'hide patterns and subvert detection'. According to Facebook, there are three phases in an adversarial learning pattern cycle that need to be detected. The first phase concerns the attack mode, wherein an adversarial pattern maker attempts to take control of events by way of spreading spam, for example, across the network. Evidently, the problem of detecting the attack phase is exacerbated by what the researchers behind FIS call the 'virality of Facebook communication' prompted into action by the numerous vectors the platform interface provides for real-time contagions to spread, including live chat, messages, wall posts, and public discussion and fake friend requests.

The second phase marks the point wherein the anomalous pattern of contagion is supposed to be detected and defences subsequently triggered. This defence phase requires a complex series of algorithmic pattern learning events occurring in FIS, which again have to function in real time to capture the flows of anomalous attacks. These events are supposed to mark out the differences between adversarial patterns and other activities spreading through the platform's many viral vectors. Events include a complex real-time repetition of classifications, feature extractions, dynamic modelling, so-called floops (making data available for classification), and blocking actions. In fact, all of these events will have to be repeated over if the ensuing third phase (the mutation phase) kicks in. This third phase is indeed the point wherein the attacker mutates the pattern in order to produce a workaround intended to avoid the anomaly detection and the defence phase. Like the old polymorphic viruses, the mutation phase is where, it would seem, distinctions made between nonadversarial and adversarial patterns often begin to vacillate.

This is the point wherein the immunologic requirement to force a distinction between nonadversarial and adversarial patterns can potentially collapse into nondistinction. There are, evidently, practical implications that follow such breakdowns. In a research paper published four years after the launch of FIS, computer scientists Dewan and Kumaraguru argue that despite claims made about the efficiency of their immune system, Facebook continued to be comprised of a range of malicious fake posts and links.[9] From a sample of 11,217 breaches captured in their study, the authors identified only 34.95% that were deleted after being flagged. Another 65% remain undetected and undeleted for at least four months after they appeared (the duration of data gathered for the research). Significantly, during this period of time, fake posts gathered 52,169 *likes* and comments from 8,783 unique users.[10]

Another related key finding in Dewan and Kumaraguru's research points out that the overwhelming majority of these undeleted malicious activities begin in concert with big breaking news events. Malicious patterns are rife following natural disasters, mass shootings, political unrest and terror attacks. Returning to the discussion in Chapter 1, then, we can see how it is often the shock of the event that enables fabrications to fill the data void. Which is to say, whenever these big events happen, adversarial actors and malicious entities exploit the 'spur in user-engagement'[11] at a point when everything is new. This is the same point at which, it seems, algorithms fail to force a distinction between nonadversarial and adversarial patterns.

The first proposition is not wholly technical. There is a rhetorical element to it too. By pointing to the promise of potential technological fixes, Facebook have hitherto fended off regulatory threats posed to their virality/growth business model. 'Now, increasingly', Zuckerberg told Congress, 'we're developing AI tools that can identify certain classes of bad activity proactively and flag it for our team at Facebook'.[12] Yet, by his own admission, Facebook are at least '5–10 years away' from detecting and totally eradicating the problem of hate speech.[13] As social media and search engines companies are forced to respond to the contagion of the Christchurch video, claims about these expedient, yet distant technological remedies, seem to have intensified. Arguably, Zuckerberg's appearance in front of Congress achieved very little aside from demonstrating Facebook's desire to control the discursive formations surrounding the immunity problem rather than fix the engineering problem itself. Certainly, when Zuckerberg admitted that in terms of ridding Facebook of race hate language, 'we're just not there',[14] he drew attention to the extent to which this historically unresolved problem has conveniently persisted alongside the astronomical economic success of the platform.[15] Ultimately, the immunity problem is consistent with the design of the platform, which is purposefully intended to facilitate the logics of virality/growth.

Hatebook

There are considerable overlaps between the technical limitations of social media immunity systems and the constant spreading of hate speech. As

Zuckerberg concedes, hate speech is 'one of the hardest' and 'linguistically nuanced' to distinguish from other kinds of speech.[16] Certainly, making such distinctions requires a tacit knowledge of the nuances of the multiple languages these platforms support throughout the world. Facebook's immune system (human and automated) has, nonetheless, struggled to overcome some seemingly basic linguistic peculiarities.

Along these lines, the Facebook immunity problem has been linked to the spreading of racial hatred and outbreaks of extreme racist violence against the Rohingya minority in Myanmar. Evidently, issues concerning the rapid take up of Facebook in Myanmar come into play.[17] For example, the lack of social media literacy in some regions seems to have made many users vulnerable to the strategic weaponization of the platform. However, in Myanmar Facebook's failing immune system takes centre stage again. For example, despite supporting Burmese text on their platform, Facebook had a distinct lack of Burmese speaking content moderators during the oppression of the Rohingya. The company employed just one Burmese speaking employee in 2014. By 2015 that number rose to just four at a time when 'Facebook had 7.3 million active users in Myanmar.'[18]

During the height of the violence against the Rohingya, Facebook failed to initially detect a particular word, Kalar, which is both a highly derogatory racial slur and the innocuous word for chickpea.[19] While some posts were quite explicit (*We must fight them the way Hitler did the Jews, damn kalars!*), other were less so (*Stuff pig's fat inside the damn kalar's mouth*).[20] Facebook's response to these kinds of postings is revealing. After becoming aware of the racist meaning of the word they started to delete all posts that featured it, only to latterly permit its use again once its dual meaning was discovered.[21] Many of these anti-Rohingya posts and comments, alongside images and videos, were collected for a Reuter's report titled *Hatebook*. The report included material that had been up on the Facebook platform 'for as long as six years'.[22] On 10 April 2018, Zuckerberg told Congress that he was hiring dozens more Burmese speakers to review hate speech posted in Myanmar.[23]

Racial Bias

Forms of racial bias also emerge from the social media immunity problem. To be sure, the failure to detect hate speech against Muslims in Myanmar stands in stark contrast to Facebook's seemingly successful deployment of AI tools to flag ISIS and Al Qaida content. 99% of this content is apparently eradicated, Zuckerberg claims, 'before any human sees it', suggesting that the rolling out of AI tools can 'proactively police and enforce safety across the community'.[24] Facebook's record of deleting far-right hate and white supremacist groups after the Charlottesville riots in 2017 has similarly drawn critical attention. Investigative journalists have noted that many banned race hate groups managed to return and set up accounts just a year after the violence erupted in the State of Virginia.[25]

Other digital platforms have made comparable commitments to machine learning technologies so as to flag and eradicate fake news, misinformation and hate speech from their platforms. Part of Google's current business model is, for example, focused on helping publishers 'take advantage of machine learning' so that they can 'quickly understand what's true and what's false online'.[26] Nonetheless, users of Google's YouTube platform have experienced similar problems when it comes to exposure to predominantly far-right race hate compared to IS type propaganda and radicalization videos. Questioned on BBC Radio 5 in July 2018, Miriam Estrin, YouTube's policy manager for Europe, the Middle East and Africa, admitted that the company 'missed the mark' by not taking down a far-right extremist video which was flagged to them over a year ago.[27]

These cases open up questions about what kind of learning patterns, markers and flags are established in proactive machine learning technologies and reactive human decision-making processes. What biases are operating in these patterns? What intrinsic discriminations are algorithmically processed? What gets *ignored* and what gets *deleted*? Moreover, where are the algorithmic boundary lines between truth, lies, propaganda, hate speech and viral hoaxes positioned in relation to the company's commitment to free speech? Why is it that this commitment seems to be more successful at weeding out Islamic hate groups, but favourably propagates the race hate, the misinformation, and fake news of white supremacists?

Proposition Two
There has been a resurgence of a perilous mode of immunopolitics which takes advantage of immunological failures to spread far-right race hate. The viral productions of white supremacy are, as such, contingent on exciting fears relating to the loss of self-identity, and subsequently intended to divide a population into racialized communities. The logic of this immunopolitics is intimately coupled to the logic of the contagion that spreads through online communities.

Immunopolitics

It is perhaps not surprising that apprehensive feelings associated with the possible collapsing of immunological borders have been historically exploited by racist regimes. The immunologic is, as such, an established divisive biopolitical means of stirring up fear concerning the potential loss of self-identity to a conveniently targeted Other. Most notably, the far right have made effective rhetorical use of a certain immunological grammar that syntactically forces a range of racial distinctions. Nonetheless, as discussed below, this rhetorical syntax is just part of a much broader biopolitical stratagem.

The immunopolitical exemplar in this case is, of course, the Nazis and their enforcement of distinctions between an inward-looking sense of racial purity and the threats posed by outside contaminations. Certainly, the entire Nazis doctrine is based on forced distinctions between, on the one hand, patriotic bloodlines, and the suppression and ultimate elimination of all alien racial contagions, on the other. Along these lines, Richard Koenigsberg draws on George Lakoff to argue that the ideology of Hitler's Nazis functioned according to metaphors that had a real cognitive purpose.[28] As Koenigsberg puts it, the metaphor that governed Hitler's malevolent rational was that of a 'nation suffering from a potentially fatal disease'.

> Everything [he] said and did revolved around this conception of Germany as a body politic that was ill. Hitler was clear about his mission: to discover and disclose the *causes* of Germany's disease (diagnosis); and then to act to cure the disease.[29]

The immunological metaphor certainly seems to play a key role in collapsing distinctions between Nazi politics and biology. It is ostensibly the point where the language of the bacterial meets the violence of racist politics. It was, it seems, his 'discovery of the Jewish virus', that Hitler considered to be 'one of the greatest revolutions of this world'.[30]

It is important to note, however, that this dark rendition of immunologic should not be grasped as solely metaphorical. In fact, it is a serious oversight to do so, since Nazi genocide manifestly resulted in a biological, not a metaphorical, mass elimination of an alienated other.[31] The Nazis mark a point in history wherein biological processes actually begin to drive and guide political action. As follows, in his commentary on Esposito's *Immunitas, Communitas* and *Bios* thesis, Frédéric Neyrat points out that Nazi politics is an 'exacerbation of biopolitics under immunological conditions'.[32] Although the rhetorical power of immunological language should not be ignored, it is through the continued racism of the Nazis' doctrine that we see how biopolitics can go way beyond its figurative mode. What Neyrat calls the Nazis' 'absolute perversion' of politics is resolved to not only force a distinction between the purity of the Aryan race and 'everything that might work against it'.[33] Ultimately, it leads to a *final solution,* which is, in effect, intended to turn a whole race of people into a biological nonentity.

Given this hideous history of biopolitical horror, there is an imperative requirement to understand how a nonmetaphorical immunologic works in the contemporary context of Christchurch and El Paso. There is a need, as such, to grasp a context-independent immunological principle, operating politically across biological, cultural, social, economic and digital contexts. Social media immune systems, for example, may well present rather crude manifestations of their biological counterparts, but the frequently imperfect process of forcing (and maintaining) distinctions persists across all of these zones of exemption, allowing for the dark logic of Nazis contagion to percolate.

Immunopolitics on social media has proven to be a complex matter since it is, in part, aimed at fearful responses to perceived threats to racialized community groups, yet it also produces a dangerous contagion. Trump is, along these lines, a major vector for this kind of immunopolitics on social media. The viral architectures of Twitter and Facebook have certainly provided this divisive kind of immunopolitics with a powerful and contagious refrain. With every tweet, it seems, Trump's passing on of this dark refrain resonates, disrupts, excites and accelerates a brand of white supremacy with alarming effectiveness. Clearly, the ways in which Trump opens up the potential of this vector to white supremacist hate speech is nothing new. For example, in the late 1980s, he appeared on television and print media similarly propagating race hate. In a moment chillingly captured in a recent TV series about the *Exonerated Five*, he told the media:

> I hate these people. Let's all hate these people, because maybe hate is what we need if we're gonna get something done.[34]

The persistent use of social media has, nonetheless, allowed for the intensification of this already well-rehearsed stirring of hatred against minority groups. Trump's early role in spreading the Obama Birther conspiracy, for example, utilized an immunologic that forced a fake distinction between the purity of being a natural born American and being born Other. His infamous tweet on July 2019, telling four black US Congresswomen to 'go back home' shows that this forced (and false) distinction continues to inform the Trump presidency. Similarly, Trump's numerous tweets about the so-called migrant Caravan are a barefaced deployment of immunopolitics intended to make his constituency fear breaches by migrants, 'mixed in' with 'criminals', 'rapists' and 'Middle Easterners' on a porous southern US border.[35] The political toxicity has reached a critical level. Evidently, these tweets have proven to be incendiary, since as the recent terror attacks in Christchurch and El Paso have demonstrated, social media expressions of a nonmetaphorical immunologic can again lead to real horror.

The Logics of Revolutionary Contagion

It would seem like the revolutionary moment is once again with the far right. However, in spite of this current dark refrain, the second proposition can be traced to a seemingly more enlightened moment of social media contagion. This earlier moment occurred at a time when the visceral register appeared to be overflowing with more joyful, affirmative political encounters. The compelling potential of new social media platforms to defeat the grip of established political systems was widely celebrated (and overhyped) in the political and media mainstream in many Western countries. Nascent forms of social media activism seemed to offer potent political tools that could penetrate the immune apparatus of entrenched regimes and their deep-rooted modes of oppression. The use of Twitter and Facebook in the Arab Spring in 2011, for example, drew much attention to the *as yet* unrealized possibilities of these platforms to spread messages of protest and animate mass support against the quasi-military regimes of previously unshakable tyrants like Hosni Mubarak in Egypt. Similarly, Obama's use of Facebook back in 2008 notably played a role in propelling the first black president into the White House. The spreading of Obama-love on social media will forever be celebrated as a first strike for cultural multiplicity against a US political system dominated by the same old white men.

Nonetheless, although the logics of these early forms of revolutionary contagion promised to rupture the political status quo, they cannot be decoupled from the current dark refrain of social media. To be sure, the role of these platforms in advances in US civil rights and civil unrest in the Middle East is consistent with the subsequent resurgence of immunopolitics and its link to the political turbulence that followed the 2008 financial crash.

Revisiting Obama-Love

Following on from Howard Dean's pioneering use of the internet in his failed 2004 campaign, Obama's campaign team were widely praised in 2008 for realizing how social media tools could be fully utilized to win an election, *against the odds*. In his victory speech Obama famously noted that he 'was never the likeliest candidate for this office'.[36] The Obama campaign victory was certainly not 'hatched in the halls of Washington'.[37] Similarly, in 2012, much mainstream media attention became focused on a range of platform tools and apps that seemed to enable Obama to bypass mainstream media, appeal directly to grassroots activist, and build a community of supporters. Yet, arguably, the disruption Obama's campaign caused to the US political system is far more nuanced than these convenient technological deterministic narratives often suggest. There are, on reflection, two alternative accounts of how the contagion of Obama-love was engineered in ways consistent with our current experience of immunopolitics.

Firstly, it is important to note that Obama-love seems to have spread online using some of the same techniques that Trump would later deploy. Although some inconspicuous ethical differences need to be teased out, Obama's political campaign certainly took advantage of tools that could build and exploit online communities. Along these lines, his team's social media tactics can now be seen as an early exercise of a comparable microtargeting operation that went on to be deployed by Cambridge Analytica. In short, the *Obama for America* app *did* collect friendship data from user's accounts without the knowledge of those friends. These contested tactics have clearly infuriated many conservatives, who have publicly argued that while Obama's use of Facebook was 'lauded by the media as being genius', the Trump campaign has in contrast been mired in scandal.[38] There are, however, some subtle, yet highly significant ethical differences in the techniques Obama's campaign used to access big data in 2008 and 2012 compared to those used by Cambridge Analytica in 2016.[39] To begin with, the capturing of a user's friendship data was done at a time when Facebook's internal regulations permitted it. Not much of an excuse, it would seem, but unlike Aleksandr Kogan's app, which was a stealthily designed campaign tool disguised as a personality quiz, Obama's app was mostly transparent with regard to its purpose of building political support. People who downloaded Obama's app in 2012 would have mostly been aware that it was a political tool. The app requested permission to access photos, news feeds and more significantly, friend lists. Importantly, people on friend lists did not give direct permission, but they were in effect targeted by their friends, not the campaign. Unlike Kogan's viral personality test, it was a not a Trojan horse, as such. Which is to say, dissimilar from Obama's target audience, who gave their permission for the app to collect data, and knew this data was part of a campaign, Kogan's app did not reveal its purpose of exploiting those who downloaded it, giving away their data, and their friend's data, to be sold on to a targeted political campaign.

Secondly, although Obama's two campaigns are often associated with social media activism, his success was derived as much from a more conventional rhetorical prowess. Obama was expert in projecting empathy through a range of media channels. In their detailed empirical study of Obama's 2012 campaign, for example, Roman Gerodimos and Jákup Justinussen argue that Facebook was not used as a means for bottom-up empowerment at all, but rather it offered Obama a 'tool of top-down promotion, focusing on [his] personality and as a means of strategically guiding followers to act'.[40] The networking of Obama-love, and its subsequent worldwide affective contagion, was part engineered by user experience designers and viral marketers.[41] It was the affective branding of Obama himself, as a mainstream politician, marketed through social media, alongside images of his family, which helped him maintain power throughout his two terms. This was not, however, simply a matter of promoting a winning personality. Obama was, in effect, the perfect brand for what Christine Harold calls 'aesthetic capitalism',[42] in the sense that he functioned to 'stir bodily propensities' and the 'mood swings' of a population. Which is to say, as Clough similarly points out, political branding of this kind provides an 'affective sense of an experience' that worms its way into memory, below consciousness, instilling what Luciana Parisi and Steve Goodman call a *preemptive logic* in the neurophysiological plasticity of the body–brain.[43]

Evidently, Trump and his supporters present the world with a very different kind of aesthetic capitalism. As discussed in Chapter 2, the brashness of the fuck your feelings campaign acts like a suppression of affect. Certainly, it is often remarked that Obama-love operated on an emotionally fine-tuned empathetic mode of communication, but Trump's utter lack of empathy for the other is no less, and perhaps even more so, visceral in tone. The now notorious photo of a smiling Trump doing a thumbs up while holding an orphan of the El Paso attack shows just how badly he does empathy.[44] Yet, clearly there is a sense of emotional affinity felt by the Trump constituency, which gets channelled through his incendiary bigoted rants on 4chan, building up hate-filled resentment towards mainstream politics and cultural multiplicity. Trump's relentless tweets shock and disrupt, while at the same time, they galvanize support from a disenfranchised population roused by his aesthetic lure.

Ultimately, Obama's hope of reshaping the American Dream as a dream of cultural multiplicity inevitably came face-to-face with the toxic environment of US politics. Trump's immunopolitics began by drumming up anxieties over Obama's race, and the perceived threat it posed to white supremist and nationalist identity. Obama's heterogenous community made up of the 'young and old, rich and poor, Democrat and Republican, black, white, Latino, Asian, Native American, gay, straight, disabled and not disabled' was evidently going to fall back into the same arc of history that Jackie Cogan rages against in *Killing Them Softly*.[45] 'Next he'll be telling us we're a community… we're all the same. We're all equal… *That we have never been.*' Cogan's USA is Trump's USA. It is 'just a collection of individuals … a collection of red states and blue states'.[46]

Obama's message of empathy was quickly followed by a murkier kind of aesthetic rebranding of politics on the right. This rebranding forced immunological distinctions to the limit. This is a situation Clough describes as 'another affective configuration and circulation of population racism'.[47] This new brand of disruptive politics connects 'populist white racial resentment to a conservative hostility to big government … along with defences of free expression'.[48] Along similar lines, Neyrat describes the almost instantaneous antagonistic response to Obama's presidency as 'typically immunological'.[49] The Birther conspiracy aside, Obama's healthcare reforms were also framed by the far right (now utterly embodied by Trump) as a threat to the immunity bubbles of individual liberty. Trump's election was similarly bolstered by immunological couched promises to build hygiene shields between the USA, the Muslim world and Mexico.

Revisiting the Arab Spring

The Arab Spring is a further example of how the potential of revolutionary contagion seems to have deviated from the initial optimism concerning social media connectivity. These platform-supported uprisings against tyranny brought about new modes of connected solidarity, but have since veered towards a fragmented community model.

Events in North Africa and the Middle East certainly began with some inspiring and empowering radical moments, some of which were accelerated by social media. The self-emulation of Mohamed Bouazizi in Tunisia, for example, seems to have provided an initial spark that allowed the stifled hostility against the Zine El Abidine Ben Ali dictatorship to overspill on the streets. It is perhaps the case that certain educated elements of this emerging protest movement were empowered by their connectivity to Twitter and Facebook. Social media seems to have allowed these protesters to spread their messages and put pressure on leaders like Mubarak. Yet, again, there are at least two reasons why these discursive narratives about the role of social media in the Arab Spring are often overhyped. To begin with, as Karppi's work on Facebook points out, there is a need to resolve a significant distinction between what it means to be connected or disconnected; certainly, in terms of how such a resolution relates to the exercise of revolutionary potential on social media.[50] The Arab Spring was a protest movement that pivoted between connection and disconnection. The protesters were in effect disempowered by short bursts of state sanctioned disconnections as much as they were empowered by social media connectivity. Throughout the protests, as Karppi points out, the 'diagram of power shifted' between the state and the protesters dependent on access.[51]

Again, the logics of social media contagion in 2011 cannot be decoupled from the current dark refrain. What started off as an infectious protest movement against engrained dictatorships soon became overrun with 'misinformation, rumours and trolls', all contesting the legitimacy of the counter community from within. The internet activist and computer engineer, Wael Ghonmin, who was at the forefront of the social media fuelled protests in 2011, recounts how his impactful Facebook page, *We are all Khaled Said*; a tribute to a man tortured to death by the police 'gathered 100,000 followers in three days and quickly became the most followed page in the Arab world'.[52] But the empowering connectivity that had previously helped to build consensus for the political struggle soon turned into an 'intense polarization...The same tool that united us to topple dictators', Ghonmin contends, 'eventually tore us apart'.[53]

Far-Right Contagion

In spite of the initial promise (and hype) surrounding these apparent moments of social media fuelled revolutionary contagion, platform architectures, it would seem, have failed to facilitate effective democratic communities. There are commercial and political reasons for this failure. To begin with, as Fuchs argues, users of these systems need to be made aware that social media is a business.[54] Users are given a false impression if they think the community links they establish and share between friends actually belong to them. As Neyrat similarly argues, these relations are not intended to 'give anything back' to the community.[55] The making of community links is, in fact, part of an economic capture and exploitation of social relations. Social media is, in effect, the commodification of community relations, some of which have already been apprehended from pre-existing links, and others that are algorithmically prompted into action, through friend recommendations, for example. For Neyrat, then, the capture of community links on social media 'presupposes an ontological expropriation'. Which is to say, the user is continuously 'being put outside of oneself'.[56]

It is also important to note that in addition to the economic shaping of community, there are political manipulations similarly dependent on ontological expropriation. Users are not only surreptitiously prompted to give away their relations for free. Relations also become integrated and organized around viral modes of community building. These expropriation tools are not just about bringing persons *outside of themselves*, as Neyrat contends. They also extract the viral potential of contagious community relations, so as to galvanize political support and build momentum. This has indeed proved to be an impoverished model of community relation, that has suited the antidemocratic goals of the alt-right and far right to extract and exploit social relations from these artificial communal spaces. By doing so, these groups can produce communities that respond to contagions of misinformation, rumours and trolling. The emergence of large-scale immunopolitical message board communities, like 4chan and 8chan, expose a masochistic collective mimicry circulating around Trump as well as the manifestos of mass shooters.

These ersatz communities are comparable to expansions of far-right immunopolitics in Europe where forced distinctions between inward looking national purity and supposed threats posed by immigrant communities to national borders spread on social media. The intention of this kind of digital populism is to stir up bigotry, homophobia and contagious racial hatred to win elections for far-right candidates like Farage, Salvini, Le Pen, Alternative for Germany (AfD), Orban, Wilders etc. Similarly, in 2018, the Brazilian Presidential election of far-right outsider, Jair Bolsonaro, marks the rise of an equally sinister mode of immunopolitics with its own recognizable social media war on cultural multiplicity in South America. Bolsonaro's campaign was similarly designed around the virality/growth model in order to stir up antidemocratic revolutionary contagions.

Again, it is important to note how the social media tactics of these far-right movements are continuous with much of the earlier logics of prodemocratic revolutionary contagion. To begin with, social media continues to offer political outsiders, whether that be Obama, a protest group in the Middle East or a far-right populist, like Bolsonaro, an affordable campaign tool to build a community of supporters. Rather than spend the huge amounts his rivals set aside for TV ads, Bolsonaro deliberately invested in developing a strong social media strategy.[57] Similar to Obama, then, Bolsonaro's team built a vast community of supporters on a social media platform; in this case, Brazil's most popular platform, Facebook's WhatsApp.[58] The virality of Bolsonaro's community is nonetheless differently assembled around a negative affective tone. The so-called Bolsominions are an aggressively influential group of devotees. They are a 'hyper-loyal volunteer army, which purges anyone who dares to question the "Mytha"', as Bolsonaro's supporters call him.[59] Their purpose is to come into direct contact with disaffected conservative voters and circulate population racism. Like Trump's campaign, they also relentlessly undermine the credibility of the mainstream media, on one hand, accusing it of liberal elitism, and of peddling fake news, while, on the other hand, they simultaneously spread their own fake news through the viral vectors of WhatsApp.

The revolutionary contagions of the far right are the result of an advanced viral media literacy. The Bolsominions spent the 2018 election campaign 'manipulating content 24/7 into memes, viral fake videos and assorted displays of 'Bolso-swarm ire', in a way the Brazilian investigative journalist, Pepe Escobar, describes as a 'properly instrumentalized … Brazilian remix of [a] Cambridge Analytica-style Hybrid War'.[60] Once on WhatsApp, disaffected conservative voters, many of whom no longer trusted the mainstream media, used the platform to substantiate rumours and find memes to share. For example, during the election over four million women had joined the #elenao Facebook group to protest against Bolsonaro's overtly violent rape culture rhetoric. In 2014, it was widely reported that he was fined for telling Congresswoman, Maria do Rosário, from the left-wing Workers Party: 'I wouldn't rape you because you don't deserve it.' The Bolsominions responded by using thousands of chat groups on WhatsApp to post photos from a recent gay pride parade of topless lesbian activists, stating that the images were taken at the #elenao protests. These misleading images were deliberately targeted at conservative minded voters with messages referring to the leader of the rival Worker's Party Fernando Haddad's lack of family values.[61]

Ignore, Delete!

Facebook's response to the political contagions of the Bolsominions is once again troubling. Before Bolsonaro was elected, Brazilian journalists had already drawn attention to the misuse of WhatsApp during the campaign. Likewise, a high profile joint study by the Federal University of Minas Gerais, the University of São Paulo and the fact-checking platform, Agência Lupa, recommended a number of proposals to try to lessen the viral reach of fake news contagions on WhatsApp ahead of the run-off elections in October 2018.[62] The study suggested that the platform limited the number of times a message could be forwarded. It proposed restrictions on the number of contacts, messages that could be sent, and the size of new chat groups. Facebook responded to the study saying there was not enough time to implement these kinds of changes. However, ahead of the US midterm elections, the platform was under pressure to at least be seen to be do something about the problem in Brazil. As its immune system struggled to contain the spreading of pro-Bolsonaro spam, hate speech, misinformation and fake news, Facebook opted for a cruder solution. On 19 October they disconnected over 100,000 Brazilian WhatsApp accounts.[63]

How do we begin to theorize the machoistic tendencies of far-right collective mimesis?

Horrific Encounters with the Data Double

Evidently, the interwoven logics of immunity, community and contagion complicate the representational and phenomenological critiques of social media, which have, for the most part, focused on the effect big data surveillance has on individual users. As discussed in the previous chapter, these conventional accounts have tended to highlight certain threats posed to personal privacy through the creation of so-called data doubles. Certainly, in recent decades, there has been an ever-expanding range of novel *phenomenal* self-concepts emerging from concerns about the incursion of data power into personal space. This list of self-concepts includes the data double, but also the data-self, the software-self and the quantified-self.[64] All of these examples function in the phenomenal tradition since they begin with the question: Who am I. However, each asks this question in the midst of a social media driven identity crisis, prompted into action by data surveillance and the threat posed to self-representation by data mimicry. For example, back in 2014, Deborah Lupton nicely summarized Haggerty and Ericson's

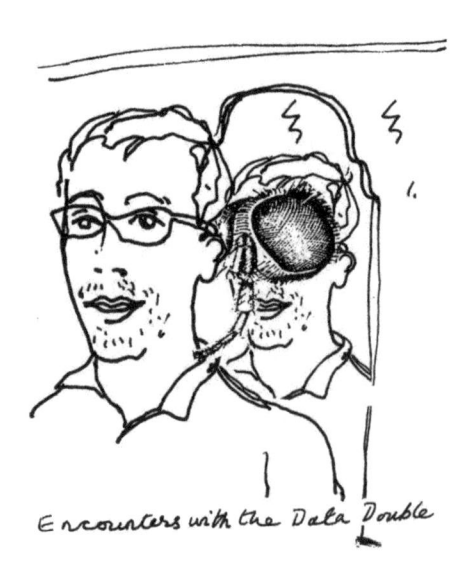

Figure 14 Encounters with the Data Double.
Illustration by Mikey B. Georgeson.

data double as 'configured when digital data are collected on individuals, serving to configure a certain representation of a person'.[65] In effect, data doubles are considered to 'have their own social lives and materiality, quite apart from the fleshy bodies from which they are developed'.[66]

If we follow a fairly conventional Platonic approach to this digitally provoked identity crisis, then we see how such a doubling effect becomes centred on the destructive influence mimesis poses to self-representation. To be sure, the question concerning the immunological exemption of self is re-posed; no longer is it simply a question of *Who am I*, but rather the question asks how a person subsists when self-representation comes under the threat of the duplicate. Would there be 'no more difference, no more distinctions', and therefore nothing to preserve the stability of *true* personal identity?[67] This is how a Platonic mimetic double is supposed to prompt a disruption of personal identity and pose an immunological threat to self-preservation, since the double is, at the same time, equivalent, but clearly different to the original. As John T. Hamilton succinctly describes the Platonic view of mimetic alienation.

> It offers an image that corresponds to the observing consciousness, inviting identification with the reflection, while spoiling, through reflection, any complete identification.[68]

We can see here how a theoretical line extends from these Platonic anxieties about representational mimesis to the alienation theories presented in the previous chapter. The Lacanian Created Self is, like this, based on a comparable concern for the survival of the purview of a person when she or he seemingly becomes lost in their own (alienating) reflection. As Elizabeth Grosz puts it:

> Lacan specifies that only through an encounter with a virtual counterpart, the double, do we acquire an identity; moreover, this identity remains irresolvably split because of an incapacity to resolve the differences between the real and the virtual body.[69]

Questions concerning the horror of the Platonic double figure writ large in literature too. Numerous authors have asked what happens to our feeling of distinct personality when we come face-to-face with a doppelgänger? Will we be, like Dostoevsky's *Double*, driven to the edge of sanity, or worse, will we, like Poe's *William Wilson*, or Sparks' Lucky Lucan, end up destroying ourselves? Or will our double be like Saramago's two-timing duplicate; a subconscious posing as our double?[70]

The Platonic response to these questions is couched in the tradition of the encounter with an evil twin or Dead Ringer. It points to a sense of self that needs protection from the collapsing of the psychic borders that follows our absorption into an environment wherein duplicates tend to multiply. Which is to say, self-identity might never recover after becoming lost in the multiplicity of its surroundings. Like this, the Platonic double is immunologic in the sense that the threat it poses to self-preservation requires an immune system response – something that ultimately upholds (keeps intact) the distinction between a personality and its merging into a milieu of mimicry.

Haggerty and Ericson's Deleuzian inspired, post-disciplinary theory of the surveillant data assemblage significantly tries to break away from the representational idiom of the Platonic double.[71] Its nonhierarchical, increasingly hidden, model of big data surveillance is a mimicry machine of sorts. As the authors put it:

> This assemblage operates by abstracting human bodies from their territorial settings and separating them into a series of discrete flows. These flows are then reassembled into distinct 'data doubles' which can be scrutinized and targeted for intervention.[72]

What makes a population observable and controllable is not therefore a replication of self, but rather a doubling of information flows. As Foot and

Gillespie similarly argue, 'what Facebook knows about its users' matters a great deal.'[73] But they only know the 'knowable information'.[74] They know a person's geolocation, their ISP, their profile information, friends and status updates. They know the links they follow and the time they spend online on other sites that host Like buttons or cookies that lead back to Facebook. This does not, however, constitute a complete double. What is missing is what is 'less legible or cannot be known about users'.[75] Foot and Gillespie call this incomplete doubling effect a production of *shadow bodies*, which emphasizes what is known and what is overlooked about a user. Any 'slippage between the anticipated user and the user herself that [the shadow] represents can be either politically problematic, or politically productive'.[76]

In contrast to Haggerty and Ericson, Karppi argues that data capture exceeds information flow.[77] As follows, we cannot disconnect what is mimicked from the instantly contagious user experiences and sentiment analysis of the Facebook Data Team (see previous chapter). Karppi's nod to Tarde suggests that we need some new reference points. Certainly, the capture of Haggerty and Ericson's data double differs considerably from a Tardean mode of collective mimicry. The latter is not simply a matter of assembling and dissembling informational flows – however incomplete. Collective mimicry is not a kind of crude copy and paste mechanism of self-identity. Nothing is resolved in the distinction Haggerty and Ericson make between the territorial settings of human bodies and their abstracted data doubles; reduced as they are to a couple of discrete data flows. These flows and felt experiences are not separated from each other in this way. On the contrary, it is the virality of social media architectures that continuously stir into action felt experiences so as to produce data flows. Without the cultivation and unremitting stirring up of contagious felt experiences, there is no data surveillance business, and no decoupled data power, as such.

Surviving in the Cracks

Given current concerns about the kind of data power expressed in the collective mimesis of the Bolsominions, there is a further need to look beyond the creation of disaffected Platonic and post-Platonic info doubles. It is my contention therefore that *current anxieties about data surveillance and collective mimesis are more effectively explained by* Caillois's impersonal spatial lures. In short, current endeavours to provoke collective mimicry surpass mere representations (or *informations*) of the self. The hateful politics of the Bolsominions emerges from a vast masochistic collective mimesis, intimately coupled to nonphenomenological assemblies of negative affective relations. Along these lines, collective mimicry does not induce the resemblances of collective experience by way of becoming disassembled from its surroundings. Following Caillois and R. D. Laing's contribution to the previous chapter, social media can be seen to lure the conformities of race hate by way of enmeshing user experiences, triggering collective, imitative impulses to like, feel and hate the same things.

This is why social media theory needs to look beyond alienated experiences, estranged (double) identities, false representations and ideological contaminations. Certainly, if theorists are to imagine social media as part of a Deleuzian assemblage of control, as Haggerty and Ericson want to, then it is perhaps more gainful to compare it to what Massumi rather profoundly calls *The Empire of Like*.[78] In typical Deleuzian fashion, then, mimicked resemblances are used to thwart the otherwise emergent mutational and differential qualities of becoming-other. Becoming-the-same is a mode of control that must maintain the intensification of shared experiences in which this mimicry is engendered. This is why theory also needs a new nonphenomenological syntax designed to think through how the becoming-the-same of experience renders the distinction between self and nonself indistinguishable. Resistance to becoming-the-same will not be achievable through the old grammar of phenomenal experience. We cannot grasp the indistinguishable moment from the subject's own personal purview of the world, on one hand, or her sense of self shaped by the object of experience, on the other. On the contrary, ultimately, to fully register the theoretical implications of this syntactic reorientation, *A Sleepwalker's Guide* must begin by addressing a significant question concerning what it means to survive in borderless encounters beyond immunopolitical regimes.

Such a survival – in between the cracks – is no longer a simple matter of preserving the self/nonself distinction. Quite the opposite, following various authors, like Caillois and Esposito, but also the immunologist, Paul Ehrlich, a new syntax needs to move on from what initially seems like a rather bleak analysis of a wide-ranging failure of immune systems to protect self-identity to consider the promises of indistinction. This is an experimental syntactic move, thwart with its own dangers. There is a hint of the horror of the Platonic double in Caillois. This is because although the concealment of distinction through camouflage would seem to offer the organism a unique opportunity to blend into its surrounding and survive, Caillois initially sees no evolutionary advantage to nonhuman mimicry of this kind. Such is the danger of collective mimicry that by wearing the mask of its predator, or by trying to blend in, a collective organism may actually transform itself into its own predators' prey, or worse, a cannibal's lunch. So, surrendering to indistinction will be a painful experience.

Similarly, the organic desire to preserve the psychic feeling of self-representation is severely disrupted by autoimmunity. Which is to say, a mode of *horror autotoxicus*, which collapses the distinction between self-representation and self-destruction into a moment of potentially deadly indistinction. It is nonetheless this failure of immunity and Caillois's more positive account of a doubly dangerous luxury of collective masochism that prompts a new theoretical alternative to be considered. *A third proposition no less!* Herein, the loss of self-representation to collective masochism may well lead to communal mimicry. This is a mode of community quite unlike our current sleepwalk towards *The Empire of Like*, embodied as it is by far-right nationalist identities of resemblance and the violence of 1930s style immunopolitics. Communal mimicry is not an acceleration of these forces! It instead celebrates the collapsing of nationalistic borders and distinctiveness into a massive-scale mimicry of cultural multiplicity. As follows, a speculative mimicry of this kind might provide the ultimate expression of a new syntax that pushes 'the apparatus of identity beyond the threshold of sameness'.[79]

Proposition Three
The third proposition visits the extremes of the immunity problem. As follows, in Caillois's theory, the failure of immunity has a doubling effect. It leads to both perilous collective mimicries and more promising moments of indistinction wherein the representational mirror is smashed and new forms of communal mimicry might emerge. In terms of social media, then, this third proposition tests the extent to which the self-destructiveness of Caillios's mode of horror autotoxicus might provide a challenge to the current dark refrain.

Redefining the Immunity Problem

As a general rule, immune systems function like border regimes. They are designed to *force distinctions* between self and nonself. The collapse of a distinction between, on one hand, an entity (e.g. a self or a body), and on the other hand, certain anomalies (e.g. a nonself or antibody), poses a risk to the stability or even the lifespan of said entity. The problem being that a failure to force a distinction between entity and anomaly means that certain protections and exemptions afforded to the entity from its perilous surroundings, begin to breakdown. The collapse of the barriers immunity provides between interiority and exteriority clearly makes the entity vulnerable to destabilizing contagions of various kind, as well as exposing it to potential predators. However, for Caillois, the principle of becoming distinct is neither the general rule of things nor does it necessarily guarantee stability.

As sketched out in the previous chapter, Caillois's study of camouflage offers a unique perspective on the immunity problem from a nonhuman context. He counters orthodox evolutionary thinking on biological subsistence attained through exemption. By blending in to their surrounding certain insects would, for example, transform themselves into plants that other insects eat. The remains of mimetic insects are indeed as abundant in the stomachs of predators as those that cannot change their visual appearance. In effect, at first glance, the dangers of camouflage seem to outweigh the immunological benefits. To be sure, by transforming themselves into the foodstuff of their own species, insects risk taking part in a horrific masochistic act of collective cannibalization!

Nevertheless, to fully grasp Caillois's contribution we need to carefully consider his methodology, which states that to answer the fundamental questions it is always necessary to resolve distinctions. On one hand, then, a redefinition of a cross-context immunity problem would need to consider how the *freedom* immunity affords the entity is replaced by dangerous moments of indistinction. Which is to say, as the borders between the entity and its surroundings collapse, distinctions become increasingly blurred, porous and folded. Dependent on which context this moment of indistinction occurs in (biological, biopolitical, psychological, technological etc.), the contaminated entity might face a loss of self-identity, integrity or even life. In the case of Caillios's insects, a tendency towards a spatial lure leads to the collapse of immunological borders, rendering the organism indistinguishable from its surroundings, and as a consequence, vulnerable to self-destructive, collective mimicry. In effect, the dispossessed entity is transformed into the nonentity, leading to the seemingly dreadful loss of division, which inevitably intensifies feelings of disorientation, fear, anxiety and even psychosis. Caillois significantly notes that the physical dissolving of immunological boundaries between an organism and its surroundings is intimately coupled to the dispossession of the mind;[80] the emptying of a subject, if you like. *Who, after all, wants to become the nonentity?*

On the other hand, though, in Caillois, the horror of self-destruction (physical and psychical), which follows on from machoistic collective mimesis, suggests a potentially radical rethinking of community. This is a community that has been compromised by all out contagion, but its collapse into indistinction nonetheless brings about something new. Along these lines, there are some notably conceptual resonances between Caillois's collective mimesis and Esposito's similar desire to reconsider community as the inverse of Nazis or neoliberal immunological modes of exemption. Which is to say, in many ways, the logics of Caillois's notion of immunity are similarly interlinked with the more affirmative logics of Esposito's community. To begin with, as Esposito contends, immunity presupposes community in the sense that the former provides a biopolitically constituted individual exemption from the 'expropriating effects' of the latter. There is 'no community without some kind of immunitary apparatus', such as that provided by law, for example.[81] For Esposito, immunity and community are a continuum. A certain kind of negative immunity is therefore grasped as thwarting the possibilities of a more affirmative version of community that otherwise might challenge the immunological excesses of these biopolitical regimes (e.g. *The War on Terror*).[82]

Moreover, though, both Caillois and Esposito show how the logics of contagion are similarly coupled to community. For example, drawing on Nietzsche's *Human All Too Human*, Esposito points to the power of social inoculation.[83] As he puts it, the biggest threat to a community's vitality is not posed by infections from the outside, but is rather produced by efforts to preserve internal stability.

> [T]he more the community is preserved intact, the more the level of innovation is reduced. The greatest danger that the community faces is therefore its own preventative withdrawal from danger.[84]

What a community needs in order to persist is not therefore immunological stability, but instead a 'viral fragment' needs to be inserted into the 'collective organism'.[85] This need for inoculation exposes the complete futility of the Nazis. Their ultimate failure emerged in their efforts to normalize the population by irradiating impurity. Hitler's use of immunological terminology, for example, saw his fight against racial impurity as 'equal to those fought by Pasteur and Koch'.[86] In effect, by trying to stabilize a specific kind of life, the Nazis needed death.[87] Notably, Esposito grasps this propensity towards death as a mode of autoimmunity. It is indeed the collective masochism of immunopolitics that comes to the fore in the Nazis. Nonetheless, further on in this discussion, I will try to make the case for a more affirmative and experiential double of the concept of autoimmunity.

For now though, we need to note that both Caillois and Esposito help us to explore the extreme of the immunity problem, grasping contagion as an affirmative way to breakdown the confines of an immunologically constructed sense of self-identity, and thus, open up the potential of an impersonal community relation based not on racial stability, but cultural multiplicity.[88] To some extent, then, the impersonal in both Caillois and Esposito does not, purposefully, coincide with a singular subjective experience (I, you or he and she). The focus is always on the collective. The outcome of this desubjectification is not, however, exactly the same proposition. Esposito's proposal is to, on one hand, reconfigure the immunitary apparatus so that it no longer fortifies the singular I, but instead provides an 'attentiveness to our encounters with others and the other'.[89] In effect, he looks to inoculation as a way to rearticulate the immunity/community continuum towards a more affirmative logic of difference. On the other hand, Caillois does not look to reconfigure immunity; instead he encourages the total collapse of immunological borders into a masochistic abyss. It is here, in this abyss of indistinction, that we encounter the three-way logics (or continuum) of immunity, community *plus* contagion itself. In short, it is the resulting indistinction, brought about by all-out contagion, that smashes the representational mirror, which persists in the immunological separation of individuals from each other.

In the context of this discussion, then, the indistinction of Caillios's collective mimesis promises an experiment that might counter a form of immunopolitics that has forced divisive distinctions between races, cultures, and creeds on social media. Given the current *War on Multiplicity*, which now comes to us in real time, via social media, direct from the White House, and the Palácio da Alvorada, this is an opportune moment to rethink the purpose of immunity, community and contagion.

Speculative Mimesis as a New Kind of Community?

The focus of this third proposition becomes something of a necessity in terms of making a break from the neoliberal and fascist captures of community that social media helps to condition. This does not mean, however, that we simply replace or oppose immunopolitics with an ideal model of community. This may provide an expedient starting place, but what is really needed is a concerted effort to rethink the concept of community anew. To begin with then, in Caillios's doubly dangerous luxury of mimesis we find something affirmative about becoming indistinct. This is Caillois's alternative resolution to his 'fundamental question' of distinction. As Hamilton argues, it is '[p]recisely because [Caillois's] mimicry blends the individual into its environment, [that] it also serves as a basis for community'.[90] So, although we seem to be in the grip of this current dark refrain of collective mimicry, which poses a persistent threat to cultural multiplicity, the loss of self-representation; this collapse into indistinction, promises experimentations with new community forms yet to come.

Along similar lines, Elizabeth Johnson takes up the case for a revolutionary kind of collective mimicry.[91] She begins by similarly noting how Caillois makes a significant jump from the physical mimicry of insects to the potential of psychic human mimicry. This is a jump into the unknown that is not without a measure of anxiety. Just as Caillois's spatial lure of the environment dissolves the body of the insect into the plant world, the human can also become lost in space to such an extent that her sense of personality becomes utterly destabilized. But, as Johnson notes, 'Caillois celebrated such insertions.'[92] He sees these dispersals of personality into space as a radical way to *dis-coordinate* and *unmoor* bodies and subjectivities. So, whereas immunity separates and divides psychical and mental capacities from their environments, the 'mimetic faculty serve[s] to unite subjects with their surroundings', and by doing so, exposes the 'artifice of difference and distinction'.[93]

Johnson's revolutionary mimesis also borrows from Michael Taussig's *Mimesis and Alterity*.[94] She positions Taussig's work as a way to sidestep the estranging forces of contagion and celebrate instead the magical force of mimesis. This is a kind of magic Taussig considers will bring humans closer to a 'sensuous living in a more-than-human world'.[95] We must add that there is nothing particularly new in this idea. Certainly, Taussig references Caillois, but also Walter Benjamin, Theodor Adorno and Max Horkheimer as fellow mimetic revolutionaries.[96] All are, as Shukin puts it, alert to how the 'mimetic faculty promised salvation from fascism and the advance of industrial capitalism'.[97] Like this, Johnson's analysis similarly points to the capacity of revolutionary mimesis to resist the kind of exemptive power immunopolitics exudes today. What is 'seductive about mimesis', she contends, is the potential freedom it offers from the aggressiveness of oppositional 'political confrontation'.[98]

Significantly, following Grosz, Johnson further argues that the possible mimetic liberation of human subjectivity does not need to constitute a *freedom from* oppression, or an immunological exemption *from* tyranny, but instead it promises the *freedom to* self-actualize.[99] This all leads to two possible modes of revolutionary mimesis; one that draws on Esposito's notion of a community that is liberated from self-identity; the other follows Taussig's magical force, which does not copy in order to become-the-same or indeed commodify, but rather mimics, copies and imitates as a way to 'explore difference, yield into and become Other'.[100]

In short, Esposito's mimetic revolution requires the smashing of the representational mirror! The mirror that reflects the I. A more direct theoretical line can be drawn from Caillois's serious undermining of personality and Esposito's contra-immunological proposition of the common life, since both are appeals to the power of the impersonal. As Neyrat puts it, Esposito tells us that we only approach something like the common life when 'if – and only if – we consider the living's characteristic of "impersonality"'.[101] The impersonal cannot be reduced, as such, to the I, or the You. It is rather an It; something that is 'undividable, from which nothing can be separated'.[102] Neyrat is quick to realize that Esposito's mission is, as follows, an 'extremely delicate' one.

> It consists of nothing less than achieving a synthesis between the negativity of the impersonal and the positivity of life![103]

Again, to achieve this synthesis, the revolutionary mimic must smash the mirror that reflects the self. This is because the mirror that reflects the self fails to reveal the self's relation to everything else. One can see how anxieties will inevitably arise once this mirror is broken and the artifice of difference and distinction is lost. The lack of an I might engender what Neyrat calls a nihilist version of community. Which is to say, when the sense of self disappears into its surroundings, it will be displaced by a sense of nothingness. The problem here is that the experience of impersonal nothingness will simply reproduce a fear that in turn 'provokes the immunitary reaction'.[104] One imagines that beneath the bluster of Trump's hate agenda is a comparable fear of nothingness! Similarly, it is perhaps this fear of nothingness that incites the white rage of the Trumpian constituency. This is a delicate move indeed! Caillois's collective masochism needs to achieve more than its challenge to the prevalent adaptationist account of mimesis. It needs to show the way in terms of how we smash the mirror of self-identity, and live beyond nothingness in a way that avoids another Trump.

What can we learn from Caillios's nonhuman? The mimicking insect smashes the representational mirror by losing itself in the spatial coordinates of its surroundings. Caillois consequently addresses the function of mimicry not as a representation of figures or space, but as Jussi Parikka contends, space becomes an 'assemblage that border[s] on disorder'.[105] This topological entanglement helps us to further ponder a notion of affective relationality that in many ways counter Lacan's mirror stage. It certainly draws attention to the porous nature of the inside/outside relation to such an extent that the representational I is replaced by a topology of entanglements. The inner and outer world of phenomenological experience is therefore collapsed into an external world of affective relationality that disturbs the border between personality and space. Again, as Parikka puts it: '[t]he reflective mind is forced to follow the noncognitive knowledge and motility of the body [...] [Caillois thus provides] a nonphenomenological mode of understanding the lived topology of the event'.[106] The question now posed concerns how can nonphenomenological understandings exist once the feeling of nothingness dissipates into collective affirmation?

Horror Autotoxicus or Feeling the Fear of Indistinction

As we have seen, Esposito describes the Nazis' choice of death as a kind of autoimmunity. However, the concept is also comparable to Caillois's collective masochism, since it too smashes the mirror that forces a distinction between self and nonself. It is, as such, a counterintuitive concept of indistinction that might allow some fresh explorations beyond the territorializations of immunological exemption. Yet, before we can tease out the potential of autoimmunity, it is important to begin by noting that the concept is not opposed to immunologic. To grasp its full purchase, we need to begin by approaching it by thinking *through* immunology. Autoimmunity refers, as such, to an immunologic phenomenon whereby an organism mounts an immune response against its own tissues; a paradoxical situation in which self-defence (immunity, protection) manifests as self-harm (pathology). Today, the term autoimmunity is used to account for any instance in which the body fails to recognize its own constituents as 'self', an error that similarly results in self-harm or injury.

Despite its location in the field of study, autoimmunity is, nonetheless, regarded as a controversial concept within immunology. It is important, as follows, to note certain flaws in Paul Ehrlich's original concept of horror autotoxicus that inspired it. In fairly crude terms, autoimmunity was initially posited as an impossibility because all organisms are so horrified by self-discrimination that they will selectively avoid self-toxicity. The later discovery of the harsh realities of autoimmune disease demonstrates deep problems in the natural preservation of an organic unity based on the overriding rule of self-tolerance. There are nonetheless those working in immunology who argue that Ehrlich's theory is misunderstood and that while self-tolerance is evidently the rule, autoimmunity is always the exception.[107] Moreover, it is further argued that rather than being a destructive incongruity of the immune system, the exception is also implicated in the maintenance of the rule.[108] In other words, the self-destructive anomaly is considered to play a productive role in the evolutionary survival of the organism.

Following Caillois, evolutionary determined equilibrium will be put aside in this discussion. The question posed here will instead ask how the paradoxical relation between self and nonself in autoimmunity problematizes the assumed emergence of a natural state of immunity. Along these lines, the defences provided by the horror of self-toxicity will, on occasion, acquiesce, and the exception will overrule self-tolerance; possibly leading to the exceptional destruction of the organism. Again, like Esposito's immunitas, autoimmunity should not be regarded as simply metaphorical. There is indeed an ongoing debate in immunology concerning the value of the self/nonself metaphor as a theoretical tool to understand how cellular organisms defend against infections. For some, the metaphor's value plunged when it became evident that cells have the potential to be simultaneously anti-self and anti-foreign. Cellular behaviour seems to defy the terms set out by the immunological metaphor. As Robert S. Schwartz puts it, 'the immune system, in short, does not operate by anthropomorphic principles such as "learn", "self", or "foreign", nor is there a sharp line between "self" and "foreign"'.[109]

Taking this challenge to immunologic a step further (*beyond the metaphor*), autoimmunity also questions how these same anthropomorphic principles are assumed to arrange social relations. In other words, similarly considered in terms of a broader concept, autoimmunity significantly complicates notions of communication, defence and regulation conventionally understood as immunologic processes. Hence, the concept prompts a novel approach that questions the ordering of social relations according to self/other relations. It tests the permeability of borders assumed to exist between self-identity and threats posed by an anomalous destructive nonself. As such, a reconfigured autoimmunity replaces immunopolitical exemption with a *politics of exception*, which can be grasped as an affirmative process of communal mimesis.

Digital Autotoxicus and Relational Media

Returning more squarely to the theme of social media, it is important to note that the role of the anomaly in digital culture has already been described as a topological autotoxicity.[110] It is something we considered to be 'a condition akin to a horror autotoxicus of the digital network', wherein the 'capacity of the network to propagate its own imperfections, exceeds the metaphor with natural unity'.[111] Like this, the topology of the digital network is grasped as the 'perfect medium' for spreading both 'perfection and imperfection'.[112] The goal now is, it would seem (given that the virality of the digital network has become deeply entangled with the social in so many profound ways), to question how a more generalized concept of autoimmunity might be applied to social arrangements, which occur when brains, bodies and technologies are increasingly in concert with each other.

Perhaps it is the case that we need to move through and beyond the imperfect communal artifice constructed by corporate social media. The social arrangements of these platforms might offer a way out! As it is, in this dark refrain, subjectivities are situated in ersatz communities ripe for economic and political expropriation and exploitation by means of virality/growth. It is in these commoditized social arrangements that anxieties relating to contagion and immunologic failure are exacerbated by a seemingly inescapable contagious corporate topological entanglement. This is a moment of anxiety a user feels when they become aware that they are part of a collective marketing virus and actively engaged in passing on the contagion by way of their relations with others. These are moments of anxiety when individuals become 'aware of their presence as part of the "informational collective" that shapes online activity' and affective experiences.[113]

So, what could the user experience become beyond this current dark refrain of social media actually be like? Future predictions are not good. Back in 2006, the information architect and design consultant, Adam Greenfield, drew our attention to a near future digital culture in which ubiquitous computing makes everyday life 'fiercely relational'.[114] Pervasive computing introduces a lived relationality that continues to be experienced when individuals become a set of values stored in a lookalike database. Profit is realized in the way in which such values, including spatial proximity to points of consumption, location traces and emotional dispositions, are matched against the values belonging to others. As computing becomes ever more ubiquitous, more immersive, and invasive, these relational values will exert a more powerful 'transformative influence' on social relations.[115] For example, forget the old postmodern nosedive down the rabbit hole of virtual reality! Once the virtual mirror is smashed, pervasive technology turns all rabbit holes inside out. In the Internet of Things, there is no longer an inside. Everything; software, hardware, sensors, triggers… becomes *Everyware*.

Greenfield is interested in the question concerning who controls the 'custody of self-consciousness'.[116] In fact, if we were to follow, as he does, Goffman's notion that users are all actors wearing a collection of masks they switch between in order to manage self-identities, then we need to grasp how relational media threatens to make the sustaining of different masks 'untenable'.[117] In the social media age, when the personal in computing moved into the social domain, these private and public performances collapse into the relational database. Which is to say, the ownership of private masks has been teased out into the public. In the near future of deep entanglement, perhaps users will all wear the same mask? This problem of becoming-the-same clearly maps onto the shift in immunological orientation highlighted in this chapter. Certainly, given the proclivity of social media, and pervasive computing, towards a darker collective mimesis, we need to look for an alternative way forward.

Anxiety

To begin with, we need to reconsider anxiety. These fearful moments of collective mimicry are perhaps akin to a Simondonian anxiety, wherein the difference between individuality and collectivity collapses into an affective state of transindividuality.[118] To begin with, the point needs to be made that although social media adapts the way in which a person experiences individuating events, following Simondon, the focus on the individual must not be confused with the constituted being. Thus as personal life increasingly shifts from individuals to the huge databases of governments and commercial organizations, the intersection between humans and technology unfolds as part of processes of individuation, which do not have to be human.[119] As Darren Ellis and Ian Tucker note, Simondon does not ontologically, as such, separate brains, bodies and technology because all are part of the experience of individuation.[120] Human and technological individuations are the threshold point at which human dreams and machines become mixed. However, this is not to say that a nightmarish tension or deep anxiety does not still exist in this coming together of bodily and technological arrangements. As they assemble, something novel and unknown emerges.

As is the case with immunology, the psychic self becomes a conceptual problem that cannot be defined by internal properties alone. It is rather an affective relation, produced through processes, not separate categories. Similarly, like Tarde's imitative subjectivity, an individual 'always-already carries some of the collective with it'.[121] The resulting anxiety is not therefore equivalent to the alienation established between immunological self and nonself, nor is it, for that matter, akin to any alienating mirror image or encounter with a double. On the contrary, this is anxiety felt as an outcome of the deep entanglements of brains, bodies and technologies, forming new collective arrangements and experiences that challenge immunological, and potentially anthropomorphic, divisions. This is not a tension-free experience, since the folded individual psyche always-already experiences collective baggage as an anxiety. In autoimmunologic terms, then, this is perhaps a new kind of horror that emerges through an experience that is both individual and collective – self and nonself – at the same time. It is similar perhaps to what Simondon refers to as the preindividual. In other words, anxiety arises through an unresolvable perceptual problem of individuation and preindividuation. This occurs because of 'the reality that the individual experiences itself as a unique subject, but at the same time recognizes itself as partially collective'.[122]

How then to overcome the anxieties ignited in the experiences of collective mimesis? How do we experience lifespans in these moments of indistinction? One consideration might be to continue to follow Simondon's solution to anxiety in the concept of the transindividual. This is not a reconstitution of individual or collective categories. As Ellis and Tucker point out, anxiety cannot be resolved inside the subject or the collective.[123] It requires a *perceptual bridge* that might enable a softer passage through the individual-collective continuum. This is a bridge that counters internal and external spaces, working across boundaries of self and collective. Moreover, the transindividual escapes spatial coordinates – it is not a grid; it is a becoming, which may indeed frustrate the colonizing spaces of market orientated mimicry. It might, as such, provide the basis for a new kind of community that does not look to perceive of something that exists outside the self as a nonself, but perceives of a 'multiplicity of perceptual worlds'.[124]

Redesigning the User Experience of Social Media

Vaidhyanathan's thesis on Facebook claims that the problems we are currently facing with regard to the threats posed to democracy and cultural multiplicity began with Zuckerberg's initial platform design. In a nutshell, there are 'two things wrong with Facebook', he claims: 'how it works and how people use it'.[125] In the first instance, Facebook works by way of user data surveillance. Along these lines, then, Vaidhyanathan follows the logic discussed in Chapter 3 concerning how the social media business model functions by way of amassing users and selling them on as products to advertisers. Secondly, Vaidhyanathan points to the problematic ways in which users *use* the platform. Many of these uses are evidently harmless, he argues. However, users also spread hate speech, white supremacist propaganda, Islamophobic and antisemitic messages. Furthermore, they use the platform to spread targeted emotional political ads and fake news that potentially undermines democratic elections. Users also use these platforms to threaten and harass other users, post revenge porn and numerous other antisocial acts.

There is, evidently, a third problem that is, in effect, betwixt the first two problems. Which is to say, in order to make its billions, Facebook have perfected a platform design that not only encourages the pernicious use of the platform, but actually uses it to virally grow its mass surveillance business model. Cynically, then, the failure of its immune system, and the tendency to outsource the immunity problem to unsuitable third-party cleaners, is a design and business choice. Vaidhyanathan's sensible solution to these three problems is that the collective political will of governments needs to resolve to combat the rhetoric of free speech Facebook takes cover under and regulate! regulate! regulate! Evidently, if social media were to be regulated like other media, then some of the above problems might eventually evaporate. However, after seeing Zuckerberg's performance in front of the US Congress in 2018 after the scandals of 2016, and the deference most of the politicians afforded him, one has to be cynical that governments, particularly in the US, will ever have the courage or collective will to follow Vaidhyanathan's sound advice.

If these governments are not willing to act, then what other options do we have? The critical analysis of dystopian media theory must not cease, of course. New problems need to be posed concerning what to do if platforms are persistently unprepared to invest in adequate immune systems, however flawed? In the current unregulated social media environment, would these platforms persist in becoming ever more immunopolitically extreme or could they, following Caillois's thesis on collective mimesis, or Esposito's notions of *Bios*, simply self-destruct or collapse into impersonal indistinction? In other words, will the hate groups of the dark refrain, who have thus far camouflaged themselves within the failed immunologics of these platforms, continue to spread forced distinctions, or could they, as Caillois contends, self-cannibalize? Could this self-destruction eventually destroy the social media business model? It is, of course, very dangerous to suggest that we wait around to see what happens.

It is, of course, overambitious, but hopeful nonetheless, to suggest another route is possible. Which is to say, if Zuckerberg is unwilling to satisfactorily self-regulate his flawed business model, he should consider instead a radical redesign of the user experience of his platform. Could this redesign take on board some of the theories discussed in proposition three? For example, how could the existing platform be redesigned to accelerate the ultimate Nazis' failure, which emerges in the efforts made to preserve racialized communities by irradiating impurity. In effect, by trying to stabilize a specific kind of purified life, the Nazis produced their own death. Along these lines, what kind of online communitas could reverse the flawed immunological mechanisms and introduce an alternative obligation to mix. Perhaps these compulsions to mix could function through new modes of enforced affirmative versions of inoculation or autoimmunity intended to breakdown the artifice between self and nonself? Since blending into the environment might serve as a basis for a new kind of community, could there not be certain user rewards for mixing and becoming ever more indistinct.

There is nothing particularly new in this rethink of virality/growth. There is a precedent in computer science where early artificial life researchers conjured with notions of benevolent contagion.[126] Viral codes were written that would clean up hard drives over night or more specifically fend off harmful viruses. What kind of benevolent viruses could Facebook's data team design that would not only fight off hate contagions, but also put an end to Nazis homogeneity? Facebook were certainly keen to be seen as the engine behind the revolutionary contagions of the Arab Spring in 2011. Why can't they act now and unleash a new revolutionary contagion that taps into the magical force of mimesis to resist the kind of exemptive power immunopolitics exudes in the current dark refrain? Experience designers could replace their failing immunity systems with inoculation and autoimmune systems that could undo conventional antagonistic anthropomorphic principles, untangling the sharp lines drawn between what is 'self' and 'foreign'. Facebook needs to replace immunopolitical exemption with a politics of exception.

Taking on board some of the theories discussed in this chapter, there seem to be three design options for a user experience couched in revolutionary mimesis. Firstly, following Esposito's notion of a community that is liberated from self-identity, designers would need to approach something like a common life of user experience. Secondly, designers might choose to follow Taussig's magical force instead, which does not copy in order to become-the-same or indeed commodify. Design needs to forget what constitutes a lookalike! Revolutionary mimesis instead copies and imitates as a way to revel in difference and yield new modes of becoming other. Thirdly, if these platforms smashed the mirrors in which the stability of self-representation is reinforced then they will need to support the subsequent anxieties many users may experience when suffering from a loss of self-identity? Could they not therefore encourage the collapsing of distinctions and unmooring of users from immunological preservation by celebrating mimesis and alterity? Ultimately, social media needs to offer a life beyond the nothingness of the Trump experience.

A Closing Word on Speculative Mimesis

To conclude the various strands of this discussion, the potential of speculative and communal mimesis needs to be considered in terms that a sleepwalker might grasp. The discussion throughout this book has been framed by the coincidence of the somnambulists from nineteenth-century crowd theory and current immersive experiences of technological nonconscious entanglements. Yet, this capricious similarity is really only part of what is being proposed. It is important to acknowledge that there are at least two kinds of sleepwalker that occupy crowd theory.

On one hand, the antidemocratic French aristocrat, Gustave Le Bon, not surprisingly considered the becoming-the-same of his sleepwalker as a tragic loss of a more refined self-identity. The conscious person in Le Bon's *The Crowd* is perceived from an initially privileged and noble position, which is subsequently stupefied by its immersion in a socialist collective unconscious. Notably, Le Bon starts from a phenomenal position of self-representation. *The Crowd* is about the personal experience of an individual nobleman, who on entering the unruly red swarm of commies, loses his sense of self-representation. This makes Le Bon's sleepwalker part of an immunopolitical stratagem intended to ward off the threats posed to the integrity of an aristocratic immune system.

If we put him in a time machine, Le Bon would be a leaver, not a remainer! To be sure, Le Bon's concern for the self-preservation of the nobleman also bears some resemblance to Freud's account of a representational mode of mimesis. Certainly, it is through the mental mimicking of external images that Freud's ego is supposed to experience itself. One's experience of one's self, established in the death drive, for instance, is changed by how the representation of the other's death is experienced. As Hamilton explains, before the Great War, Freud considered the lack of experience of death made the ego blissfully unaware of, it would seem, what it was like to live or die.[127] After the war, however, the abundant images of death provided the ego with a representational vision of its own life and death.

> One's life has been preserved, at least for now. In denying death, in shunting off infinitely for later consideration, one robs oneself from the opportunity to believe in self-preservation.[128]

On the other hand, though, Tarde's sleepwalker exists in the mimetic tension between becoming-the-same and alterity. As follows, his speculative contagious overspills are not rendered immunological exempt. On the contrary, contagion becomes key to the arrangement of everyday social relations. Along these lines, Tardean topological entanglements do not simply become contagious; *they are contagions.* So, like Caillios's space of mimicry, the Tardean arrangement of everyday relationality established between humans and the environments they inhabit are determined by universal imitative radiations. Like this, Tarde argued that the psychological sense of 'myself' is an illusion produced by the contamination of others.[129] In other words, the self is understood to imitate the other to a point at which the relation between self and other – so important to both immunologic and anthropomorphic principles – collapses into a social cosmos of speculative mimesis. Speculative mimesis is the axiomatic rule of the entire Tardean social field. It actually marks out the space of individuality; what Caillois similarly calls the feeling of personality. But this feeling is an illusion of self-representation formed in speculative mimesis. The somnambulist is a dream of separateness from the social surrounding.

An important point to conclude on here is that like Tarde's social somnambulist, communal mimesis is formed in speculative mimesis. As Hamilton points out, for Caillois collective mimesis is not an 'entirely negative concept'. The 'basis for community' occurs fundamentally because the mimicking individual becomes blended into the commonness of its environment. Communal mimesis celebrates a kind of 'nonprivate' commonness, which is not stabilized by the immunopolitics of 'self-preservation' but instead requires the loss of self.[130]

5

Deeper Entanglements

This discussion concludes by moving beyond the nonconscious entanglements of the social media paradigm to explore the potential promises and perils of an immersive future of somnambulistic user experiences. It would seem that the sleepwalker is increasingly becoming intertwined with new kinds of ubiquitous technology, linked to an ever-expanding experience economy. These novel, all-pervasive experiences are enabled through the apparent insertion into the wider environment of sensor-driven and location-sensitive computing power. These technologies offer a range of altered *reality* experiences, including virtual, augmented and mixed contexts of use. Pervasive computing is not however a rerun of the kind of consensual hallucination users were supposed to experience with virtual reality. Immersion is not a rabbit hole through which users escape the real world. On the contrary, as briefly discussed in the previous chapter, these ubiquitous experiences are transformative, since the insertion of computing into the environment turns virtual reality *inside out*.[1] The user experience is assumed to be unfolding in what has been called the Internet of Things (IoT), wherein brains and bodies encounter a range of newly animated, mostly invisible, nontask and proximity-based user experiences.

The subject matter under discussion is initially grasped through the lenses of human–computer interaction (HCI) and user experience design (UX). Both disciplines are clearly caught in a moment of acute transition. On the horizon already, there are embedded sensory experiences, including *more-than-human* interactions with (and between) AIs, drones and robotics. However, the main focus of the discussion is not simply on technological change. It instead explores transformations in the user experience of computing power by looking to resolve an important distinction. This is in fact probably the most significant distinction addressed in the book. Certainly, my somewhat overly ambitious proposal is to try to overcome the ultimate bifurcation that forces a distinction between mind and matter. Which is to say, the chapter is inspired by Whitehead's desire for a nonbifurcated theory of nature in which the subject and the object of study are not grasped as lifeless abstracts of perception experienced *in mind*, but instead become fused together in the events of a lively matter-mind entanglement. The discussion is particularly enthused by the contrast Whitehead makes between a kind of matter that is, on one hand, *lifeless*, and apprehended by the mind, and one that is, on the other hand, *alive*, and therefore apprehending.[2]

Along these lines, the discussion opens up a dialogue with a comparable concept Andrew Murphie (following Whitehead's *Nature Alive*) has called *Media Alive*.[3] My aim here is similarly to challenge some of the traditions in the study of human communication and media technology, which have been, as Murphie points out, largely informed by the bifurcation between mind and matter. Bifurcated thinking has certainly been prevalent in communications and interaction models and practices and embedded in important concepts and discussions on technical development and the social impacts of media technology.[4] As we will see below, the desire to collapse such a fundamental distinction between mind and matter certainly goes against the grain of much of the literature in the study of HCI and UX, wherein there is still the remnants of a forced distinction made between the active human experience of media (phenomenal perceptions, attentional work, mental modelling etc.) and what Murphie calls 'the supposedly not quite as active world' of media in itself.[5]

My intention here is to engage with the concept of Media Alive as a means to upset many of the scholarly conventions that have informed the study of HCI and UX. Such an approach requires a much broader concept of user experience than those commonly explored in what has been called the *phenomenological matrix* of the HCI discipline.[6] Significantly, then, a Whiteheadian concept of user experience is developed on, which does not belong to the user, the computer, or the newly enlivened environments in which these components come together. What is alive is instead considered to be the deeper entanglement of experience itself.

After a brief survey of the various implications of these newly animated media immersions on interface visibility, intelligence and the nonhuman world, the discussion focuses on the concept of embodied interaction. This is a concept of human experience with computing power that underpins the phenomenological matrix of HCI. What I hope to show by reviewing this material is the limitation of its theoretical frame in terms of how it grasps Media Alive. As follows, in the latter part of the chapter, the conventions of this matrix are contrasted with an experimental nonbifurcated approach to user experience. This part of the discussion introduces a series of Whiteheadian conceptual tools, intended to probe nonbifurcated experiences. These tools include a further development of the nonphenomenological syntax introduced in Chapter 3, a spatial analysis comparable to Caillios's topological milieu, and a concept of *prehended* user experience.

Media Alive?

So, in what ways are media considered to be alive, and what are the implications of new immersive vitalities on such a concept? If we are to follow recent discourses from the technology sector, we can see how pervasive digital media have been positioned as a considerable expansion of user experience beyond the social computing paradigm. There are many potential consequences that might occur following this deepening of the human–computer entanglement. To begin with, the widespread insertion of media technology into the objects and surfaces of the user's environment will expand the reach of data power and ignite new anxieties about privacy and autonomy. Perhaps the sleepwalker already has one foot firmly standing in an immersive future, wherein all kinds of experiential data are gathered from interactions with pervasive computing power. Along these lines, experiences are readily captured through interactions with everyday things like cars, fitness gadgets and training shoes, watches, kettles, mirrors, speakers, furniture, pavements and streetlamps.

The sleepwalker will also have to contend with the consequences of the disappearance of computing power into the environments they inhabit. Seamless interactions with computerized things mean that the visual conventions of graphical user interfaces (GUIs) will become of less importance. Likewise, the insertion of miniaturized hardware sensors with connected software capacities into everyday things will affect the conventions of the subject/object relation with media technology in profound ways. In effect, encounters with IoT will be increasingly hidden from users. Furthermore, events will be triggered by nontask interactions, fleeting moments of contact, and new kinds of accidentally engendered glitches. These encounters with computing will also become more sensitive and feely. Biometric detection systems will, as such, capture data about the affective valence of bodies and faces responding to environmental stimuli, igniting new concerns about data privacy and human autonomy.

Another common concern about pervasive computing is the assumed challenge it poses to the autonomy of human intelligence and intention.

The disappearance into the environment of machine learning, and other AI technologies, will potentially pose a threat to the centrality of human cognitive processes, like memory, perception, and attention. Computing power, which has been conventionally grasped as an augmentation of human cognition, will generate user experiences that occur outside of human cognition. In the complex passage and variation of events, past engagements with IoT, including noncognitive experiences, such as bodily movements, for example, will be prompted back into action in the present. In other words, via machine learning technologies, noncognitive experiences will work in the background as patterns that generate inferred future experiential performances.[7] Experiences can, as such, be processed through machine to machine communitive networks without the need for human attention or input. Yet, these patterns will also feed into new propositions, subsequent, and potentially subcritical, cognitive judgements, again without the need for human participation, but nevertheless steering human impulses and actions.

As we will see below, media theorists have expressed concern about these newly animated environments, particularly, with regard to how the agential power of an all-pervasive operational level of computing threatens to blur the divide between communicative humans and technological objects. This is certainly one way in which immersive media somnambulism can be conceived. As Hansen argues:

> [T]oday's digital networks possess the capacity to gather and to exploit all kinds of data without us having any knowledge, and, to a great extent, any possibility for knowledge, of such activity.[8]

Although a seemingly autonomous IoT looks set to open up the user experience to encompass all worldly interactions, we also need to admit to the continuity of a deeper nonconscious entanglement that is just as closed as the previous paradigm. Media Alive is therefore just as likely to be shaped by the propagation of mimicked human stupidity, bigotry and failed immunity, as it is by a transcendent system of smart intelligence that exceeds the human will to power.

Another implication we need to contemplate here is that the deep nonconscious entanglements of IoT (however smart or stupid) will not be contained to human–computer or indeed computer–computer relations in isolation. The blending of computing power into the wider environment has already impacted more broadly on the nonhuman world. *Media Alive has well and truly converged with Nature Alive.* Computational power is engaged with the widespread capturing of entangled experiences relating to endangered animal life, eroding and rotting landscapes, and human manufactured climate change. The sciences are yielding a vast nonhuman experiential dataset. This kind of media-nature aliveness is in many ways paradoxical since it potentially offers to, on one hand, bolster the amount of scientific data that traces and evidences the destructive impacts of the Anthropocene. However, on the other hand, widespread computing increases the toxic, assemblages of material extraction, human conflict, and proliferation of nonrecyclable devices that feed into the destructive immanence of human and nonhuman experience. *Media Alive plays its considerable role in Nature Deceased.*

Trapped in the Phenomenological Matrix

The irony of the emergence of a nonhuman Media Alive is that the subject matter of HCI and UX remains resolutely phenomenological. These tendencies in the field of HCI single it out as an example of bifurcated thinking writ large. Although in recent decades, the theoretical frame has shifted away from its origins in ergonomics (body–machine coupling), and latterly a second paradigm solely constrained to cognitive processes (mind–machine coupling), a so-called third paradigm of HCI is firmly rooted in a *phenomenological matrix* that divides mind and nature.[9] At the centre of this matrix is the concept of embodied interaction. Harrison et al., for example, contend that how we come to 'understand the world, ourselves, and interaction' in these new pervasive contexts crucially derives 'from our location in a physical and social world as embodied actors'.[10] To understand the philosophic implications of embodied interaction, HCI researchers have turned to phenomenology. Paul Dourish, for example, sees these new embodied contexts as intimately linked to the technological changes he first observed in the latter part of the twentieth century.[11] To begin with, in the 1970s, GUI technology introduced a visualization of computing that prompted a representational turn in the study of interaction, typified by cognitive task-based testing and mental models utilized in the cognitive paradigm. Yet by the 1980s, the growth in digital network communication added new importance to the social in interaction design, prompting a trend in research towards analysing distributed notions of cognition. Subsequently, in the 1990s, when computing first begins to break out of the screen and make its way into the physical environment in the shape of tangible technologies, attention is drawn towards the limits of the cognitive approach. It is these two latter developments in the context of computer use (social and tangible), which

Dourish argues, require a new HCI framework focused on embodiment and grasped through the twentieth-century phenomenological tradition.[12]

Embodiment is defined in a way that makes it useful to the HCI researcher, mainly because it provides a 'property of being manifest in and of the everyday world' in which interactions take place.[13] This property is not, however, simply restricted to physical things, like computers or mobile devices, but can include participatory patterns, like conversations between 'two equally embodied people' set against 'a backdrop of an equally embodied set of relationships, actions, assessments and understandings'.[14] This backdrop owes an initial debt to Husserl's phenomenology, insofar as it is seen as part of a transition away from an experience of the world grasped through the realm of abstract ideas (idealism) to one derived from the experience of concrete phenomena. However, more attention is given to Heidegger and Merleau-Ponty in third paradigm HCI research. In the first instance, Heidegger famously tried to escape Husserl's 'mentalistic model that placed the focus of experience in the head'.[15] This is, evidently, important to the third paradigm's similar transition from the cognitive realm of mental modelling to embodied interaction, whereby interaction is no longer considered in the head (or mind), 'but out in the world... that is already organized in terms of meaning and purpose'.[16] Certainly, Heidegger's ontological worldview is not taken as a given – it arises through interaction.

Dourish is not the first to utilize Heidegger for HCI purposes. Below, he refers to Winograd and Flores earlier adoption in 1986 of the Heideggerian distinction between *ready-to-hand* and *present-at-hand* to explain a distinctly first paradigm user experience of interacting with a mouse.

> [C]onsider the mouse connected to my computer. Much of the time, I act through the mouse; the mouse is an extension of my hand as I select objects, operate menus and so forth. The mouse is, in Heidegger's terms, ready-to-hand. Sometimes, however, for instance on those occasions when I reach the edge of the mousepad and cannot move the mouse further, my orientation towards the mouse changes; now, I become conscious of the mouse mediating my action, and the mouse becomes the object of my attention as I pick it up and move it back to the centre of the mousepad. When I act on the mouse in this way, being mindful of it as an object of my activity, the mouse is present-at-hand.[17]

This switching between automatic interaction and mindful attention suggests that the mouse only really exists; because of the way, it becomes present-at-hand through embodied interaction. The point is that the mindful activity of using the mouse is constitutive of ontology, not independent of it (Dourish 1999). The mouse comes into being in the mind, because, it would seem, it is part of an embodied experience of being in the world.

This notion of mindful embodiment is further developed by Dreyfus,[18] who brings in the phenomenology of perception developed by Merleau-Ponty.[19] Here, we find that perception itself is an active process, carried out by an embodied subject. As a result, third paradigm HCI research begins to focus on a somewhat dualistic distinction between the 'physical embodiment of a human subject, with legs and arms, and of a certain size and shape' and a 'cultural world' from which subjects extract meaning.[20] From this stance, the importance of developing 'bodily skills and situational responses', alongside mindful acts (or 'cultural skills'), which in turn respond to the user's embeddedness in this 'cultural world', comes to the fore.[21] It is in between bodily and mindful interactions that abilities and understandings of computing are developed.

It must be further noted that there is a considerable social component to this notion of interaction. On one hand, then, we find the presence of the phenomenological body of the user subject, who, on the other hand, simultaneously becomes the 'objective body' experienced and understood by others in the cultural worlds they encounter.[22] From this point on, HCI researchers start to draw on Merleau-Ponty's phenomenal perception of embodied and cultural worlds to develop, for example, 'a taxonomy of embodied actions for the analysis of group activity'.[23]

Although escaping Husserl's mental prison of the head to explain how experience emerges from fleshy human interaction with the world, human perception remains stubbornly (and problematically) central to the phenomenologist's ontology. Whether or not it is in the head or embodied in the world, HCI phenomenology similarly begins with the notion that it is the human who has the experience. In other words, *where the action is* can be grasped ontologically as it is sensed (in the head, in the hand or through some other bodily interaction) to the human.

In Whiteheadian terms then, the matrix not only traps experience in a bifurcated relation between mind and matter, but it also constrains the terms of reference one can apply to experience to the subject-predicate-object syntax. Which is to say, it is always the subject (the user) who experiences the object (i.e. computational device). To use Whitehead is to therefore challenge such a position and develop tools that can take a radical departure from the phenomenological tradition.

A Whiteheadian Sleepwalk in HCI

In order to disturb this tendency towards bifurcation in HCI, this discussion needs to begin with Whitehead's ostensibly uncanny notion that experience did not start with subjective human consciousness.[24] Which is to say, the world, and the cosmos it floats in, did not simply begin with the arrival of conscious human experience. It is not human consciousness that draws attention to experience. It is, on the contrary, experience that draws attention to an anomalous human worldview limited by its internal perception of the here and now. It is important to avoid, as such, a solipsistic theory of mindful perception, which erroneously bifurcates from the concreteness of the passage of nature from which it emerged. Whitehead's sleepwalk (see Chapter 2), accordingly, offers a constraining philosophical point of departure, since it is not phenomenal human consciousness that sheds light on experience, but experience in the actual world that draws attention to the aberration that is human consciousness. In other words, it is very important that the place and time (the here and now) of interaction is no longer simply understood as an anthropomorphic phenomenal experience, but rather grasped through a set of tools that refuse the bifurcation between mind and the material nature of what is experienced. As follows, in Whitehead's early process philosophy, the embodied location of points in time and positions in space suggested in the phenomenological matrix are not regarded as well-formulated problems, since they overlook the complex 'temporal thickness' and intensity of the durational quality of the actual occasions (or events) of experience.[25]

Of course, HCI researchers may well want to question the value of an approach that side-lines the human, or more specifically, human consciousness. However, this stance is important to grasping the sleepwalker's experience, since the transient perception of the somnambulistic user, captured in the here and now of experience, only represents a small slice of the passage of events occurring in the actual world. Arguably, as a consequence, the focus on human perception, in isolation, neglects to grasp the full extent of changes to the technological infrastructure that redefine where the action is in terms of a more-than-human experience. In other words, interaction researchers need to move on from their sole concern with what is *ready-to-hand* or *present-at-hand* (i.e. the mouse example above) to consider collective and autoaffective experiences of technology.

It is important to add that a Whiteheadian sleepwalk does not simply reject human perception. On the contrary, human perception needs to be seen as taking into account what occurs in the passage of events.[26] Perception and event are not prized apart in any way, shape or form. This is not, however, the same as saying that perception produces the reality of experience. Perception does not decide if things are more or less real! Which is to say, in a Whiteheadian frame, embodied interaction only goes as far as declaring mere instants of percipient, and sometimes specious, events in experience. What the Whiteheadian sleepwalker profoundly tells us is that it is, inversely, the process of reality that produces subjectivity.

Conceptual Tools for Nonbifurcated Experience

A Whiteheadian sleepwalk helps us rethink the status of human consciousness in HCI. While the phenomenologist brings in a bifurcation between the perceiving human mind, embodiment, and experience in the actual world, the somnambulist eschews theories that force such a bifurcation. The phenomenologist, for example, takes what is experienced in the actual world as the here and now. What is ready-in-hand, as we have seen, becomes a position in space and a point in time from which meanings can be constructed from what is present-in-hand. However, this perception of the here and now of experience can be recast as a misplaced abstraction of a far more complex relation to reality experienced through a concrete passage of events. For Whitehead, then, the data of experience are not in mind. The actual world is not apprehended by the mind; on the contrary, the mind is part of the passage of events in the actual world. Significantly then, as I have argued throughout, it is not that mindfulness does not exist; evidently, it does, but the mind only has a *foothold* in experience rather than a *command post*.[27]

Whitehead resolved not to limit his philosophical outlook to theories that made such a bifurcation happen. He looked, as such, to develop new concepts of experience that are not exclusively the property of human perception, but rather inclusive and interlocked with the actual world humans are a part of. Of course, this is a complex task to undertake, thwart with so many homemade traps. I suggest, as such, that we try to follow three trap-avoiding steps. It is necessary to, first, undo the subject predicated philosophies developed over epochs of human consciousness; to completely disengage from the solipsistic sense that humans are the masters of subjectivity when it comes to observing real material substances or the formulation of ideas that describe them. It also means overcoming the language games we have absorbed into our minds that explain our subjective experience of the real world in such limited ways.

Second, and clearly related to HCI, we need to challenge the rigidity of subject–object relations as the only way to think about the ontology of spatial interaction. Third, Whitehead prompts us to move beyond purely spatial concepts of interaction to radically approach experience in terms of the passage of events.

Freeing Experience from the Syntax Trap

As a development on the new syntax I tried to set out in Chapter 3, the Whiteheadian sleepwalker asks us also to test the limits of phenomenal language. This is a syntactic redesign, which is, like the tools of physics, intended to better probe the dynamics of the actual world without putting human experience at the centre of things. Moreover, language, as it has been developed in the bifurcation of mind and nature, is clearly designed to only handle a static world, and fails, as such, to express the dynamics and aliveness of reality.[28] In his endeavour to refuse bifurcation, Whitehead criticized the orthodox linguistic concept of *having an experience* of an object, since it is erroneously determined by the mould of the subject–predicate. That is to say, the subject (the knower) is always situated by the experience of the object (the known). As Victor Lowe argues, the subject–predicate mould is 'stamped on the face of experience', so that the experient is always the subject who is qualified by the sensations of the objective world.[29] This is how phenomenal language traps experience in the unidirectional relation between the private subject and the public object.

The Whiteheadian sleepwalker's intervention into the trappings of language is of use to our current study of user experience for two main reasons. First, we see how the subject predicate trap is already set in the research focus on situated interactions, where, for example, it is the user who experiences the smooth ergonomics of the mouse, so that the subject user is situated by their experience of the public object. As a counterintuitive alternative, Whiteheadian subjects can be made into objects, and inversely, objects into subjects. The notion that objects can experience subjects, as is the case when a well-designed mouse experiences the hand of the user, should not be, however, an entirely alien design concept in tangible computing, ergonomics or experience design. By drawing on Whitehead's reinvention of terms like feeling, emotion, satisfaction, and enjoyment, design theorists should be able to develop effective ways to account for the relationalities of experience not yet adequately realized, so that it might be possible to conjure up a concept of the mouse feeling the warmth of the user's hand. Significantly, the subject does not simply know the object, but is provoked into knowing by the experience of the object. Furthermore, in the new IoT contexts of interaction a user who encounters an object can become the subject of interaction. It might be the case then, as Hayles similarly argues, that in twenty-first-century media subject agency has ceded control to the technological object; that is to say, the binary divide between active, communicative subjects and passive, silent, fixed objects, no longer works.[30] HCI researchers will also have to take into account objects that have become sociable, sidestepping human awareness or taking the place of humans altogether.[31] Ultimately though, rethinking experience as neither predicated by subject nor object makes way for immanent relations in which subjective forces are not predetermined as the knowers of objects, but focus attention instead on the shifting relations in which each experiences the other.

Second, in Whitehead, we encounter a viable alternative to Heidegger's solution to Husserl's problematic concept of experience as locked inside the head. For Whitehead, experience is said to be 'the self-enjoyment of being one among many, and of being one arising out of the composition of the many'.[32] This is not a self-satisfying moment in time beginning in the head, brain, mind or body. Experience may indeed be related to human experiences, but it cannot be decoupled from the interlocking relations of an assemblage of brains, minds and bodies which are found to be in a much deeper entanglement with nature. As Whitehead puts it:

> [W]e cannot determine with what molecules the brain begins and the rest of the body ends. Further, we cannot tell with what molecules the body ends and the external world begins. The truth is that the brain is continuous with the body, and the body is continuous with the rest of the natural world. Human experience is an act of self-origination including the whole of nature, limited to the perspective of a focal region, located within the body, but not necessarily persisting in any fixed coordination with a definite part of the brain.[33]

Clearly, this assemblage does not limit experience to any privileged sense organ (the brain or the sensation of a body), or a higher level of consciousness (the all-perceiving mind with the capacity for language). Although Whitehead concedes that human consciousness may well be an exhibit of the 'most intense form of the plasticity of nature',[34] there is no dichotomy between the human and what is experienced, and ultimately, in this nonbifurcated sensemaking assemblage, nature is closed to mind.

Space is Interaction

Whitehead fundamentally changes the concept of spatial interaction by introducing a process philosophy in which it is the passage of events that is experienced. To be sure, early on in his so-called pre-speculative epistemological phase Whitehead sought to develop a relational theory intended to overturn the ancient Greek's notion of absolute space.[35] This nascent trajectory of his work begins with a mathematician's interest in overturning orthodox geometry. The problem for Whitehead is the geometric point! His relational theory of space thus notes how time is missing or constrained to points in the Euclidean geometric grid. He argues that things do not occur in points in space; points are not ultimate entities, but abstractions of complex durations. We need to, therefore, forget a concept of space defined as the place, where we find bodies at certain fixed points in time, acting on other bodies. Interaction is not a property of space. Bodies are not in space because they interact. Space is, *in itself*, a certain kind of process of interaction. Interaction in space is not, as such, defined by one point effecting another, for example, the hand meeting the mouse, but is a coming together of a coherent population of interacting bodies into a society of events. It is this process of coming together, what Whitehead would go on to call concrescence, which requires attention and needs explaining as best we can.[36]

The theoretical reframing of human–computer interaction may well have to start with a redefinition of interaction as an immanent relation in which it is not points in time or space that are experienced, but durations. Again, this rethinking of interaction fundamentally changes the terms of phenomenological HCI research. Where the action is does not bring us to a location determined by the perceiving mind or where a body interacts with a computer, but space itself is interaction. Here, we can see how ergonomics may well have been onto something that both cognitive and phenomenological HCI went on to ignore. Instead of concentrating on perceptive locations of interaction in space – i.e., the points in space where hands (and minds) meet the mouse – ergonomic experts engaged in capturing (and breaking down) computer tasks into discrete activities in time. Albeit an oversimplification of a passage of time lacking in the thickness required by Whitehead's theory of events, the ergonomic study of interaction is not limited to a notion of perception fixed to a geometric grid.[37]

Like phenomenal HCI, the Whiteheadian sleepwalker endeavours to escape from the same Cartesian structures that underpin the second cognitive paradigm. To do this, Whitehead borrows from William James's concept of pure experience to make a contra-Cartesian move.[38] However, we must first clearly distinguish here between the phenomenological contra-Cartesian position Dourish takes in his thesis *Where the Action Is* and Whitehead's event analysis.[39] On one hand, Dourish is critical of the cognitive paradigm's convention of grasping interaction through a mind–computer metaphor that seems to have lost its relation to a body.[40] As we have seen, embodied interaction is not just information in the mind; it is also experienced in the hand. On the other hand, though, Whitehead does not regard mind or body as the situation, where interaction occurs, but rather draws attention to how both are composed in a passage of events. The I of the mind (and the body from which it seems to belong) does not determine who we are, since in the duration of events, both body and mind are swept up in the present before slipping into the past. Therefore, unlike Descartes' dualism, the mind does not determine who we are. Again, this is not the command post of experience we find in the phenomenological matrix. The mind always comes later! The experience does not, therefore, belong to the mind. The mind's perceptual judgements, as well as its apparent capacity for memory and attention, can only testify to the passage of events from its percipient foothold – in the duration of events.[41]

From an events perspective, then, we can begin to look at perception in a very different light from the phenomenological subject and her interaction with concrete objects in abstract points of time and space. Perception needs to be approached not by way of what is ready or present-in-hand, but by way of what is in passage; in what Whitehead calls a percipient event.[42] Therefore, unlike the phenomenal mind that puts concrete objects to death, because they are only ready-to-hand or miraculously brings them back to life, since they are here right now and present-at-hand, in mental space, it is the event itself that becomes the concrete fact of experience. There would be no objects to perceive, no mindfulness of objects, without the passing of these concrete events. The object perceived is not, therefore, what is concrete or what brings about the abstractions of consciousness. Whiteheadian objects are not concrete substances from which abstract properties arise; on the contrary, objects are abstractions.[43]

In an events analysis, it is not enough to say here is the mouse, since it will be perceived in a complex array of abstract objects, including how it is sensed through a clicking noise even if it is not seen, as well as the haptic physicality and perception of shape or even viewed under a microscope as a mass of molecules, and so on. Abstract objects are not experienced merely in the now either. They provide a uniqueness and continuity that presents the foothold the mind needs in the events that pass it by; there is the mouse and there it is again! It is not, as such, an object in a given space. It is a mouse event or pattern of interaction that produces the subjective reality of the mouse. Ontologically, the mouse is not, therefore, hidden from consciousness, but it is declared in the percipient encounter with events.[44] To put this another way, it is not the abstract properties of the concrete object that declares the mouse, but rather the mouse is an abstract object perceived of in the unified concrescence of the events that declare it.

The subject who perceives the mouse is not the author of the event, or the author of the many variations in mouse events. However, we must not simply replace subject/object with object/event relations. We need to think of interaction as a society or a nexus of events in passage that provide ingression to objects, so that the object is expressed in the event and the event expressed in the object.[45] As Stengers puts it, every duration of an event 'contains other durations and is contained in other durations'.[46] This is the relational temporal thickness of Whitehead's event that cannot be grasped in individual points in time or space. As follows, we need to recall that making the subject the author of this kind of mouse event reintroduces bifurcation. The human mind (however exceptional its plasticity in nature) cannot experience the whole event. The subject does not decide on events (whether the mouse is here or not here), as such. The events decide the subject. The subject's point of view (this percipient window on experience) belongs to an 'impersonal web' of events.[47] To put it another way, events are not a privileged conscious point of view the user adopts. Users may well occupy the here, but it is their relation to the now that sweeps them up in a complex flow of events in which they might confuse the observational present for something that exceeds the mere foothold the mind has in all of this complexity.

To counter the phenomenal mind, which finds meaning in the symmetry of the here and now, Whitehead introduces us to the asymmetry of the here and now. Yes, the percipient event locates us in the here but this here does not move in tandem with the now. The durational now scoops up the here producing infinite variation. It is indeed, as Stengers points out, the *and* in the here and now that really matters in terms of meaning making.[48] This is what relates the asymmetrical sense of an observational present (the here) to the now in durational passage. This is Whitehead's cogredience, which would later be developed more fully in process philosophy as the vector-like concept of prehension.[49]

Prehending HCI

The need for prehension begins with a problem regarding how humans confusingly perceive what is here with real things that are supposed to exist at a distance, as there. Prehension, according to Lowe, therefore, provides the 'thread' of process and reality.[50] It is the vector that makes events into concrescent unities, and analysable, as such. The prehension takes us beyond the here and now of phenomenality. So, unlike the idealist's answer to this problem, wherein the abstraction of space by the mind results in a solipsistic subjective perception, we find instead a production of reality in what is felt is always becoming: the past (objective datum – what is prehended) is alive and well in the present derivation (subjective form – how it is prehended).[51] Prehensions thus provide a way of grasping how what is *there* becomes something *here*. In other words, a prehension is the relation established between events in which the past has a stake in the composition of what is new. Again, it is not simply the *here* and *now* (immediate present) that matters to Whitehead, but how prehension sweeps past events up into a unity (or nexus) in which something *there* becomes something *here* (causal efficacy). Following Whitehead's nonbifurcated event analysis, then, the mouse cannot be said to be in or out of mind because the past (what is prehended as the mouse) is always in the now (this is how the mouse becomes a subjective form). In short, the mouse is experienced as a flow of events (a process), whereby the past event flows into the present event.

Prehension might help HCI researchers to go beyond Dourish's criticism of the cognitive paradigm by not only radically inverting the notion that action in the world necessarily comes after concrete experiences of objects (the mouse) followed by an abstraction (the mouse in hand or mind), but also questioning the very concept of social context. As Blackwell argues, much of the study of situated and embodied interaction misses the new technical landscape in which social context is engendered by machine learning systems.[52] Machine learning codes operate on 'grounded' data, and their 'cognition' is based wholly on information collected from 'the real world'.[53] These systems directly interact with social context insofar as they collect data from social media, cookies and relational databases, making the user experience increasingly inferred. For Blackwell, the critical issue at stake now is that by making humans into data sources in the service of machine learning systems, it is no longer simply a problem of grasping human cognition as situated in the machine, but instead, we need to recognize the inhumane character of a 'cognition' emerging from a new technological context. Prehension can, as such, help us to reconceive of user experience beyond the subjective relations of the *here* and *now* (beyond those interactions with that mouse too!) by looking to a spatiotemporal concept of the event experienced *over there* (by a machine) becoming experienced *here* (by the human) and able to therefore anticipate an action sometime in the future.

Developing a Critical Media Theory of Experience

This focus on prehension considerably overlaps with similar concerns in critical media theory. For example, Rebecca Coleman's work on pre-emergent and emergent media cultures draws on Raymond Williams to point to an experiential media grasped as 'a series of practices, activities, flows and events' that, as Williams says, are not 'fully articulated' but hover 'at the edge of semantic availability'.[54] Significantly, Coleman positions this experiential media culture as part of the displacement of the human within the datalogical network, on one hand, and a tendency to 'affect or prehend novelty, on the other'.[55] This is not a media culture that simply represents the user, as set out in the cruder renditions of the data-double model (see Chapters 3 and 4), or is it merely orientated towards what the user has done. According to Coleman, experiential media is more focused on the immediacy of what users are doing and what they may do. This is a 'future-oriented' prehension in the sense that it does not observe use, but rather experiences the events of use.

On a similar note, Hansen argues that there has been 'a shift in the economy of experience itself' wherein media systems that once addressed humans first are now registering the environmentality of the world itself, prior to, and without any necessary relation to, human affairs.[56] As follows, Hansen draws important attention to the difficulties of developing a robust nonbifurcated analysis of experiential media. His argument is evidently a complex one, but the main conclusion seems to concern how the current wave of digital media technology refuses conscious human minds access to the processing of the environmentality of the world. This is because, what Hansen calls the 'higher order perceptual experiences' of the human are no longer implicated in the making of the operational levels of digital culture, including data gathering and mining.[57]

At the first look, this account seems like a plausible explanation for what happens when experiential media, weaponized by the latest operations of digital technology, captures and commodifies a more broadly understood concept of experience. Human consciousness is, in effect, cut out!

Nonetheless, as Greg Seigworth points out, Hansen's approach seems to open up an 'experiential gap or an interval between the body's perceptual apparatuses and the making of worldly sensibility'.[58] Like this, the latter is supposed to be produced solely by technical machines. But as Seigworth points out, this conception produces a 'troubling kind of ahistorical suspension or hiatus'.[59] It ignores, as such, 'longer stretches of temporal continuity' in which 'durations' persist 'alongside any array of ruptures/ gaps/delays'.[60]

Ultimately, these human concerns for the loss of human consciousness in digital culture, echoed by others, like Katherine Hayles, perhaps miss Whitehead's more profound and constraining concept of nonbifurcated experience. It is surely not the case that a nonbifurcated twenty-first-century media can be determined by more or less human consciousness. On the contrary, experience is generative in the circuitries of pervasive media, which records and patterns mind and nature in concert with each other. Indeed, the experience of the *there*, and *there it is again*, media event is transformed in pervasive digital media, but only in respect to the novel digital objects that now ingress with the thickness of durational passage.

Conclusion

Significantly, immersive, always-on, big-time data gathering operations capture more experience than a mere mouse click could ever do, but we have our media history confused if we think that there was ever a time when the human mind had a more privileged status in media spaces. Media theory accounts that bemoan the loss of human consciousness from media systems are reminiscent in this sense to the alien in Nicolas Roeg's 1976 film, *The Man Who Fell to Earth*. Throughout the film, we see how Thomas Newton, played by David Bowie, experiences all of the events of the analogue media world into which he fell. Sitting in front of multiple TV screens, Newton seems to completely inhabit the symmetry of the here and now. 'Get out of my mind, all of you... Leave my mind alone, all of you. Stay where you belong!' he shouts at the screens.[61] However, notwithstanding Bowie's convincing extra-terrestrial conceptual persona, humans are not aliens of this kind. We cannot detach our experiences of media objects (sensed or otherwise) from the entangled thickness of duration. Our experience of media does not operate like Newton's command post – experiencing everything in the here and now! In other words, while it does seem to be the case that experience capitalism is, via large scale data gathering and machine learning, implicated in the processing of more and more experience (including nonhuman experience), it is important to stress that so-called higher order human experiences are not bifurcated from actual experience. Minds are not absent from the matter-flow. They are not cut out of the loop of actual experience, but instead human experiences are immanent to a complex maelstrom of deeply eventful entanglements that confound notions of predicated subjective conscious experience or objective reality.

To conclude, then, any resistance to experience capitalism should not be concerned with trying to reinsert human consciousness into a hidden operational level of computation. In other words, the struggle should not be founded on a perceived loss of human judgement in the face of a new dehumanizing technological context. Humans have never had a command post in the loop between conscious interaction and the technological nonconscious. On the contrary, following a nonbifurcated line, we might need to admit to the impossibility of such a task and focus instead on the sleepwalker's mere foothold in the durational viscosity of events.

Outro Disrupting the Dark Refrain

Figure 15 A Sleepwalker's Time Machine.
Illustration by Mikey B. Georgeson.

Returning to the musicological theme of the intro, this outro aims to suggest various ways in which the sleepwalker might disrupt the dystopic ostinato of the dark refrain. Options are limited. However strong the desire to turn conceptual work into praxis is, no one concept will ever kill all fascists. There is no one killer app or coherent campaign message here. *A Sleepwalker's Guide* does not advocate a binary delete or ignore choice. There is no 'do or die' rhetoric! Resistance to the dark refrain is not a matter of deciding to disconnect. As recent critics of social media have pointed out, large scale disconnect campaigns, like the post-Cambridge

Analytica #deletefacebook, end up as a number of resistance options 'hardly anyone chooses'.[1] We are also reminded that 'deactivation is the opposite of activism'.[2] More profoundly, I think, we need to listen to the comments made by our students concerning the impossibility of disconnection. They have grown up connected. Theirs is *not* to do or die, or indeed, make a rudimentary on/off judgement call. To disconnect, to disengage, or even to detox from connectivity, means they could potentially disappear into a social vacuum.

If a concept cannot ultimately destroy or dismantle this deadly chorus, then what can it do? To begin with, what I propose is that the sleepwalker can offer a conceptual care system, including a roll out of further related concepts that support a more complex series of user judgements. To be sure, in the intro I fleetingly mentioned the plight of some improvising musicians, who at some point in their freeform jam became stuck in a rhythmic habitual rut. Along these lines, we now need to help users to remove the pegs that fix experience to rigid routines and enslavements. This care system requires a conceptual toolkit for future experiments and lines of flight that might at very least make the repetitive refrain stutter or fade away.

Somnambulism challenges the ways in which judgements are assumed to be made. As follows, although clearly influenced by Tarde's nonconscious associations, *A Sleepwalker's Guide* began and ended by positing Whitehead's aesthetic fact as an alternative mode of judgement. This theoretical move is intended to help users to explore the relation between felt experiences and cognitive processes as it becomes entangled in the resonations of rumours, conspiracy and fabrication. Like this, Whitehead's aesthetic facts provide a kind of nonconscious mood music. These are facts that are neither beholden to the positivistic rationality of an individual nor do they become lost in the immersions of a stupid crowd. Aesthetic facts are, in contrast, a speculative kind of composition, experienced on broader spectra of virtual and real potentialities. This mood music evidently predates the powerful lures of social media, but the viral platforms through which these facts currently spread have intensified their tune and made them even more catchy.

There are many user vulnerabilities to be found on the sleepwalker's spectra of experience, including those related to fake news, but the most pressing problem concerns the anxieties felt when the user experience is seized by the *Empire of the Like*.[3] As follows, the repetition produces an ersatz condition of self–other similarity or the becoming-the-same of the dark refrain. It expropriates, nurtures and exploits the collective nonconscious, coupling it to a surveillant assemblage, which hoovers up data from user engagements, collective moods and contagious affects. What gets sucked up the data pipe ends up stored in opaque black boxes, full of abstract, relational lookalikes. Because of the proprietary nature of these black boxes, we can only theorize about the experiences of the lookalikes inside.

The influence of aesthetic facts on the sleepwalker can be further explored using affect theory. Or, more precisely, the power of the aesthetic lure can be grasped in the problematic spat affect theory has with the cognitivists.[4] This is a problematic spat since the latter's erroneous location of judgement as limited to personal consciousness is often offset by certain affect theorist's woolly focus on a romantic concept of personal feeling.[5] To better understand how the dark refrain affectively tones the user experience through pre-personal feelings, affect theory needs to be deployed more robustly. An affect theory of social media needs to get to grips with the various commercial incursions into user sensitivities and those feely tricks and hooks that politically target the timelines of the collective nonconscious. Nonetheless, ultimately, it is the cognitivists who misapprehend affect theory's lack of focus on the command post of human consciousness as an error or theoretical omission. On the contrary, following Whitehead's much broader mobilization of impersonal felt experiences, new materialism's rendering of affect manages to deftly reframe the fabled cognitive command posts of attention, perception and memory, and recast them as mere footholds in an aesthetic ontology.

To explore this aesthetic ontology the sleepwalker has been transformed into a fully fledged fictioning machine. This is a machine that is, at first, pointed towards the brutal logics of positivist accounts of truth, as well as the absurdity of the postmodernist's post-truth thesis. However, we now need to consider more fictioning applications. The calls are out. Not just more calls for papers, but calls for action! In this way, affect theory and art practice can come together in ways that challenge the dark refrain by producing new shocks. Crucially, though, the shock event of the fictioning machine must not be designed to wake the sleepwalker. The goal is neither wakefulness nor sleep. The barriers sleep provides between the *Bios* and capitalism may well help to protect users from digital labour's attack on the dream. The user experience is indeed a 24/7 dream machine, and evidently, we all need a good night's sleep. But the struggle against experience capitalism's occupation of the dream occurs mainly in the outer margins of sleep; not in the nonphenomenology of deep sleep. One has to ask, again, what use is a deactivated activist? If dreams are to play a role in wrestling back control from the dark refrain, then, perhaps we need to make more of our daydreams and everyday reveries. We need to make dreams more intensive and social.[6] Sleep itself needs to become more peripatetic and ambulant.

A Sleepwalker's Guide argues that the trickery of experience capitalism does not start with ideology or end in the commodification of the self. On the contrary, the illusions start and end in the ramping up of affective intensities to a point where the already full visceral registers of shared experience begin to resonate and overflow. This does not mean that Roland Barthes's famous mythologies of capitalism have simply expired.[7] It's just that the symbolic level of experience; those Platonic ideas-in-form, cannot be disassociated from the visceral register. We will not expose the ideological tricky of social media advertising by donning Neda's sunglasses in John Carpenter's film, *They Live*. Vision might seem to be the sense that is atop of the decision-making stack, but to understand how virality/growth works on judgement, students need to first feel the trickery of affect. After that, they will need to protect their skin and gut, before they cover their eyes!

The leitmotif of the dark refrain (its affective branding) is found in the endlessly repeated utterances of nationalistic declarations of greatness, bringing sovereignty back home, anti-immigrant sentiments and racist hate speech. In Chapter 4, it is proposed that this recurrent theme tune of the dark refrain is located somewhat *indistinctly* between immunity and virality. Like this, Trump is described as both an immunopolitical expression of white sameness and a viral host for a white supremacist contagion. Following Esposito and Caillois's influence on proposition three in the fourth chapter, the *Sleepwalker's Guide* argues for a new kind of online community composed outside of the failed immune systems, virality/growth and ontological expropriations of shared user experiences. Along these lines, the third proposition proposes a new UX design template for a social media platform, based on the principles of inoculation and autoimmunity. Ultimately, this new model of online community requires a benevolent virus since if the brain of the racist craves cognitive consonance (more of the same) then let it become infected by cultural dissonance.

The final chapter expanded on this new UX design by challenging the phenomenological matrix in human–computer interaction (HCI) research and its preference for a version of experience intentionally apprehended by human consciousness. In sharp contrast to HCI, the Whiteheadian concept of experience does not provide for a trustworthy command post in the microflows of the event. *A Sleepwalker's Guide* thus proposes an alternative series of nonphenomenological, proto-conceptual tools that might help to explore media aliveness and new ways of feeling the immanence of experience. Importantly, Whitehead's experience does not belong to a mind. Our student's perceptual judgements, and their capacity to pay attention and remember, really only testify to these microflows as this kind of percipient foothold in reality. Their judgements may seem like they are fixed in the *here* and *now* of a spatialized mindful experience. However, decisions have always been made *over there* before they arrive *here* in perception. This is now increasingly the case as judgements are processed through multiple inferential computational time machines (see figure 15). Looking beyond the social technological paradigm to a pervasive computational future, then, we find, in the place of user participatory design, an anticipatory mode of user experience. Pervasive provides a version of media alive focused on what Rebecca Coleman calls the immediacy of what users are doing and what they may do. This is a 'future-oriented' prehension in the sense that it does not observe use, but rather experiences the events of use.[8]

Most significantly, *A Sleepwalker's Guide* has called for a new syntax of experience. Indeed, even if the cognitivists do not accept Whitehead's cosmic theory of decentred user experience, there is a need to free the user experience from the syntax it is currently trapped within. Finally, then, we can draw on one last musicological reference point. Which is to say, when Jim Hendrix asks *Are You Experienced?* he doesn't mean it in the sense that we need to take ownership of our experiences. For Hendrix, getting your mind together means crossing over to a different kind of mindful experience that does not bifurcate from nature. The Jimi Hendrix Experience was already in the sunrise and at the bottom of the sea. But *Are You Experienced?* is definitely not a romantic song. It is a nonphenomenological song. This is experience with the brain's delimiter switched off.[9] It is, we assume, an acid laced *Mind at Large* experiencing large doses of cognitive dissonance that decentres the feeling of consciousness inside the head and transfers it to a felt experience of immanence. It seems that Hendrix knew of a new syntax that might ultimately lead to a new user experience. We need to start to write some new songs of experience; some new somnambulist songs.

Notes

Intro

1. The first (*Virality*) drew attention to new modes of contagious communication. The second (*The Assemblage Brain*) explored how the disciplinary *interferences* of the neurosciences, art and philosophy could be assembled to 'make sense' of the user experience paradigm. See Sampson, Tony D. 2012. *Virality: Contagion Theory in The Age of Networks*. Minneapolis: University of Minnesota Press and Sampson, Tony D. 2017. *The Assemblage Brain: Sense Making in Neuroculture*. Minneapolis: University of Minnesota Press.
2. Ibid. 80–6.
3. Ibid. 76.
4. For a useful insight into Tarde and his influences see Tonkonoff, Sergio. 2017. *From Tarde to Deleuze and Foucault: The Infinitesimal Revolution*. London: Palgrave Macmillan.
5. Neyrat, Frédéric. 2018. *Atopias: Manifesto for a Radical Existentialism*. New York: Fordham University Press.
6. Dowdell, E. B. and Clayton, B. Q. 2018. 'Interrupted sleep: College students sleeping with technology'. *Journal of American College Health*: 1–7.
7. Crary, Jonathan. 2013. *24/7: Terminal Capitalism and the Ends of Sleep*. London, Brooklyn: Verso, 30.
8. Ibid. 17.
9. For example, I'm sure many other writers will have experienced those arbitrary sentences that creep into sleep in the early hours of dreamy sleep and repeat themselves until you wake up.
10. See for example, Norman, Donald A. 2007. *Emotional Design: Why We Love (Or Hate) Everyday Things*. New York: Basic Books. So also, discussion at the end of Chapter 3.
11. As I argued in *The Assemblage Brain*, following Deleuze and Guattari, conceptual personae are philosophical tools. Plato used Socrates for such purposes, and Nietzsche introduced many personae: Zarathustra, Dionysus, Overman et al. In *What Is Philosophy?* Deleuze and Guattari introduce their own conceptual persona of the idiot who is well deployed to slow down the discourse of school teacher. See Sampson. 2017. *The Assemblage Brain*, 24.

12 Ibid. 75–6.
13 Inspiration for the dark refrain comes from the ritornello or refrain concept as discussed in Deleuze, Gilles and Guattari, Felix. 1987. *A Thousand Plateaus*. Minneapolis: University of Minnesota Press, 310–50.
14 Ibid. 3. See also discussion on a similar viral communication model in Genosko, Gary. 2012. *Remodeling Communication: From WWII to the WWW*. Toronto: University of Toronto Press.
15 Simecek, Karen. 2019. 'Affect theory'. *The Year's Work in Critical and Cultural Theory*. https://doi.org/10.1093/ywcct/mbz010.
16 Laing, R. D. (1967) 1983. *The Politics of Experience*. New York: Pantheon Books.
17 Genosko, Gary. 1998. *Undisciplined Theory*. London: Sage, 91–6.
18 Tarde cited in Sampson, Tony D. 2012. *Virality*, 36.
19 Caillois, Roger. 'Mimetism and psychasthenia'. Claudine Frank, and Camille Naish (eds.). 2003. *The Edge of Surrealism: A Roger Caillois Reader*. Durham [NC]: Duke University Press.
20 Stokes, Adrian Durham cited in Williams, Meg Harris (ed.). 2014. *Art and Analysis: An Adrian Stokes Reader*. London: Karnac, 112–13.
21 Crary, Jonathan. 2001. *Suspensions of Perception: Attention, Spectacle, and Modern Culture*. Cambridge, MA: MIT Press, 97.
22 Genosko, Gary. 1998. *Undisciplined Theory*, 96. Georgeson's work explores matter-flow. The artist wakes up twenty minutes earlier than normal and writes/draws pages or streams of consciousness.
23 Ibid.
24 Greenfield, Adam. 2006. *Everyware: The Dawning Age of Ubiquitous Computing*. Berkeley: New Riders.
25 Ruyer, Raymond. 2016. *Neofinalism*. Minneapolis: University of Minnesota Press.
26 Grosz, E. A. 2018. *The Incorporeal: Ontology, Ethics, and the Limits of Materialism*. New York: Columbia University Press, 219.
27 Ibid.
28 Ibid.
29 Ibid.
30 Clough, Patricia Ticineto. 2000. *Autoaffection: Unconscious Thought in The Age of Teletechnology*. Minneapolis: University of Minnesota Press.

1 Feeling Facts and Fakes

1 Whitehead, Alfred North. 1985. *Process and Reality: An Essay in Cosmology*. New York: Free Press, 185.
2 Burrows, David and O'Sullivan, Simon. 2019. *Fictioning: The Myth-Functions of Contemporary Art and Philosophy*. Edinburgh: Edinburgh University Press and keynote in Bath.

3 See O'Sullivan, Simon. 2017. 'Mythopoesis or fiction as mode of existence: Three case studies from contemporary art'. *Visual Culture in Britain*. 18 (2): 292–311. https://www.simonosullivan.net/articles/Mythopoesis_or_Fiction_as_Mode_of_Existence.pdf
4 Whitehead. *Process and Reality*, 185.
5 Whitehead, Alfred North and Russell, Bertrand. [1910] 1963. *Principia Mathematica*. Cambridge: Cambridge University Press.
6 The following references to Andrew Murphie's *Media Alive* keynote talk at the Affects, Interfaces, Events conference in Aarhus in 2018 are from the author's notes. See conference website. https://aie.au.dk/aie-2018/
7 Murphie. *Media Alive*.
8 Whitehead, Alfred North. 1971. *The Concept of Nature*, Tarner lectures delivered in Trinity College, November 1919. Cambridge: Cambridge University Press.
9 Whitehead, *Process and Reality*, 179. There are similar attacks made on positivism in Whitehead, Alfred North. 2010. *Modes of Thought*. New York: Free Press.
10 Murphie. *Media Alive*.
11 See Dennett D. C. and Roy D. 2015. 'Our transparent future'. *Scientific American*. 312 (3): 64–9.
12 Whitehead. *Modes of Thought*, 23.
13 Graves, Lucas and Amazeen A. Michelle. 2019. 'Fact-checking as idea and practice in journalism'. https://oxfordre.com/communication/view/10.1093/acrefore/9780190228613.001.0001/acrefore-9780190228613-e-808
14 See for example, in the UK, House of Commons Digital, Culture, Media and Sport Committee Disinformation and 'fake news': Final Report, 14 February 2019. https://publications.parliament.uk/pa/cm201719/cmselect/cmcumeds/1791/1791.pdf
15 See for example, Wardle, Claire, and Derakhshan, Hossein. 2017. *Information Disorder: Towards an Interdisciplinary Framework for Research and Policymaking*. Strasbourg Cedex Council of Europe, Council of Europe Report. https://rm.coe.int/information-disorder-report-november-2017/1680764666
16 Mooney, H. (2018). '"Fake news" and the sociological imagination: Theory Informs practice'. Forty-sixth National LOEX Library Instruction Conference Proceedings (Library Orientation Series No. 51). https://deepblue.lib.umich.edu/bitstream/handle/2027.42/143532/LOEX2018_MooneyFakeNewsSocImagination_vFinalDeepBlue.pdf?sequence=1&isAllowed=y
17 Wardle and Derakhshan. *Information Disorder*.
18 Mooney. 'Fake news'.
19 Lewandowsky, S., Ecker, U. K. H. and Cook, J. 2017. 'Beyond misinformation: Understanding and coping with the "post-truth" era'. *Journal of Applied*

Research in Memory and Cognition. 6 (4): 353–69. https://doi.org/10.1016/j.jarmac.2017.07.008 and https://research-information.bristol.ac.uk/files/152516154/Pages_from_JARMAC_2017_59_Revision_1_V1.pdf
20 Susman-Peña, T. and Vogt, Katya. 2017 'Ukrainians' self-defense against information war: What we learned from learn to discern'. IREX. https://www.irex.org/insight/ukrainians-self-defense-against-information-war-what-we-learned-learn-discern
21 E.g. Simon, Herbert A. 1996. *The Sciences of the Artificial* (3rd edn) Cambridge, MA: MIT Press, 21.
22 N. Katherine Hayles. *Unthought: The Power of the Cognitive Unconscious*. Chicago; London: University of Chicago Press, 12–14.
23 Collins, Harry. 2013. *Tacit and Explicit Knowledge*. Chicago; London: University of Chicago Press.
24 N. Katherine Hayles. *Unthought*, 10–11.
25 Ibid. 10.
26 Harry Collins speaking at the Tacit Engagement in the Digital Age conference, 26–8 June 2019. A joint conference by the 'Re-' Interdisciplinary Network (CRASSH) and the AI and Society Journal. Hosted by Cambridge University. Author's notes. See conference website. https://cms.mus.cam.ac.uk/conferences/tacit-engagement-in-the-digital-age
27 Clough, Patricia Ticineto. 2000. *Autoaffection Unconscious Thought in the Age of Teletechnology*. Minneapolis: University of Minnesota Press; Thrift, Nigel. 2004. 'Remembering the technological unconscious by foregrounding knowledges of position'. *Environment and Planning D: Society and Space*. 22 (1): 175–90; Hayles, Katherine N. 2006. 'Traumas in code'. *Critical Inquiry*. 33 (1): 136–57; Grusin, Richard. 2010. *Premediation: Affect and Mediality after 9/11*. New York; London: Palgrave Macmillan.
28 Clough. 2000. *Autoaffection*.
29 Clough, Patricia Ticineto. 2018. *The User Unconscious: On Affect, Media, and Measure*. University of Minnesota Press, xxxi–xxxii.
30 Ibid. xxxv–xxxvi.
31 Connolly, William E. 2017. *Aspirational Fascism: The Struggle for Multifaceted Democracy under Trumpism*. Minneapolis: University of Minnesota Press, 20.
32 Ibid. 21.
33 Sampson. *The Assemblage Brain*, 153.
34 Dewan, Prateek and Ponnurangam Kumaraguru. 2017. 'Facebook Inspector (FbI): Towards automatic real-time detection of malicious content on Facebook'. *Social Network Analysis and Mining*. 7 (1).
35 Massumi, Brian. 2016. *Politics of Affect*. Cambridge: Polity, 53–4.
36 Massumi, Brian. 2010. 'The future birth of the affective fact: The political ontology of threat'. Gregg, Melissa and Seigworth, Gregory J. (eds.). *The Affect Theory Reader*. Durham and London: Duke University Press, 54.
37 Ibid.

38 Massumi. *Politics of Affect*, 53.
39 Whitehead. *Modes of Thought*, 60–1.
40 https://www.bloomberg.com/news/articles/2017-11-16/inside-google-s-struggle-to-filter-lies-from-breaking-news
41 Las Vegas Sheriff Joe Lombardo cited in Ortiz, Jorge L. 'Las Vegas sheriff: Investigation into mass shooting shows no conspiracy or second'. *USA TODAY*, 3 August 2018. https://eu.usatoday.com/story/news/nation/2018/08/03/sheriff-las-vegas-investigation-mass-shooting/898643002/
42 Lazzara, Gina. 'Las Vegas authorities shut down social media rumors of more than one shooter'. 10 News, San Diego 4 October 2017. https://www.10news.com/news/national/authorities-debunk-social-media-rumors-of-more-than-one-shooter-1
43 See for example organizations like Snopes who trace the online spreading of fake news. https://www.snopes.com/fact-check/las-vegas-shooting-rumors-hoaxes-and-conspiracy-theories/
44 Silverman, Craig. 'Fake Antifa Twitter accounts are trolling people and spreading misinformation'. BuzzFeed, 30 May 2017. https://www.buzzfeednews.com/article/craigsilverman/fake-antifa-twitter-accounts
45 Text from the official Melbourne Antifa Facebook page. https://www.facebook.com/melantifainfo/posts/1723859081252211
46 Bell, Colin. 'The people who think mass shootings are staged'. BBC News Website. 2 February 2018. https://www.bbc.com/news/blogs-trending-42187105
47 Johnson, Stephen. 'One of our comrades has made those Trump supporting dogs pay: Left-wing "Melbourne Antifa" extremists condemned for praising Las Vegas shooter after he shot dead 59 people'. *Daily Mail*, 4 October 2017. https://www.dailymail.co.uk/news/article-4942668/Melbourne-Antifa-extremists-praises-Las-Vegas-shooter.html
48 boyd, Danah and Golebiewski, Michael. 'Data voids: Where missing data can easily be exploited'. *Microsoft Research and Data and Society*, May 2018. https://datasociety.net/wp-content/uploads/2018/05/Data_Society_Data_Voids_Final_3.pdf
49 Ibid. 2.
50 Ibid.
51 Ibid. 4.
52 Ibid. 3–4.
53 Ibid. 4.
54 Ibid. 5.
55 Ibid. 5.
56 Nate Dame, a search specialist, cited in 'Inside Google's struggle to filter lies from breaking news'. *The Daily Hunt*. Friday 17 November. https://m.dailyhunt.in/news/india/english/financial+chronicle-epaper-

finance/inside+google+s+struggle+to+filter+lies+from+breaking+news-newsid-76490805
57 The character Morpheus in Silver, Joel. 2018. *The Matrix*. Warner Bros Entertainment Inc.
58 Cadwalladr, Carole. 'Daniel Dennett: "I begrudge every hour I have to spend worrying about politics"', *Guardian*, 13 February 2017. https://www.theguardian.com/science/2017/feb/12/daniel-dennett-politics-bacteria-bach-back-dawkins-trump-interview
59 Ibid.
60 William E. Connolly. 'Fake News and "Postmodernism": The Fake Equation'. Discussion on Connolly's *Contemporary Condition* blog, May 2018. http://contemporarycondition.blogspot.com/2018/05/fake-news-and-postmodernism-fake.html
61 Gove made this statement on Channel 4 television after the political editor for Channel 4 News, Faisal Islam, pointed out that his support for a campaign that claimed that Britain sends £350 million to the EU every week, which could be better spent on the National Health Service, was wholly inaccurate. Islam accused Gove of importing the post-truth politics of Donald Trump.
62 Hanlon, Aaron. 'Postmodernism didn't cause Trump. It explains him', *Washington Post*, 31 August 2018. https://www.washingtonpost.com/outlook/postmodernism-didnt-cause-trump-it-explains-him/2018/08/30/0939f7c4-9b12-11e8-843b-36e177f3081c_story.html?noredirect=on&utm_term=.1d7fd9e2b04f
63 Ibid.
64 Ibid.
65 Dennett and Roy. 'Our transparent future'.
66 Connolly. 'Fake news and "postmodernism"'.
67 Ibid.
68 Connolly. *Aspirational Fascism*, 21.
69 Connolly. 'Fake news and "postmodernism"'.
70 Ibid.
71 Ibid.
72 Ibid.
73 Ibid.
74 Massumi, Brian. 'The autonomy of affect'. *Cultural Critique*, 31, *The Politics of Systems and Environments, Part II*. Autumn, 1995, 91.
75 Connolly. 'Fake news and "postmodernism"'.
76 Ibid.
77 Connolly, William E. 2017. *Aspirational Fascism*, 21.
78 Whitehead. *Process and Reality*, 184–5.
79 Debaise, Didier. 2017. *Nature as Event: The Lure of the Possible*. Durham: Duke University Press, 81.
80 Whitehead. *Process and Reality*, 184.

81 Debaise. *Nature as Event*, 78.
82 Ibid. 80–3.
83 Ibid. 81–2.
84 Whitehead. *Process and Reality*, 184–5.
85 Whitehead. *Modes of Thought*, 52–3. Italics added.
86 Ibid.
87 Stengers, Isabelle. 2014. *Thinking with Whitehead: A Free and Wild Creation of Concepts*. Cambridge, MA; London: Harvard University Press.
88 Following Whitehead. *Modes of Thought*, 60–1.

2 On the Viral Spectra of Somnambulism

1   Wiene, Robert. [1920] 2002. *Cabinet des Dr. Caligari*. New York, NY: Kino International.
2   Ibid.
3   Kracauer, S. 1947. *From Caligari to Hitler: A Psychological History of the German Film*. Princeton, NJ, US: Princeton University Press.
4   Ibid. 65.
5   Whitehead, Alfred North. 1985. *Process and Reality: An Essay in Cosmology*. New York: Free Press, 161.
6   Anderson, Victoria. 'We must not sleepwalk into trusting fake news'. *The Big Issue*, 31 March 2017. https://www.bigissue.com/opinion/victoria-anderson-must-not-sleepwalk-trusting-fake-news/
7   Soros, George. 'Europe is sleepwalking into oblivion' *Financial News*, 12 February 2019. https://www.fnlondon.com/articles/george-soros-europe-is-sleepwalking-into-oblivion-20190212
8   See 'Artificial intelligence: Professor Toby Walsh on 10 ways society will change by 2050'. *ABC News*, 7 August 2017. https://www.abc.net.au/news/2017-08-07/artificial-intelligence-the-top-10-predictions-toby-walsh/8775034
9   Anderson, Victoria. 'We must not sleepwalk into trusting fake news'.
10 World Economic Forum. *Global Risks Report 2019: 14th Edition*. http://www-115weforum.org/docs/WEF_Global_Risks_Report_1,901pdf
11 Sampson, Tony D. 2012. *Virality: Contagion Theory in the Age of Networks*. Minneapolis: University of Minnesota Press, 36.
12 See further discussion on Tarde in Sampson. *Virality* and Sampson, Tony D. 2016. *The Assemblage Brain Sense Making in Neuroculture*. Minneapolis; London: University of Minnesota Press.
13 Le Bon, Gustave. [1885] 1976. *Psychologie des Foules*. Paris: Retz.
14 Andersen, Kurt. 2018. *Fantasyland: How America Went Haywire: a 500-year History*. London: Ebury Press, 2018
15 Durkheim, Émile. [1885] 1982. *The Rules of the Sociological Method*. New York: Free Press. See chapter V.

16 McLuhan, Marshall. 1962. *The Gutenberg Galaxy: The Making of Typographic Man*. Toronto: University of Toronto Press, 32.
17 Braga, Adriana. 2016. 'Mind as Medium: Jung, McLuhan and the Archetype'. *Philosophies*. 1 (3): 220–7. https://www.mdpi.com/2,2919,405/-117/-115/102/htm
18 McLuhan, Marshall. 1969. *Counter Blast*. Toronto: McClelland and Stewart, 31.
19 Kroker, Arthur. 1995. 'Digital humanism: The processed world of Marshall McLuhan'. *CTheory*. http://ctheory.net/ctheory_wp/digital-humanism-the-processed-world-of-marshall-mcluhan/
20 Lévy, Pierre. 1998. *Becoming Virtual: Reality in the Digital Age*. New York: Plenum, 85–7.
21 For example, Parag Khanna. 'When cities rule the world'. Parag Khanna's website. https://www.paragkhanna.com/home/when-cities-rule-the-world
22 I use 'esque' here because I think it highly debatable that McLuhan saw much light in the collective consciousness.
23 Hern, Alex. 'Cambridge Analytica Files: Cambridge Analytica: how did it turn clicks into votes?', *Guardian*, 6 May 2018. https://www.theguardian.com/news/2018/may/06/cambridge-analytica-how-turn-clicks-into-votes-christopher-wylie
24 Ibid.
25 Youyou W., M. Kosinski and D. Stillwell. 2015. 'Computer-based personality judgements are more accurate than those made by humans'. *Proceedings of the National Academy of Sciences of the United States of America*. 112 (4): 1036–40.
26 Matz S. C., M. Kosinski, G. Nave and D. J. Stillwell. 2017. 'Psychological targeting as an effective approach to digital mass persuasion'. *Proceedings of the National Academy of Sciences of the United States of America*. 114 (48): 12714–19. One has to add here that such a measure is ludicrously based on a measurement of assumption that a spouse knows more than a sibling etc.
27 In a DCMS letter to Facebook, following Schroepfer's appearance, the Chair of the Fake News Committee, Damien Collins MP, listed some forty unanswered questions. These included questions about the exact percentage of users Facebook tracked and how much data Facebook had on so-called dark ads, which appeared during the EU referendum in the UK in 2015. Schroepfer also failed to say when Mark Zuckerberg knew about Cambridge Analytica and claimed not to know how many other developers were using or selling data on to third parties. All transcripts and videos of the DCMS Misinformation and Fake News committee are archived here: https://www.parliament.uk/business/committees/committees-a-z/commons-select/digital-culture-media-and-sport-committee/inquiries/parliament-2017/fake-news-17-19/

28 Ibid. See https://www.parliament.uk/documents/commons-committees/culture-media-and-sport/180501-Chair-to-Rebecca-Stimson-Facebook-re-oral-evidence-follow-up.pdf.
29 Halpern, Sue, 'Cambridge Analytica and the perils of psychographics'. *The New Yorker*, 30 March 2018. https://www.newyorker.com/news/news-desk/cambridge-analytica-and-the-perils-of-psychographics
30 See all transcripts and videos of the DCMS Misinformation and Fake News Committee. Archived here: https://www.parliament.uk/business/committees/committees-a-z/commons-select/digital-culture-media-and-sport-committee/inquiries/parliament-2017/fake-news-17-19/
31 Ibid.
32 Ibid.
33 See discussion in the introduction to Sampson, Tony D., Stephen Maddison and Darren Ellis. 2018. *Affect and Social Media: Emotion, Mediation, Anxiety and Contagion*. London: Rowman and Littlefield International.
34 Cadwalladr, Carole. 'Cambridge Analytica's ruthless bid to sway the vote in Nigeria'. *Guardian*, 21 March 2018. https://www.theguardian.com/uk-news/2018/mar/21/cambridge-analyticas-ruthless-bid-to-sway-the-vote-in-nigeria
35 Bracho-Polanco, Ed, 'How Jair Bolsonaro used "fake news" to win power'. *The Conversation*. 8 January 2019. https://theconversation.com/how-jair-bolsonaro-used-fake-news-to-win-power-109343
36 Escobar, Pepe. 'Welcome to the jungle: Jair Bolsonaro brings perfect storm of fascism and neoliberalism to Brazil'. *MintPress News*, 30 October 2018. https://www.mintpressnews.com/jair-bolsonaro-brings-perfect-storm-of-facism-and-neoliberalism-to-brazil/251224/.
37 See extended discussion on Tarde in Sampson. *Virality* and Sampson, *The Assemblage Brain*.
38 Tonkonoff, Sergio. 2017. *From Tarde to Deleuze and Foucault: The Infinitesimal Revolution*. London: Palgrave Macmillan.
39 See Matei Candea (ed.) 2010. *The Social after Tarde: Debates and Assessments*. London: Routledge.
40 Tonkonoff. *From Tarde to Deleuze and Foucault*, 25.
41 Tarde, Gabriel. 1895. *Monadologie et Sociologie*. Paris: Les Empêcheurs de Penser en Rond.
42 Tonkonoff. *From Tarde to Deleuze and Foucault*, 10–12.
43 Ibid. 93. Deleuze cited in.
44 Ibid. 27.
45 Sampson. *Virality*, 37.
46 See for example explicit references to Tarde in Lisa Blackman or Tiziana Terranova's work. One might assume, on reading Tonkonoff, that Tarde has a distinct lack of sisters.
47 Tonkonoff. *From Tarde to Deleuze and Foucault*, 47.

48. Ibid. 105–10.
49. Sampson. *Virality*, 185. Crary cited in.
50. As previously discussed with Parikka, Jussi. '"Tarde as Media Theorist": an interview with Tony D. Sampson, by Jussi Parikka'. *Theory, Culture and Society* Website. 25 January 2013. https://www.theoryculturesociety.org/tarde-as-media-theorist-an-interview-with-tony-d-sampson-by-jussi-parikka/
51. Sampson. *Virality*, 167. Tarde cited in.
52. Tonkonoff. *From Tarde to Deleuze and Foucault*, 49.
53. Robert De Niro speaking on the Graham Norton Show on Friday 11 October 2019 on BBC 1.
54. All references to Andersen's book are taken from this abridged version in 'How America lost its mind: The nation's current post-truth moment is the ultimate expression of mind-sets that have made America exceptional throughout its history'. *The Atlantic*, 28 December 2017. https://www.theatlantic.com/magazine/archive/2017/09/how-america-lost-its-mind/534231/
55. Ibid.
56. Ibid.
57. Ibid.
58. Ibid. Andersen blames postmodern intellectuals, post-positivists, poststructuralists, social constructivists, post-empiricists, epistemic relativists, cognitive relativists, descriptive relativists.
59. Ibid.
60. Ibid.
61. Lévy. *Becoming Virtual*.
62. Andersen. 'How America Lost Its Mind'.
63. Ibid.
64. See further analysis of Tarde's monadic sociology in Sampson. *The Assemblage Brain*, 185.
65. Gabriel Tarde. *Monadology and Sociology*. Melbourne: Re.Press, 2012, 8–9.
66. Ibid. 36.
67. See further discussion on the steering of Tardean accidents in Sampson. *Virality*, 99.
68. Vaidhyanathan, Siva. 2019. *Antisocial Media: How Facebook Disconnects Us and Undermines Democracy*. Oxford: Oxford University Press.
69. Ibid. 174. It is also necessary to add that in 2019 Twitter banned advertising from its network.
70. Ibid.
71. Ibid.
72. Ibid.
73. Ibid.
74. Ibid.

75 Andersen. *Fantasyland: How America Went Haywire*, 426–7. Italics added.
76 Connolly, William E. 2017. *Aspirational Fascism: The Struggle for Multifaceted Democracy under Trumpism*. Minneapolis: University of Minnesota Press, 15.
77 Andersen. 'How America lost its mind'.
78 Dominik, Andrew. 2013. *Killing Them Softly*. Elite Film.
79 Ibid.
80 See Lee Edelman in Berlant, Lauren and Edelman, Lee. 2013. *Sex, or the Unbearable*. Durham: Duke University Press, 17.
81 Dominik. *Killing Them Softly*.
82 Ibid.
83 See The K-12 school shooting database. https://www.chds.us/ssdb/incidents-by-year/
84 NRA Video on NRATV YouTube. https://www.youtube.com/watch?v=43wKT9NzPdA
85 Connolly. *Aspirational Fascism*, 14–15.
86 Ibid. 8.
87 Ibid. 26.
88 Ibid. 6.
89 Ibid. 15.
90 Massumi, Brian. 2015. *The Politics of Affect*. Cambridge: Polity, 210–11.
91 Connolly. *Aspirational Fascism*, 26–7.
92 Kelly, Richard. 2002. *Donnie Darko*. [United States]: 20th Century Fox Home Entertainment. Version of script creatively referenced. https://www.dailyscript.com/scripts/donniedarko.pdf
93 Williams, James. 'Whitehead's curse'. Gaskill, Nicholas and Nocek, A. J. (eds.) 2014. *The Lure of Whitehead*. Minneapolis: University of Minnesota Press, 249–66.
94 Ibid.
95 Ibid.
96 Version of Kelly's Donnie Darko script. https://www.dailyscript.com/scripts/donniedarko.pdf
97 Tonkonoff. *From Tarde to Deleuze and Foucault*, 53.
98 Le Bon, Gustave. *The Crowd* and Freud, Sigmund, 1951. *Group Psychology and the Analysis of the Ego*. New York: Liveright.
99 Ginsberg made a number of references to 'fascist sleepwalkers. See for example, Allen Ginsberg interviewed by Allan Gregg in 1997 (ASV #28) published on the Allen Ginsberg Project website, 11 January 2012. https://allenginsberg.org/2012/01/allen-ginsberg-interviewed-by-allan-gregg-1997-asv-28/
100 Clough, Patricia Ticineto. 2000. *Autoaffection: Unconscious Thought in the Age of Teletechnology*. Minneapolis: University of Minnesota Press; Thrift, Nigel. 2004. 'Remembering the technological unconscious by

foregrounding knowledges of position'. *Environment and Planning D: Society and Space.* 22 (1): 175–90; Hayles, Katherine. N. 2006. 'Traumas in Code'. *Critical Inquiry.* 33 (1): 136–57; Grusin, Richard. 2010. *Premediation: Affect and Mediality after 9/11.* New York; London: Palgrave Macmillan.
101 Hayles, Katherine. 2017. *Unthought: The Power of the Cognitive Nonconscious.* Chicago; London: University of Chicago Press, 119.
102 Ibid. 65–6.
103 Whitehead. *Process and Reality,* 145.
104 Thrift, Nigel. 2007. *Non-Representational Theory: Space, Politics, Affect.* New York; London: Routledge, 7.
105 See Clough. *Autoaffection* and *The User Unconscious.*
106 Massumi. *The Politics of Affect,* 211.
107 Ibid. 210.
108 Ibid. 210.
109 Ruyer, Raymond. 2016. *Neofinalism.* Minneapolis: University of Minnesota Press.
110 Stengers, Isabelle. 2014. *Thinking with Whitehead: A Free and Wild Creation of Concepts.* Cambridge, MA; London, England: Harvard University Press.
111 Whitehead. *Process and Reality,* 176.
112 Grosz, E. A. 2018. *The Incorporeal: Ontology, Ethics, and the Limits of Materialism.* New York: Columbia University Press, 216.
113 Whitehead. *Process and Reality,* 161.
114 Following Caillois, Roger. 'Mimetism and psychasthenia'. Claudine Frank, and Camille Naish (eds.), 2003. *The Edge of Surrealism: A Roger Caillois Reader.* Durham [NC]: Duke University Press, 91.
115 Fuller, Matthew. 2018. *How to Sleep: The Art, Biology and Culture of Unconsciousness.* London; New York: Bloomsbury Academic, 1.
116 Ibid.
117 Ibid. 2.
118 But of course, not all wakefulness is reflective.
119 Clough, *The User Unconscious,* 88.
120 Amin, Ash, and N. J. Thrift. *Cities and Ethnicities.* 2002. London: Sage Publications.
121 Clayton, Martin; Sager, Rebecca and Will, Udo (2005). 'In time with the music: The concept of entrainment and its significance for ethnomusicology'. *European Meetings in Ethnomusicology,* 70.
122 Debaise, Didier. 2017. *Nature as Event: The Lure of the Possible.* Durham: Duke University Press, 53.
123 Ibid. 55.
124 Deleuze, Gilles. 2006. *The Fold.* London: Continuum, 2006, 78.
125 Ibid.
126 Ibid.
127 Debaise. *Nature as Event,* 53.

128 Ibid. 54.
129 Connolly. *Aspirational Fascism*.
130 Ibid. 16.
131 Ibid. 15.
132 Ibid. 17.
133 Kroker, Arthur. 2014. *Exits to the Posthuman Future*. Cambridge: Polity, 11–12.
134 It is important to note that while drafting this chapter, Facebook introduced a policy change in March 2019 supposedly banning support for far-right extremism following the Christchurch terror attack. See Beckett, Lois. 'Facebook to ban white nationalism and separatism content: Company previously allowed such material even though it has long banned white supremacists', *Guardian*, Wednesday 27 March 2019. https://www.theguardian.com/technology/2019/mar/27/facebook-white-nationalism-hate-speech-ban

Coda Christchurch; El Paso

1 New Zealand Police (@nzpolice), 15 March 2019.
2 Abbruzzese, Jason and Zadrozny, Brandy. 'Streamed to Facebook, spread on YouTube: New Zealand shooting video circulates online despite takedowns: The video continues to spread across the internet, illustrating how difficult it is to keep graphically violent images away from the public'. NBC News, 15 March 2019. https://www.nbcnews.com/tech/tech-news/streamed-facebook-spread-youtube-new-zealand-shooting-video-circulates-online-n983726
3 Silverman, Craig and Lytvynenko, Jane. 'The Eerie Absence of Viral Fakes After The New Zealand Mosque Attacks: The shooter's media plan was so comprehensive, and his content spread so quickly, that there was little room for fakes to fill the void'. Buzzfeed News, 15 March 2019.
4 Varela, Julio Ricardo, 'Trump's anti-immigrant 'invasion' rhetoric was echoed by the El Paso shooter for a reason: The president's words – and those of his supporters – have contributed to a societal fear of immigrants, especially Hispanic immigrants'. 5 August 2019. https://www.nbcnews.com/think/opinion/trump-s-anti-immigrant-invasion-rhetoric-was-echoed-el-paso-ncna1039286

3 The Virality of Experience Capitalism

1 The marketing manager from Snapchat said they were interested in learning from the 'findings and recommendations' of my 'publicly available work' on virality. After several emailed exchanges it soon

became clear that Snapchat were less interested in some of the more sociologically nuanced aspects of the virality thesis. Indeed, the exchange ended politely with Snapchat telling me how fascinating they found my work to be.
2   Laing, R. D. [1967] 1983. *The Politics of Experience*. New York: Pantheon Books.
3   I have to express thanks to Charles Talcott for this term, which he used to describe part of my invited talk on collective mimesis at the American University of Paris in May 2019.
4   Inexpensive since a successful viral ad is supposed to spread by itself.
5   Goriunova, Olga. 2013. 'New Media Idiocy'. *Convergence: The International Journal of Research into New Media Technologies*. 19 (2): 223–35.
6   Escobar, Pepe. 'Welcome to the Jungle: Jair Bolsonaro Brings Perfect Storm of Fascism and Neoliberalism to Brazil'. *MintPress News*. 30 October 2018. https://www.mintpressnews.com/about-mint-press-news/
7   Palme Dutt, R. 'The question of fascism and capitalist decay'. *The Communist International*, 12 (14): 20 July 1935. Marxists Internet Archive: https://www.marxists.org/archive/dutt/articles/1,679/question_of_fascism.htm
8   See discussion in Esposito, Roberto. 2008. *Bíos: Biopolitics and Philosophy*. Minneapolis, MN: University of Minnesota Press, See translator's introduction.
9   For example, a comparison between the biopolitics of the Nazis and neoliberalism is made in Esposito, *Bíos*. See translator's introduction, xxxvi.
10 Toffler, A. 1996. *Future Shock*. New York: Bantam Books.
11 Ibid. 208–9.
12 Holbrook, Morris B. and Elizabeth C. Hirschman. 1982. 'The experiential aspects of consumption: Consumer fantasies, feelings, and fun'. *Journal of Consumer Research*. 9 (2): 132–40.
13 Pine, Joseph B. and Gilmore, James H. [1999] 2011. *The Experience Economy*. Boston: Harvard Business Press.
14 Ibid. 56.
15 Goffman, Erving. 2007. *The Presentation of Self in Everyday Life*. London: Penguin Books.
16 For example, Norman, Donald A. (2004) 2007. *Emotional Design: Why We Love (or Hate) Everyday Things*. New York: Basic Books.
17 Langlois, G. and Elmer, G. 2013. 'The research politics of social media platforms'. *Culture Machine* vol. 14. Open Humanities Press. http://www.culturemachine.net/index.php/cm/article/viewArticle/505 (2013). See also Langlois, Ganaele and Greg Elmer. 2019. 'Impersonal subjectivation from platforms to infrastructures'. *Media, Culture and Society*. 41 (2): 236–51. Here they further argue that 'as social media

and digital media giant corporations move away from an enclosed platform model towards a distributed, impersonal infrastructure, the mining of individual data and the shaping of individual attitudes is increasingly geared towards establishing relationships between user data and a plethora of nonhuman, environmental data. Such an infrastructure invokes impersonal subjects, and thus requires a new politics of relationality'.

18 Greenfield, Adam. 2006. *Everyware: The Dawning Age of Ubiquitous Computing*. Berkeley: New Riders.
19 See also Langlois, Ganaele and Elmer, Greg. 2019. 'Impersonal subjectivation from platforms to infrastructures'.
20 Smythe, Dallas W. 1975. Critique of 'The Consciousness Industry'. *Journal of Communication*. 27 (1): 197–232.
21 Ciaccia, Chris. 'How much does facebook make off you? The amount may surprise you'. *Fox News*, 9 April 2018. https://www.foxnews.com/tech/how-much-does-facebook-make-off-you-the-amount-may-surprise-you
22 Ibid.
23 Zuboff, Shoshana. 2015. 'Big other: Surveillance capitalism and the prospects of an information civilization'. *Journal of Information Technology*. 30 (1): 75–89.
24 Andreou, Athanasios et al. 'Measuring the Facebook advertising ecosystem'. *Proceedings of the Network and Distributed System Security Symposium*, San Diego, United States. 2019. 1. https://hal.archives-ouvertes.fr/hal-01959145/file/Andreou-etal_FacebookAds_NDSS2019.pdf
25 Ibid.
26 Ibid. 8.
27 Marx–Engels Correspondence 1893. 'Engels to Franz Mehring'. Archived here: https://www.marxists.org/archive/marx/works/1893/letters/93_07_14.htm. Italics added.
28 Williamson, Judith. 1978. *Decoding Advertisements: Ideology and Meaning in Advertising*. London: Marion Boyars, 1978.
29 Ibid. 63–4.
30 Caillois, Roger. 'Mimetism and psychasthenia'. Frank, Claudine and Naish, Camille (eds.), 2003. *The Edge of Surrealism: A Roger Caillois Reader*. Durham [NC]: Duke University Press, 28.
31 Fuchs, Christian. 2017. *Social Media: A Critical Introduction*. London: Sage.
32 Ibid. 284, 301–6.
33 Ibid. 77.
34 Ibid. 14.
35 Drenten, Jenna. 2012. 'Snapshots of The self: Exploring the role of online mobile photo sharing in identity development among adolescent girls'. *Online Consumer Behavior: Theory and Research in Social Media, Advertising, and E-Tail*. Angeline G. Close (ed.), New York: Routledge, 15.

36 Ibid. 6.
37 Williamson, *The Created Self*, 48.
38 Massumi, Brian. 2016. *Politics of Affect*. Cambridge: Polity.
39 Ibid. 9–10.
40 Ibid. 85.
41 Ibid. 85.
42 Clough, Patricia Ticineto. 2018. *The User Unconscious: On Affect, Media, and Measure*. University of Minnesota Press, 86. Top of Form
43 Mellamphy, Nandita Biswas, Dyer-Witheford, Nick. Hearn, Alison, and Matviyenko, Svitlana. 2015. 'Apps and affect'. Editorial introduction to issue 25 of *The Fibre Culture Journal: Digital Media, Networks, Transdisciplinary Critique*. http://fibreculturejournal.org/wp-content/pdfs/FC25_FullIssue.pdf
44 See for example further discussion in Sampson. *The Assemblage Brain*, 99–100, and the introduction to Sampson et al. 2018. *Affect and Social Media: Emotion, Mediation, Anxiety and Contagion*.
45 Karppi, Tero. 2018. *Disconnect: Facebook's Affective Bonds*. Minneapolis: University of Minnesota Press, 114–17.
46 Krauss, Rosalind E. 2008. *The Optical Unconscious*. Cambridge, MA: MIT Press. 155.
47 Ibid.
48 Grosz, Elizabeth A. 2001. *Architecture from Outside: Essays on Virtual and Real Space*. Cambridge, MA: MIT Press, 36.
49 Krauss. *The Optical Unconscious*, 155.
50 Ibid.
51 Ibid.
52 Caillois, Roger. 'Mimetism and psychasthenia', 28.
53 Grosz. *Architecture from Outside*, 37–8.
54 I am aware here that Laing's general approach to experience in *The Divided Self* and *The Self and Others*, for example, is quite unlike the Whiteheadian notion of experience I am forwarding here. For example, in *The Self and Others* he says that the term experience he employs does not exist without an experiencer, and vice versa, an experiencer does not exist without experience. See R. D. Laing. 1961. *The Self and Others*. London: Penguin, 29.
55 Laing, *Politics of Experience*, 20. Italics added.
56 Ibid. 25.
57 Ibid. 25–6.
58 Ibid. 18.
59 Ibid. 12.
60 Ibid. Italics added.
61 Ibid. 80. Italics added.
62 Ibid. 80.

63 Barad, Karen. 2007. *Meeting the Universe Halfway: Quantum Physics and the Entanglement of Matter and Meaning.* Durham: Duke University Press.
64 This how the founder of the Facebook data science team, Cameron Marlow, describes its purpose on his LinkedIn profile: https://www.linkedin.com/in/cameronfactor
65 Simonite, Tom. 'What Facebook Knows'. *MIT Technology Review.* 13 June 2012. https://www.technologyreview.com/s/428150/what-facebook-knows/
66 Ibid.
67 Ibid.
68 Ibid.
69 Ibid.
70 Ibid.
71 Ibid.
72 Ibid.
73 'The Digital, Culture, Media and Sport Committee questions Dr Aleksandr Kogan from the Department of Psychology at the University of Cambridge, as part of its inquiry into fake news'. 24 April 2018. https://www.parliament.uk/business/committees/committees-a-z/commons-select/digital-culture-media-and-sport-committee/news/fake-news-aleksandr-kogan-evidence-17-19/
74 Ibid. It is interesting to further note that Joseph Chancellor, a co-founder of GSR with Kogan, was employed by Facebook as a quantitative researcher on the User Experience Research team, just two months after leaving GSR. See DCMS Disinformation and 'fake news': Final Report, 39. https://www.parliament.uk/business/committees/committees-a-z/commons-select/digital-culture-media-and-sport-committee/news/fake-news-report-published-17-19/ It is important to say that any direct involvement in the scandal by Cambridge University has been dispelled. Certainly, at the hearing Kogan confirmed the Facebook data collection work was carried solely by his company, Global Science Research (GSR), who sold it on to Cambridge Analytica's parent company SCL for use in the Trump campaign. 'We [GSR] basically did a market research project' Kogan explained to the hearing. The first stage of GSR project cost SCL $800,000 and involved a recruiting company hired by GSR to find and pay 200,000 Facebook users to do a personality test. Significantly, by simply logging on to the test these 200,000 users not only authorized access to their personal data, but opened up access to substantially larger amounts of data gathered from their network of friends. The second stage of the project involved SCL paying a further £230,000 for Kogan to 'use the data to drive predictions about people's personalities'. Again, this data analysis was carried out by GSR, not Cambridge University. Nonetheless, according to Kogan's evidence, there was a wrangle over

a budget of around £2million initially floated by SCL to pay for the two stages of the research. Kogan claims he was due to work in collaboration with Cambridge University's Psychometrics Centre, who would provide the prediction models. However, SCL were not, according to Kogan, prepared to pay the $500,000 the Centre asked for access to these models. It was this outcome that resulted in Kogan, he claims, setting up GSR to carry out the entire project.

75 See account in Sampson, Tony D., Maddison, Stephen and Ellis, Darren. 2018. *Affect and Social Media: Emotion, Mediation, Anxiety and Contagion*. London: Rowman and Littlefield International.

76 Ibid. The researchers who carried out the experiment found that when they reduced the positive expressions displayed by other users they produced less positive and more negative posts. Likewise, when negative expressions were reduced, the opposite pattern occurred. Although the recorded levels of contagion were rather paltry, the researchers concluded that the 'emotions expressed by others on Facebook influence our own emotions, constituting experimental evidence for massive-scale contagion via social networks'. See also Kramer A. D., Guillory J. E. and Hancock, J. T. 2014. 'Experimental evidence of massive-scale emotional contagion through social networks'. *Proceedings of the National Academy of Sciences of the United States of America*. 111 (24): 8788–90.

77 Ibid.

78 Matz S. C. et al. 2017. 'Psychological targeting as an effective approach to digital mass persuasion'. *Proceedings of the National Academy of Sciences of the United States of America*. 114 (48): 12714–19.

79 Keltner, Dacher, Aleksandr Kogan, Paul K. Piff, and Sarina R. Saturn. 2014. 'The Sociocultural Appraisals, Values, and Emotions (SAVE) Framework of Prosociality: Core Processes from Gene to Meme'. *Annual Review of Psychology*. 65 (1): 425–60.

80 Ibid.

81 It was reported here in March 2018 https://www.cambridge-news.co.uk/news/cambridge-news/kogan-facebook-cambridge-analytica-data-14426886.

82 Keltner et al. 'The sociocultural appraisals, values, and emotions (SAVE) framework of prosociality'.

83 Ibid.

84 Ibid.

85 Vaidhyanathan. *Antisocial Media*, 173–4.

86 Ibid. 173.

87 Ibid. 8.

88 Ibid. 173.

89 This link to intensity and viral reach is reflected in the anti-Euro content produced by RT and Sputnik, for example, which had 134 million

potential impressions, in comparison with a total social reach of just 33 million and 11 million potential impressions for all content shared from Vote Leave website and Leave.EU website. See DCMS Disinformation and 'fake news': Final Report.
90 Huang, Julie Y. et al. 2017. 'Catching (up with) magical contagion: A review of contagion effects in consumer contexts'. *Journal of the Association for Consumer Research.* 2 (4): 430–43, 430.
91 Ibid. 434.
92 Ibid. 439.
93 Karppi, Tero. *Disconnect,* 13.
94 Burke, M., C. Marlow, and T. Lento. 2009. 'Feed me: Motivating newcomer contribution in social network sites'. *CHI -CONFERENCE-.* 2: 945–54.
95 Ibid.
96 Karppi. *Disconnect,* 34.
97 Kosinski, M., D. Stillwell, and T. Graepel. 2013. 'Private traits and attributes are predictable from digital records of human behavior'. *Proceedings of the National Academy of Sciences.* 110 (15): 5802–5.
98 Haggerty, Kevin D. and Richard V. Ericson. 2000. 'The surveillant assemblage'. *British Journal of Sociology.* 51 (4): 605–22.
99 Ibid.
100 Karppi. *Disconnect,* 35.
101 Ibid. Tarde as discussed in Karppi.
102 Stengers, Isabelle. 2014. *Thinking with Whitehead: A Free and Wild Creation of Concepts.* Cambridge, MA; London, England: Harvard University Press, 70–1.

Segue A Dark [Viral] Refrain

1 Published in April 2019, The Online Harms White Paper further supports a new regulatory regime by presenting staggering research showing the extent to which immunity on social media has dramatically failed. 'Close to half of all [UK] adults', the White Paper claims 'have seen hateful content in the past year'. https://www.gov.uk/government/consultations/online-harms-white-paper
2 Block, Hans, and Moritz Riesewieck. 2018. *The Cleaners.* Lighthouse Home Entertainment.
3 Haggart, Blayne and Tusikov, Natasha. 'What the UK's Online Harms white paper teaches us about internet regulation'. *The Conversation,* 18 April 2019. https://theconversation.com/what-the-u-k-s-online-harms-white-paper-teaches-us-about-internet-regulation-115337

4 Immunity, Community and Contagion

1. Esposito, Roberto. 2008. *Bíos: Biopolitics and Philosophy*. Minneapolis, MN: University of Minnesota Press, 166
2. Thanks to the first reviewer of the first draft of this text who usefully teased out some of these questions from what was a fairly dense line of argumentation.
3. See Facebook's PR video: 'Facing facts: An inside look at Facebook's fight against misinformation. https://spectacle.is/video/facing-facts-an-inside-look-at-facebooks-fight-against-misinformation
4. Testimony of Mark Zuckerberg, Chairman and Chief Executive Officer, Facebook. Hearing before the United States Senate Committee on the Judiciary and The United States Senate Committee on Commerce, Science and Transportation, 10 April 2018. https://www.judiciary.senate.gov/imo/media/doc/04-10-18%20Zuckerberg%20Testimony.pdf
5. Symantec Technical Brief: The Digital Immune System: Enterprise-Grade Anti-Virus Automation in the 21st Century. https://www.symantec.com/content/dam/symantec/docs/security-center/white-papers/digital-immune-system-01-en.pdf
6. Ward, Mark 'Why some computer viruses refuse to die' on BBC News (online). https://www.bbc.co.uk/news/technology-44564709
7. Facebook immune system. Facebook research paper. https://research.fb.com/wp-content/uploads/2011/04/facebook-immune-system.pdf
8. Ibid.
9. Dewan, Prateek, and Ponnurangam Kumaraguru. 2017. 'Facebook Inspector (FbI): Towards automatic real-time detection of malicious content on Facebook'. *Social Network Analysis and Mining*. 7 (1).
10. Ibid.
11. Ibid.
12. Testimony of Mark Zuckerberg.
13. Ibid.
14. Ibid.
15. Ibid.
16. Ibid.
17. The widespread use of Facebook in Myanmar is in part due to the liberalization of telecom businesses introduced to the country by Aung San Suu Kyi. The falling cost of accessibility to mobile phones, for example, meant that many people who had never used social media were able to download the Facebook app, which unlike other platforms significantly supported Burmese text. By 2016 there were over 9.5million Facebook users in Myanmar. See for example Trautwein, Catherine. 'Facebook free basics lands in Myanmar'. *The Myanmar Times*, 6 June 2016. https://www.mmtimes.com/business/technology/20685-facebook-free-basics-lands-in-myanmar.html.

18 Stecklow, Steve. *Hatebook: Why Facebook is Losing the War on Hate Speech in Myanmar*, Reuters Report filed on 15 August 2018. https://www.reuters.com/investigates/special-report/myanmar-facebook-hate/
19 Subedar, Anisa. 'The country where Facebook posts whipped up hate'. BBC News (Online), 12 September 2018. https://www.bbc.co.uk/news/blogs-trending-45449938
20 Stecklow, Steve. *Hatebook*.
21 Ibid
22 Ibid.
23 Testimony of Mark Zuckerberg.
24 Ibid.
25 Wong, Julia Carrie. 'A year after Charlottesville, why can't big tech delete white supremacists?', *Guardian*, Wednesday 25 July 2018. https://www.theguardian.com/world/2018/jul/25/charlottesville-white-supremacists-big-tech-failure-remove
26 Google News Initiative: Building a stronger future for journalism. https://newsinitiative.withgoogle.com/
27 Miriam Estrin speaking to BBC Radio 5 Live's Anna Foster. See 'YouTube: Not removing far-right video "missed the mark"'. BBC News (online), 24 July 2018. https://www.bbc.com/news/av/44939032/youtube-not-removing-far-right-video-missed-the-mark
28 Koenigsberg, Richard. 'Genocide as immunology: The psychosomatic source of culture'. Online essay on the Library of Social Science Website, 2005. https://www.libraryofsocialscience.com/ideologies/resources/koenigsberg-genocide-as-immunology/
29 Ibid
30 Hitler cited in Esposito. *Bíos*, 117.
31 See, for example, Frédéric Neyrat's commentary on Roberto Esposito's *Communauté, Immunité, Biopolitique: Repenser Les Termes de la Politique* which begins by drawing special attention to the immunological conditions of Nazisim. These conditions are significantly not metaphorical. To be sure, the rhetorical power of immunological references cannot be ignored, but it is through the racism of the Nazis that we see how biopolitics goes way beyond its representational mode in politics. What Neyrat calls a 'absolute perversion' of politics is resolved not only to force a distinction between the 'purity of the Aryan race' and 'everything that might work against it'. But the Nazis distinction goes way beyond division to eventual biological elimination. See Neyrat, Frédéric. 2010. 'The birth of immunopolitics'. *Parrhesia*. 10: 31–8. https://www.parrhesiajournal.org/parrhesia10/parrhesia10_neyrat.pdf
32 Ibid. 33. Italics from the original.
33 Ibid.
34 DuVernay, Ava. 2019. *When They See Us*. Los Gatos: Netflix, Inc.

35 See for example Trump's Tweet posted on 22 October 2018. 'Sadly, it looks like Mexico's Police and Military are unable to stop the Caravan heading to the Southern Border of the United States. Criminals and unknown Middle Easterners are mixed in. I have alerted Border Patrol and Military that this is a National Emergency. Must change laws!' https://twitter.com/realdonaldtrump/status/1054351078328885248?lang=en
36 From Transcript of Obama's 2008 victory speech in Chicago. https://edition.cnn.com/2008/POLITICS/11/04/obama.transcript/
37 Ibid.
38 Megan McCain, speaking on the ABC Channel programme *The View* on Tuesday, 20 March 2018.
39 See Tobias, Manuela. 'Comparing Facebook data use by Obama, Cambridge Analytica'. Politifact website, Thursday, 22 March 2018. https://www.politifact.com/truth-o-meter/statements/2018/mar/22/meghan-mccain/comparing-facebook-data-use-obama-cambridge-analyt/
40 Gerodimos, Roman and Jákup Justinussen. 2015. 'Obama's 2012 Facebook campaign: Political communication in the age of the like button'. *Journal of Information Technology and Politics*. 12 (2): 113–32.
41 Sampson, Tony D. 2012. *Virality: Contagion Theory in the Age of Networks*. University of Minnesota Press. See also Sampson, Tony D. 2012. 'Tarde's phantom takes a deadly line of flight – from Obama Girl to the assassination of Bin Laden'. *Distinktion: Journal of Social Theory*. 13 (3): 354–66.
42 Christine Harold cited in Clough, Patricia Ticineto. 2018. *The User Unconscious: On Affect, Media, and Measure*. Minneapolis; London: University of Minnesota Press, 43.
43 See Clough's discussion on political branding, including references to Luciana Parisi and Steve Goodman in Clough. *The User Unconscious*, 43.
44 Permission for the photo was granted by the baby's uncle (a Trump supporter) who wanted to meet with the President to see if he 'feels maybe some kind of remorse for statements that he's made'. https://www.businessinsider.com/trump-gave-thumbs-up-photo-baby-orphaned-el-paso-shooting-2019-8?r=US&IR=T
45 Dominik, Andrew. 2013. *Killing Them Softly*. Elite Film.
46 Ibid.
47 Clough. *The User Unconscious*, 57.
48 Ibid.
49 Neyrat. 'The birth of immunopolitics', 34.
50 Karppi, Tero. 2018. *Disconnect: Facebook's affective bonds*. Minneapolis: University of Minnesota Press, 123.
51 Ibid. The main reason the internet disconnect only lasted for five days was because of the enormous cost it incurred to the Egyptian economy.
52 Shearlaw, Maeve. 'Egypt five years on: Was it ever a "social media revolution"? Tahrir Square's spirit of change was infectious, but activists

looking back say Facebook and Twitter were just tools, never the driving force', *Guardian*, Monday 25 January 2016. https://www.theguardian.com/world/2016/jan/25/egypt-5-years-on-was-it-ever-a-social-media-revolution. See also Wael Ghonmin's Ted Talk. https://www.ted.com/talks/wael_ghonim_let_s_design_social_media_that_drives_real_change#t-773832

53 Ibid.
54 Fuchs, Christian. 2017. *Social Media: A Critical Introduction*. London: Sage.
55 Neyrat. 'The birth of immunopolitics', 33.
56 Ibid.
57 Escobar, Pepe. 'Welcome to the jungle: A troubling new era has begun in Brazil with the election on Sunday of the far-right Jair Bolsonaro as president'. Global Research, 31 October 2018. https://www.globalresearch.ca/welcome-to-the-jungle/5658515
58 Ibid.
59 Ibid.
60 Ibid.
61 Mier, Brian. 'WhatsApp: Bolsonaro's hate machine'. *Brasil Wire*, 5 October 2018. http://www.brasilwire.com/whats-up-fascism-phone-app-delivers-probable-bolsonaro-victory/
62 The authors of the report published an article in *The New York Times*. See Tardáguila Cristina., Fabrício Benevenuto and Pablo Ortellado. 'Fake news is poisoning Brazilian politics. WhatsApp can stop it', *New York Times*, 17 October 2018. https://www.nytimes.com/2018/10/17/opinion/brazil-election-fake-news-whatsapp.html. See also summary of report in Portuguese: https://piaui.folha.uol.com.br/lupa/wp-content/uploads/2018/10/Relat%C3%B3rio-WhatsApp-1-turno-Lupa-F-USP-2F-UFMG.pdf
63 Frier, Sarah and Camillo, Giulia. 'WhatsApp bans more than 100,000 accounts in Brazil election'. *Bloomberg*, 19 October 2018 and updated on 20 October 2018. https://www.bloomberg.com/news/articles/2018-10-19/whatsapp-bans-more-than-100-000-accounts-in-brazil-election?fbclid=IwAR2ci2PWKab6e-l_kTq-cxnuXqGmz72LR3jv4UnNC0JjYugTaVUI8qSneao
64 See for example, Lupton, Deborah. 2016. *The Quantified Self: A Sociology of Self-Tracking*. Cambridge: Polity, 2016.
65 Lupton, Deborah. 'Self-tracking cultures: Towards a sociology of personal informatics'. Peer reviewed conference paper. OzCHI '14 : Proceedings of the 26th Australian Computer-Human Interaction Conference : Designing Futures, the Future of Design, 3–5 December 2014. https://core.ac.uk/download/pdf/30345240.pdf
66 Ibid.
67 Hamilton, John T. 2015. 'The luxury of self-destruction: Flirting with

mimesis with Roger Caillois'. Daniel Hoffman-Schwartz, Barbara Natalie Nagel and Lauren Shizuko Stone (eds.) 2015. *Flirtations: Rhetoric and Aesthetics this Side of Seduction*. New York: Fordham University Press, 106–15.
68   Ibid. Cited from online version. See Hamilton, John T. 2012. 'The luxury of self-destruction: Flirting with mimesis with Roger Caillois'. Presented at Flirtations: Rhetoric and Aesthetics This Side of Seduction, a Poetics and Theory/ Comparative Literature Workshop, Draper Program, New York University, 3 March 2012. https://dash.harvard.edu/handle/1/14065783
69   Grosz, Elizabeth A. 2001. *Architecture from Outside: Essays on Virtual and Real Space*. Cambridge, MA: MIT Press, 79.
70   See Dostoyevsky, Fyodor. 2008. *Notes from Underground; The Double, and Other Stories*. New York: Barnes and Noble Classics; Poe, Edgar Allan. 1903. 'William Wilson'. *Booklovers Magazine*. 2 (4): 355–68; Spark, Muriel. 2001. *Aiding and Abetting*. United Kingdom: ISIS Publishing; Saramago, José. 2005. *The Double*. London: Vintage.
71   Haggerty, K. D. and R. V. Ericson. 2000. 'The surveillant assemblage'. *British Journal of Sociology*. 51: 605–22.
72   Ibid. 606.
73   Foot, K. A., Boczkowski, P. J. and Gillespie, T. (2014). *Media Technologies: Essays on Communication, Materiality, and Society*. Cambridge, MA: MIT Press, 174.
74   Ibid.
75   Ibid.
76   Ibid.
77   Karppi. *Disconnect*.
78   See discussion in Massumi, Brian. *A User's Guide to Capitalism and Schizophrenia: Deviations on Deleuze and Guattari*. Cambridge, MA: MIT Press, 96–7.
79   Ibid. 88
80   Caillois, Roger. 'Mimetism and psychasthenia'. Claudine Frank, and Camille Naish (eds.), 2003. *The Edge of Surrealism: A Roger Caillois Reader*. Durham [NC]: Duke University Press, 99–100.
81   Esposito, Roberto. 2011. *Immunitas: The Protection and Negations of Life*. Cambridge: Polity, 16.
82   See Timothy C. Campbell's introduction to Esposito, Roberto. 2008. *Bíos: Biopolitics and Philosophy*. Minneapolis, Minnesota: University of Minnesota Press, xi–xxix.
83   Esposito. *Bíos*, 105
84   Ibid.
85   Ibid. 106
86   Ibid. 122. Hitler cited in.
87   Ibid. 117.

88 Ibid. 193–4.
89 Ibid. xli. Campbell's introduction to.
90 Hamilton. 'The luxury of self-destruction'. 6.
91 Johnson, Elizabeth R. 2016. 'Reconsidering mimesis: Freedom and acquiescence in the Anthropocene'. *South Atlantic Quarterly*. 115. (2), 267–89.
92 Ibid. cited from version archived on Durham Research Online, 13. http://dro.dur.ac.uk/23131/1/23131.pdf
93 Ibid. 13–14.
94 Taussig, Michael. 2017. *Mimesis and Alterity: A Particular History of the Senses*. London: Taylor and Francis, 2017.
95 Johnson. 'Reconsidering mimesis', 10.
96 Ibid. 10–13.
97 Ibid. 4.
98 Ibid.
99 Ibid.
100 Ibid. 10. Taussig cited in.
101 Neyrat. 'The birth of immunopolitics', 35.
102 Ibid.
103 Ibid.
104 Ibid.
105 Parikka, Jussi. 2010. *Insect Media: An Archaeology of Animals and Technology*. Minneapolis: University of Minnesota Press, 97.
106 Ibid. 100.
107 Nagy, Zoltan A. *A History of Modern Immunology: The Path Towards Understanding*. New York, NY: Elsevier, 2014, 241.
108 Ibid. 241.
109 Schwartz, Robert S. 'Review of the immune self: Theory or metaphor?' *New England Journal of Medicine*. 332, (1995): 1176–7. http://www.nejm.org/doi/full/10.1056/NEJM199504273321718
110 Parikka, Jussi, and Sampson, Tony D. *The Spam Book: On Viruses, Porn and Other Anomalies From the Dark Side of Digital Culture*. New Jersey: Hampton, 2009.
111 Ibid. 15.
112 Ibid.
113 Ellis, Darren and Tucker, Ian. *The Social Psychology of Emotion*. London: Sage, 2015, 178.
114 Greenfield, Adam. *Everyware: The Dawning Age of Ubiquitous Computing*. New York, NY: New Riders, 2006, 81.
115 Ibid. 84.
116 Ibid. 86.
117 Ibid. 86–7.
118 Ellis and Tucker. *The Social Psychology of Emotion*, 171–9.
119 Ibid. 172.

120 Ibid. 173.
121 Ibid. 174.
122 Ibid. 175.
123 Ibid. 175.
124 Ibid. 174
125 Naughton, John. 'Anti-social media: How Facebook disconnects us and undermines democracy' by Siva Vaidhyanathan – review, *Guardian*, Monday 25 June 2018. https://www.theguardian.com/books/2018/jun/25/anti-social-media-how-facebook-disconnects-us-undermines-democracy-siva-vaidhyanathan-review
126 Sampson, T. 2004. 'A virus in info-space'. *M/C: A Journal of Media and Culture*, 7. http://www.media-culture.org.au/0406/07_Sampson.php. See also discussion in Parikka, Jussi. 2007 (2016). *Digital Contagions*. Peter Lang, 214–15.
127 Version of Hamilton's article in edited book – 'Flirtations: Rhetoric and aesthetics this side of seduction'.
128 Hamilton. 'The luxury of self-destruction'. 1.
129 Tarde, Gabriel. 2001. *Penal Philosophy*. New Jersey: Transactional Publisher, 116–18.
130 Hamilton. 'The luxury of self-destruction'. 6.

5 Deeper Entanglements

1 Greenfield, Adam. 2006. *Everyware: The Dawning Age of Ubiquitous Computing*. Berkeley: New Riders.
2 Whitehead, Alfred North. 2010. *Modes of Thought*. New York: Free Press, 127–69.
3 Andrew Murphie's *Media Alive* keynote talk at the *Affects, Interfaces, Events* conference in Aarhus, 29–30 August 2018. See conference website. https://aie.au.dk/aie-2018/
4 Ibid.
5 Ibid.
6 Harrison, Steve et al. 'The three paradigms of HCI'. Paper presented at the Conference on Human Factors in Computing Systems, 2007. https://people.cs.vt.edu/~srh/Downloads/TheThreeParadigmsofHCI.pdf
7 Blackwell, A. 2015 'Interacting with an inferred world: The challenge of machine learning for humane computer interaction'. *Proceedings of The Fifth Decennial Aarhus Conference on Critical Alternatives*, 169–80.
8 Hansen, Mark. 2015. *Feed-Forward: On the Future of Twenty-First-Century Media*. Chicago: University of Chicago Press, 71.
9 See further discussion in Sampson, Tony D. 2017. *The Assemblage Brain: Sense Making in Neuroculture*. Minneapolis: University of Minnesota Press.
10 Harrison, Steve. et al. 'The three paradigms of HCI', 6.

11 Dourish, Paul. 2004. *Where the Action Is*. Cambridge, MA: MIT Press.
12 Ibid. 15–22.
13 Dourish, Paul. 1999. 'Embodied interaction: Exploring the foundations of a new approach to HCI', 2. Paper published online. https://s3.amazonaws.com/academia.edu.documents/42681423/embodied99.pdf?response-content-disposition=inline%3B%20filename%3DEmbodied_interaction_Exploring_the_found.pdf&X-Amz-Algorithm=AWS4-HMAC-SHA256&X-Amz-Credential=AKIAIWOWYYGZ2Y53UL3A%2F20190828%2Fus-east-1%2Fs3%2Faws4_request&X-Amz-Date=20190828T091838Z&X-Amz-Expires=3600&X-Amz-SignedHeaders=host&X-Amz-Signature=ee0a625fcdbda5324a3d29c42be51500699a53ddf66d84798fe5b5fde99b3637
14 Ibid. 8.
15 Ibid. 9.
16 Dourish. *Where the Action Is*, 108
17 Ibid. 109. Winograd and Flores (1986) cited in.
18 Ibid. 114. Dreyfus (1996) cited in.
19 Merleau-Ponty, M. 1962. *Phenomenology of Perception*. London: Routledge.
20 Dourish. *Where the Action Is*, 114.
21 Dourish. 'Embodied interaction', 10.
22 Dourish. *Where the Action Is*, 115.
23 Ibid. 115.
24 Whitehead, A. N. (1920) 2004. *The Concept of Nature*. New York: Dover.
25 Ibid. 56.
26 Stengers, Isabelle. 2014. *Thinking with Whitehead: A Free and Wild Creation of Concepts*. Cambridge, MA; London, Harvard University Press, 147.
27 Ibid. 67.
28 Urban, W. M. 1951. 'Whitehead's philosophy of language and its relation to his metaphysics'. Schilpp, P. A. (ed.) *The Philosophy of Alfred North Whitehead*. New York: Tutor Publishing Company, 304.
29 Lowe, Victor. 1951. 'The development of Whitehead's philosophy'. Schilpp P. A. (ed.) *The Philosophy of Alfred North Whitehead*. Tutor Publishing Company, 106.
30 Hayles N. K. 2009. 'RFID: Human agency and meaning in information intensive environments'. *Theory Culture and Society*. 26 (2–3): 47–72.
31 Mitew T. 2014. Do objects dream of an internet of things? *Fibreculture Journal*. Issue 23. http://twentythree.fibreculturejournal.org/fcj-168-do-objects-dream-of-aninternet-of-things/
32 Whitehead, Alfred North. 1985. *Process and Reality: An Essay in Cosmology*. New York: Free Press, 145.
33 Whitehead cited in Dewey. John. 1951. 'The philosophy of Whitehead'. Schilpp, P. A. (ed.) *The Philosophy of Alfred North Whitehead*. New York: Tutor Publishing Company, 644.

34 Whitehead, A. N. 1967. *Adventures of Ideas*. New York: Free Press, 78.
35 Lowe. 'The development of Whitehead's philosophy', 53–4.
36 Ibid. 104.
37 Stengers. *Thinking with Whitehead*, 52.
38 Ibid. 70.
39 Dourish. *Where the Action Is*, 127, 191.
40 Ibid. 7.
41 Stengers. *Thinking with Whitehead*, 75.
42 Whitehead. *The Concept of Nature*, 107–8.
43 Stengers. *Thinking with Whitehead*, 90–1.
44 Ibid. 46.
45 Whitehead. *The Concept of Nature*, 144–52.
46 Stengers. *Thinking with Whitehead*, 52.
47 Ibid. 65.
48 Ibid. 67.
49 Whitehead. *The Concept of Nature*, 108–9.
50 Lowe. 'The development of Whitehead's philosophy', 97.
51 Whitehead, Alfred North. 1985. *Process and Reality*, 236–43.
52 Blackwell. 'Interacting with an inferred world'.
53 Ibid.
54 Coleman, Rebecca. 2018. 'Social media and the materialisation of the affective present'. Sampson, Tony D., Maddison, Stephen and Ellis, Darren. 2018. *Affect and Social Media: Emotion, Mediation, Anxiety and Contagion*. London: Rowman and Littlefield International, 71–2.
55 Ibid.
56 Hansen, Mark. *Feed-Forward*, 8.
57 Ibid. 81.
58 Seigworth G. J. 2015. 'Structures of digital feeling'. A keynote address at the University of Buffalo. http://www.academia.edu/26759922
59 Ibid.
60 Ibid.
61 Roeg, Nicolas. 2007. *The Man Who Fell to Earth*. Universal.

Outro Disrupting the Dark Refrain

1 Karppi. *Disconnect*, 146–7.
2 Vaidhyanathan. 'Don't delete Facebook. Do something about it'. *New York Times*, 24 March 2018. https://www.nytimes.com/2018/03/24/opinion/sunday/delete-facebook-does-not-fix-problem.html
3 See discussion in Chapter 4; and Massumi, *A User's Guide to Capitalism and Schizophrenia*, 96–7.
4 See for example, chapter 3 of Hayles, *Unthought* and Hayles, N. Katherine and Sampson, Tony D. 2018. 'Unthought meets the assemblage brain: A

dialogue between N. Katherine Hayles and Tony D. Sampson'. *Capacious: Journal for Emerging Affect Inquiry.* 1 (2): 60–84, 2018

5 See for example, Andrea Long Chu's dialogue with McKenzie Wark on the weakness of affect theory. 'The sun is the size of a human foot: An interview with Andrea Long Chu'. 29 October 2019. On the Public Seminar website. http://www.publicseminar.org/essays/the-sun-is-the-size-of-a-human-foot/?fbclid=IwAR23XULptV3qN5VGXfSLZ3LbS_Qg-NhV6DxxtOZNFdGpj0_ZAHbZ4-L4POQ

6 Manley, Julian. 2019. *Social Dreaming, Associative Thinking and Intensities of Affect.* [S. L.]: Palgrave Macmillan.

7 Barthes, Roland. [1957] 2013. *Mythologies.* New York: Hill and Wang.

8 Coleman. 'Social media and the materialisation of the affective present'. In Sampson et al., 71–2.

9 See further discussion on The Mind at Large concept (i.e. Bergson and Huxley) and delimiters in neuroculture in Sampson, *The Assemblage Brain.* 198–9.

Index

absolute sensation 68–9
actual occasion 34, 158
actual world 158–9, 160
Adorno, Theodor 140
advertising 46, 82–3, 85, 100, 103, 172, 183n69
aesthetic delight 11–12, 36
aesthetic experience 18–19, 35–6, 38
aesthetic facts 1, 13–15, 19, 22, 24, 26, 31–2, 35–9, 47, 57, 62–3, 74, 170–1
aesthetic figures 7, 12, 41
aesthetic ontology 8, 12, 16, 60–1, 171
affect theory 22, 88–9, 91, 95, 171–2, 202n5
Agência Lupa 131
artificial intelligence (AI) 18–20, 41, 112, 115–16, 154
algorithms 20, 24, 28–31, 36, 45, 71, 74, 83–4, 88–90, 92, 96–8, 103–4, 106–7, 111, 116–19, 121, 129
algorithms rabbit holes 11, 15, 29
alienation 60, 79, 85, 88, 94–6, 108–10, 132–3, 122, 135, 146
Alternative for Germany (AfD) 5, 129
Althusser, Louis 50
ambulant 6, 43, 66, 69, 71–3
Amin, Ash 71
anaesthetic register of feeling 60–1
Andersen, Kurt 43, 52–9, 70, 183n54, 183n58, 183n
Antifa 26–7, 29, 30–31
antisocial contagion 103–4
 see also prosocial contagion
antivirus (AV) 116–17
anxiety 5, 20, 41, 74–5, 94, 102, 127, 133, 134, 137, 140, 144–6, 149, 153, 170
Arab Spring 124, 127–8, 148
Are You Experienced? 173
 see also Hendrix, Jimi
Aryan race 123, 194n31
assemblages 55–6, 96, 107, 110, 133, 135, 142, 161, 170–1,

Assemblage Brain, The 73, 174n1, 174n11
aspirational fascism 21–2, 32, 57, 59
 see also fascism
autoaffection 10, 21, 37, 69, 73, 90, 158
autobiographical self 19
autoimmunity 113, 115, 136, 138–9, 142–6, 148, 172

Bakshy, Eytan 99–100
Barad, Karen 89, 98
Barthes, Roland 85, 88, 172
Baudrillard, Jean 33
becoming-the-same 5, 85, 135, 145, 149–50, 170
behaviour 19, 28, 42, 45–7, 75, 78, 83, 91, 94–7, 100, 102–3
behavioural science 3, 46–8, 81, 98–9, 105, 107
Bell, Colin 27
Benjamin, Walter 140
Bergson, Henri 50
bifurcation 9, 68, 151–2, 157–60, 164, 168, 173
 see also nonbifurcation
big lie strategy 11, 20, 22, 27, 34–5, 38, 54, 56, 58, 62, 74
Bios 122, 147, 171
Birther conspiracy 54, 123, 127
Blackwell, Alan 165
Bolsominions 130–1, 134–5
Bolsonaro, Jair 5, 48, 79, 129–31
Bouazizi, Mohamed 128
Bowie, David 167
boyd, dana 28–31
Braga, Adriana 44
Brexit 5, 33, 57
brutal fact 8, 11–14, 15–16, 34–7, 171
Burrows, David 12
Bussoti, Sylvano 5
Buzzfeed 77

Index

Caillois, Roger 4, 7, 9, 79, 86, 90–4, 96, 97, 110, 114–15, 134–43, 147–8, 150, 172
Cambridge Analytica 5, 45–8, 76, 100, 102, 125, 130, 170, 181n27
camouflage 7, 79, 86, 91–2, 115–16, 135, 137, 147–8
care system 58, 170
Carpenter, John 172
Cartesian thinker 72–3, 162–3,
Cesare the Somnambulist (fictional character) 41, 65
Christchurch terror attack 76–7, 111, 119, 123–4, 186n134
Chun, Wendy 21
Cleaners, The (documentary) 111–12, 147
Clough, Patricia 4, 10, 21, 37, 67, 70, 73, 89–90, 127
Cogan, Jackie (fictional character) 60–1, 127
cognition 1, 13–14, 17–19, 37, 47, 67–8, 70, 73, 74, 90, 154–5, 165–6
cognitive command post 68–9, 109, 171
Coleman, Rebecca 166, 173
collective consciousness 43–5, 55, 181n22
collective masochism 9, 113, 129, 135–8, 141, 142
collective mimesis 41–3, 50, 63, 75, 80, 85, 131, 134–5, 138–9, 145–7, 150
collective nonconscious 1, 3, 8, 10, 16, 21, 36–7, 39, 40–3, 47, 63, 65–8, 70–2, 74–5, 82, 84, 98, 171
Collins, Harry 18–20
community 6, 9, 61, 76, 81, 84, 114–15, 121, 123, 125, 127–31, 136, 138–41, 144, 146, 148–50, 172
communitas 115, 122, 148
conceptual personae 2–4, 15, 40–2, 48, 63–4, 70 73, 167, 174n11
Connolly, Willian E 22, 32, 34–5, 62–3, 74
conspiracy theory 11, 13, 18, 20, 27, 30–1, 36, 52–8, 170
contagion theory 2, 6–7, 50–1, 56, 105, 114–15
Crary, Jonathan 2–3, 7, 51,
created self 85, 89, 93
crowd theory 2, 42–3, 65–6, 149

Damasio, Antonio 19
dark refrain 4–6, 41–2, 44–5, 48, 52, 75–6, 78–9, 109–13, 114–15, 123, 124, 128, 136, 140, 144, 147–8, 169–73
data doubles 106–7, 131–34, 166

data power 105–6, 131, 134, 153
data voids 8, 15, 18, 24, 27–31, 74, 119
de Chardin, Pierre Teilhard 44
De Niro, Robert 52
Debaise, Didier 37, 73
deep nonconscious entanglement 19–21, 154
Dehaye, Paul-Olivier 47
Deleuze, Gilles 1–2, 5, 34, 49–50, 72–3, 174n11, 175n13
Dennett, Daniel 32–4, 53
Department of Culture, Media and Sport (DCMS) 46–7, 100, 181n27
dialectical 1, 79–10
digital immune system (DIS) 117
distinctions 7–9, 11, 14–15, 69, 96, 97, 114–20, 122–3, 127, 129, 132, 136–9, 147–9
do Rosário, Maria 130
Dominik, Andrew 59, 61
Donnie Darko (film) 64–5, 71
Dostoevsky, Fyodor 133
Dourish, Paul 155–7, 163, 165
Drenten, Jenna 87–8
Durkheim, Emile 43–4, 49, 55
dystopian media theory 1, 3–4, 147

Ehrlich, Paul 135, 142–3
El Paso terror attack 76–7, 123–4, 126
Ellis, Darren 145–6
Elmer, Greg 81–2, 187n17
embodied interaction 152, 155–7, 159, 163, 165
emotions 15, 47, 60, 88–9, 91, 101, 102, 104–5
Empire of Like 135–6, 170
Engels, Friedrich 85, 88
entrainment 5, 71–2, 95, 96, 102–3,
Ericson, Richard V 106–7, 134–5
Escobar, Pepe 48, 130
Esposito, Roberto 4, 135, 138–9, 141, 142, 172
event philosophy 13, 64, 158–60, 162–8
see also shock events
Exonerated Five 123
experience capitalism 3, 78, 80–2, 88, 90, 97, 105, 107, 109, 167–8, 172
expropriation 6, 81–2, 129, 138, 144, 170–2

Facebook 5, 26–7, 29, 46–7, 56, 76–7, 82–3, 91, 98–107, 111, 116, 117–20, 123–8, 130–1, 134, 146–8

Facebook Immune System (FIS) 117–19
fake news 12, 15–17, 20–38, 46, 48, 74, 130–1
Fantasyland 43, 52–9
far-right contagion 80, 128–30
fascism 6, 34, 59, 75, 79–80, 139–40
feeling 12, 15–16, 36–7, 61, 69, 72–3, 89, 93, 97, 109, 136, 173
fictioning machines 12, 27, 29, 36, 40, 57, 61, 64, 171
  see also machine fictioning
foothold (in the event) 15, 38, 69, 159, 163–4, 168, 173
Foucault, Michel 49–50
Frank the demon rabbit (fictional character) 64–5, 71, 150
Freud, Sigmund 66, 95,
Fuchs, Christian 87, 128–9
fuck your feelings 59–62
Fuller, Matthew 70, 73

gangster 52, 54, 56, 59–60
Gestalt 7, 9, 93
Ghonmin, Wael 128
Gillespie, T 133–4
Gilmore, James 81
Ginsberg, Alan 66
global brain thesis 44–5, 53
Goffman, Ervin 82, 88
Golebiewski, Michael 28–31
Goodman, Steve 126
Google 11, 28–9
Gove, Michael 33, 179n61
Grand, Sue 21
Gatsby (fictional character) 7
Greenfield, Adam 82, 144–5
Grosz, Elizabeth 9, 69, 89, 93–4, 133, 140–1
Guattari, Felix 1–2, 5, 174n11

Haggerty, Kevin 106–7, 134–5
Hamilton, John T 132, 140, 150
Hanlon, Aaron 33
Hansen, Mark 154, 166
Hatebook 119–20
Hayles, N Katherine 19–20, 67–8, 69, 161, 167
Heidegger, Martin 95, 156
Hendrix, Jimi 173
here and now 173, 158–9, 164–6
Hitler, Adolf 120, 122, 138
Horkheimer, Max 140
horror autotoxicus 136, 142–3, 144

human–computer interaction (HCI) 151–2, 155–65, 172
Husserl, Edmund 156–7, 161
hypnosis 41–3, 47–8, 50, 51, 59, 64–5, 67

ideology 85–6, 88–9, 122, 172
ignore/delete 9, 112–13, 115, 131, 169
imitation 50–1, 53, 84, 91–2, 135, 146, 150
immunity problem 5, 9, 14, 78, 92, 112–13, 114–20, 136–40, 142, 142, 147–8, 154, 172, 192n1
immunitas 115, 122, 143
immunopolitics 4, 6, 9, 80, 114–15, 121–4, 125, 127, 129, 136, 138–40, 148, 150
impersonal 1, 4, 12, 14, 16, 19, 20–1, 29, 37, 47, 78–9, 82, 89, 91, 94, 110, 134, 139, 141, 164, 171, 187n17
indistinction 2–3, 6–7, 14–15, 35, 62, 70–2, 94, 97, 107–9, 115, 135–48
intensity, 12–13, 15, 16, 22, 23, 35, 36–37, 71, 78, 104, 109, 158, 191n89
internet of things (IoT) 151, 153–4, 161
irrational 12–15, 43, 52–3, 57, 62–3, 66, 70

Jefferson, Thomas 61
Johnson, Elizabeth 140
judgements 11, 15–20, 32–9, 52–3, 57, 63, 66, 74–5, 154, 163, 170, 173

Karppi, Tero 91, 107, 128, 134
Kelly, Richard 64
Killing Them Softly (film) 59–61, 127
Koenigsberg, Richard 122
Kogan, Aleksandr 45–6, 100, 102, 125–6, 190–91n74
Kracauer, Siegfried 41, 64
Kramer, Adam 99–101
Krauss, Rosalind 92–3,

Lacan, Jacques 85–6, 88, 91, 93, 133, 142
Laing, R. D. 4, 6, 78, 90–1, 94–7, 110, 135, 189n54
Langlois, Ganaele 81, 187n17
Las Vegas (mass shooting) 15, 24–7, 29
Le Bon, Gustave 149, 65–6, 70, 149
Leibniz, Gottfried 22, 49
Lévy, Pierre 44, 53
line of flight 4–6, 9, 34, 170
lookalike audience 83–4, 88, 92, 96–8, 106–7, 110, 144, 149
Lowe, Victor 160, 165
Lupton, Deborah 131–2

lure of experience (feeling) 16, 18, 36–8, 47, 91, 94

machine fictioning 12, 17–18
  see also fictioning machines
machine learning 20, 28, 36, 46, 97–8, 112, 115–17, 121, 154, 165–8
magical contagion 104–5
Manet, Édouard 7
Man Who Fell to Earth (The) (Film) 167
Marlow, Cameron 99–100, 190n64
Martin, Trayvon 29
Martinez, Natalie 77
Marxist media theory 85, 88
mass shooting phenomena 5, 15, 18, 22–30, 76–7, 111, 119
Massumi, Brian 22–3, 68, 89, 135
McLuhan, Marshall 44
mechanical habit 3, 5, 7, 19, 42
media alive 9, 152–5, 173
Merleau-Ponty, Maurice 156–57
microsociology 42, 49–51, 54–6
monads 22, 49, 54–6
more-than-human 21, 43, 65, 75, 90, 140, 151, 158
Murphie, Andrew 9, 13, 20, 152
Myanmar 120, 193n17

National Rifle Association (NRA) 61
nature alive 152, 154, 155
new materialism 22, 40, 42, 43, 51, 63–4, 66–8, 89–92
Neyrat, Frédéric 2, 122–3, 127, 129, 141, 194n31
Nietzsche, Friedrich 50, 95, 174n11
Nonphenomenological 6, 9, 43, 51, 78–9, 89–91, 94, 97–8, 109–10, 135, 142, 153, 172–3

O'Sullivan, Simon 12
Obama, Barack 54–5, 61, 123–7, 130
OCEAN model 46

paradoxes 17, 35, 61–2, 70
Parikka, Jussi 142, 183n50
Parisi, Luciana 89, 126,
perception 7, 9–10, 12, 24, 37, 59, 67, 69, 73, 93, 151–2, 157–9, 162–3, 165, 171, 173
personality traits 46–8, 57, 59, 97, 102
pervasive technology 3, 9, 44, 82, 144–5, 151, 153–5, 167, 173

phenomenology 9, 21, 43, 69, 78–9, 90, 93, 131, 142, 152, 155–7, 158, 162–3
Pine, Joseph 81, 82
platform architecture
Plato's cave 72–3
Platonic double 94, 107, 132–5
Politics of Experience (The) 78, 94–6
  see also R. D. Laing
positivism 11–13, 15, 32–6, 40, 53–4, 57, 61, 63, 170
post-truth 11–16, 21, 31–3, 38, 171
postmodernism 11, 15, 32–5, 53, 171
prehension 164–6
present-at-hand 156, 158, 163
Principia Mathematica 12–13
Proceedings of the National Academy of Sciences (PNAS) 101
prosocial contagion 102–3
psychographics 46–7, 97–8
psychological self 43, 51

quantified-self 131

racial bias 121
racism 5, 6, 29–30, 52, 54, 59, 75, 77, 96, 112, 115, 120, 122, 172
rationality 1, 2, 14–16, 43, 51, 52–3, 58, 60, 70, 88, 89, 170
ready-to-hand 156, 158, 163
relational media 144–5
representation 11, 15, 32, 33, 35, 37, 49, 85–6, 88, 97, 106–7, 131–3, 136, 139, 141–2, 149–50
resonation 11, 16, 22–5, 32, 35, 38, 54, 56, 62–3, 74, 96, 123, 170, 172,
reverie 2, 41, 52, 66, 70
revolutionary contagion 4, 6, 114, 124–31, 148
rhythm 5, 42, 71, 88, 91, 103, 112–13, 170
Roeg, Nicolas 167
Rohingya 120
rumours 8, 11, 15, 18, 24–8, 31, 35–6, 39, 54, 130
Russell, Bertrand 13, 16
Ruyer, Raymond 9–10, 68–9

search engines 8, 15, 17, 22, 26–31, 53, 74, 118, 119
search engine optimization (SEO) 22, 27–31, 35, 38, 53, 77
Seigworth, Greg 166–7
self-concept 1, 43, 78–9, 82, 84, 85–91, 94–6, 107–10, 131

self-enjoyment 43, 68–9, 72–4, 109, 161
self-other similarity 84, 92, 97–8, 103, 170
Shakespeare, William 12, 36
sharing 31, 75, 76–7, 79, 81, 84, 87–91, 95–9, 103–6, 111, 116
shock event 15–16, 18, 21–5, 28–32, 34–8, 62, 72, 74, 77, 111, 171
Simondon, Gilbert 145–6
sleep 2–3, 66–73, 171–2
smart 2, 19, 45, 154,
Snapchat 78, 186–7n1
spectra of experience 11, 14–15, 18, 40, 43, 51, 61, 72, 170
speculative mimesis 79, 139, 149–50
speculative philosophy 13, 34–5, 37
Stengers, Isabelle 38, 109, 164
strongmen (populist) 154, 57, 74–5, 80, 110
syntax trap 160

Tarde, Gabriel 2, 48–56, 63, 84, 107, 134, 150
Taussig, Michael 140–1, 149
thing-self 21, 71
Thomas Newton (fictional character) 167
Thrift, Nigel 20, 67, 71
time machine 64, 169, 173
Toffler, Alvin 80–1
Tonkonoff, Sergio 49–51, 174n1
Trump, Donald 6, 11, 21–3, 32–5, 45, 52, 54–60, 62–3, 74, 77, 123–7, 129, 130, 141, 149, 172
Tucker, Ian 145–6
Twitter 22, 30, 54–8, 62, 76–7, 79, 112, 123, 124, 128

user engagement 2, 5, 6, 81–3, 96, 97, 103, 105–6, 113, 119, 144, 154, 171

user experience 1–10, 13, 21, 31, 40, 42, 43, 46, 68, 78, 81–4, 90, 92, 97–100, 104, 107, 108, 110, 112, 126, 134–5, 144, 146, 149, 151–6, 160, 165–6, 170–3, 174n1
user unconscious 21, 54, 56, 90
UX design 151–3, 172
UX industry 81–2

Vaidhyanathan, Siva 56, 103–4, 146–7
virality/growth 9, 78–84, 91, 96–9, 104, 110, 113, 114, 115, 119, 129, 144, 148, 172
visceral register of experience 3, 14, 19–20, 22, 24, 43, 47, 52, 58, 62–3, 72, 74, 89, 124, 172

wakefulness 2–4, 6, 7, 40, 42–3, 44, 63–70, 171, 185n18
WhatsApp 48, 79, 130–1,
white rage 22, 55, 57–9, 61, 63, 141
white supremacy 29–30, 77, 121–3, 127, 147, 172, 186n134
Whitehead, A.N. 4, 8–9, 11–14, 16, 17, 24, 32, 34, 35–39, 43, 47, 60, 64, 68–9, 72–4, 94, 109, 110, 151–3, 157–67, 170–73
Wikipedia 28–9
Williams, James 64
Williams, Raymond 166
Williamson, Judith 85–9, 93, 95, 106
Wylie, Christopher 46–7

YouTube 61, 76, 79, 112, 121

Zuboff, Shoshana 83
Zuckerberg, Mark 47, 76, 116, 119–20, 147–8, 181n27